FREEDOM TO PRACTISE

PERSON-CENTRED APPROACHES TO SUPERVISION

EDITED BY

KEITH TUDOR

AND

MIKE WORRALL

PCCS Books
Ross-on-Wye

First published 2004
Reprinted 2010

PCCS BOOKS
2 Cropper Row
Alton Road
Ross on Wye
HR9 5LA
UK
Tel +44 (0)1989 763900
contact@pccs-books.co.uk
www.pccs-books.co.uk

Text: this collection © Keith Tudor and Mike Worrall
the chapters © individual authors

Cover photograph © Peak District National
Park Authority/Ray Manley

Freedom to Practise:
Person-centred approaches to supervision

British Library Cataloguing in Publication Data.
A catalogue record for this book is available from the British Library.

ISBN 1 898059 59 4

Cover design by Old Dog Graphics
Cover photograph of Kinder Scout from www.peak-pictures.com
Printed by ImprintDigital, Exeter

Blackburn
College

Library
01254 292120

DEDICATION

To Louise and Pam, who provide us with and remind us of wider views in life.

ACKNOWLEDGEMENTS

Our thanks go to all the contributors for their work and willingness to be
edited; to Robin Shohet and Joan Wilmot for their close reading, enthusiasm
and generous comments; and to Maggie Taylor-Sanders and Pete Sanders for
their work, support and patience.

ALSO BY THE SAME EDITORS

Freedom to Practise, Volume II:
Developing person-centred approaches to supervision

ISBN 978 1 898059 97 4

CONTENTS

colour changing
pastel to bold

held not confined

fluid in honesty
growing asking changing

held not confined

being energy, questions, difference
moving out of safe to scary

held not confined

meeting self changing self
a place of feeling

held not confined

Seni Seneviratne
November 2002

INTRODUCTION

KEITH TUDOR AND MIKE WORRALL

Given the widespread subscription to the person-centred approach within the field of counselling, and given the almost universal acceptance of the need for supervision of counselling and psychotherapeutic practice, the lack of literature on person-centred supervision seems surprising. Rogers himself paid little attention to supervision and, of the early writers, only Patterson (1964, 1983, 1997) has written consistently about supervision from a person-centred perspective. More recently, Villas-Boas Bowen (1986), Mearns (1995), Conradi (1996), Merry (1999, 2001), Lambers (2000) and Worrall (2001) have contributed to our understanding of person-centred supervision. These individual contributions have added parts to this body of knowledge, although as disparate contributions. One of our intentions for this book is to bring together current ideas about the person-centred approach and about supervision in order to be more systematic about our thinking about supervision and in order to develop the approach.

In Part One we look at person-centred philosophy and theory in relation to the practice of supervision. In Chapter 1, based on Rogers' (1959) own description of his 'systematic thinking', we offer a tentative structure for a theory of person-centred supervision. As a part of this we ask whether the conditions Rogers hypothesised as necessary and sufficient for therapeutic change are relevant also in supervision. One of Rogers' major contributions to the field of psychotherapy (see, for example, Rogers, 1951) was to put the client's experience of therapy on the map. In a later paper (Rogers, 1958) he refers to the necessity that the client

1

receives the therapist's unconditional positive regard and empathic understanding as the 'assumed condition'. Following this, we think it's important to include some description of supervision from a supervisee's point of view. This is apparent in a number of chapters: Deborah Gibson provides this specifically in Chapter 2; Seni Seneviratne discusses this in Chapter 6; and in Chapter 14 Rachel Freeth, a psychiatrist, reflects on her own experience of person-centred supervision.

Holloway (1995) points out that supervision was not recognised as a unique practice, distinct from training, until the 1980s. Once recognised, the generic literature on supervision has expanded, and has identified and developed a number of aspects of this activity including: the *functions* of supervision (Kadushin, 1976; Proctor, 1988); the respective *roles* of supervisor and supervisee (e.g. Zalcman and Cornell, 1983); the notion of *development* in supervision (e.g. Stoltenberg and Delworth, 1987); the *process* of supervision (e.g. Casement, 1985, 1990; Hawkins and Shohet, 1989, 2000); the *organisation* of supervision (e.g. Page and Wosket, 1994) and *tasks* of supervision (Carroll, 1996); and the *context* of supervision (e.g. Carroll and Holloway, 1999). Hess (1980) and, more recently, Jacobs (1996) have both edited volumes which explore the issue of theoretical orientation in supervision. Jacobs' *In Search of Supervision* shows a number of therapists commenting on his work with a particular client. In it Conradi (1996) writes from the perspective of a person-centred therapist and supervisor— although, by her own acknowledgement, she is also heavily influenced by Jungian analytic psychology. In Chapter 3 we review this generic literature from a person-centred perspective. We continue this review in Chapter 4, which we devote to two particular process models of supervision, on the grounds that each is both widely known and significantly influential.

Despite the current interest in integration—often, in our view, eclecticism by another name—most training in counselling and psychotherapy (at least in Britain) is still orientation-specific. It is, for instance, a requirement of the British Association for Counselling and Psychotherapy that accredited training courses show allegiance to one 'core theoretical model'. The United Kingdom Council for Psychotherapy is itself organised in 'Sections' by theoretical allegiance. Both enshrine and, arguably, reify the importance of theoretical coherence. Good therapists, however, from whatever theoretical orientation, seem to us to have more in common with each other than do those who, at least on paper, share common theoretical ground with each other. We think that what matters here is the authentic congruence between personal philosophy and elected theoretical orientation, and that this is infinitely more important than an apparent congruence which, at worst, is little more than confluence with an accrediting body. In Chapter 5 we take up the challenges of issues, questions and dilemmas in supervision from a personal, professional and person-centred perspective and conclude with what we identify as a number of domains of supervision, and a discussion of the congruence between the practitioner's personal philosophy, and the philosophy, theory and practice of their chosen approach.

Part One, then, lays the foundations of a person-centred approach to supervision. Part Two consists of a number of dialogues and developments in the field. We begin with Seni Seneviratne's chapter on race, culture and supervision, which explores one particular aspect of the context of supervision. She emphasises, amongst other things, the need for supervisors to acknowledge the historical component of cross-cultural relationships and the importance of fluidity in how we construe 'culture'. In Chapter 7 Jo Valentine looks at supervision in an organisational context. She emphasises the need for supervisors to understand in some detail the context in which their supervisees work, and challenges the assumption that line management and clinical supervision need to be offered separately. The next two chapters take strands of thinking that, respectively, arise from (Chapter 8) and are compatible with (Chapter 9) person-centred theory and practice, and look at them in the context of supervision. Greg Madison takes Gendlin's ideas about focusing and suggests ways in which focusing might inform the practice of supervisors both within and beyond the person-centred approach. In Chapter 9 Penny Allen summarises the practice of Interpersonal Process Recall, based on the work of Kagan, and shows how it sits comfortably with person-centred principles. The last two chapters in this Part look at what else may be going on in supervision, and at what else supervision might be. Rose Cameron describes her awareness of 'subtle energy' in supervision. She shows how such awareness can enhance the quality of contact between supervisor and practitioner and, by implication, between practitioner and client. In Chapter 11 Tony Merry writes about supervision as a form of heuristic research. While he recognises that many practitioners are resistant to or uncomfortable with the idea of research, he also suggests that, at best, supervision is itself a form of personal and facilitated research.

Patterson (1983, 1997) and others assert that it is necessary for the supervisee to be operating from the same theoretical base as the supervisor. To advocate or advance one theoretical orientation always carries the danger of rigidity and sectarianism—both processes and politics at odds with the person-centred approach. Whilst we favour personal and philosophical congruence, and the theoretical coherence and consistency which supports this, we also embrace diversity. Furthermore, we are with Schon (1983) in wanting to facilitate the 'reflective practitioner', one who is critical and independent. Cornell and Zalcman (1984), writing in the international *Transactional Analysis Journal*, describe this process of facilitation as one of 'engaging therapists in actively questioning their conceptual framework and correlating their ideas with their clinical observations'.

This, they say, 'will compensate greatly for the biases and limitations of any given psychotherapy method' (p. 113). They suggest that this 'will result in more effective therapists who are more likely to continue their own learning and substantially contribute to the further development of psychotherapeutic theory and practice' (ibid., p. 113). In this sense good supervision is good supervision and, indeed, both of us have experience of good supervision, training and therapy from practitioners of theoretical orientations other than the person-centred approach. No doubt too, there are practitioners who have had experiences of bad supervision from supervisors who are or who identify themselves as person-centred or who consider themselves as supervising in a manner which is congruent with their theoretical orientation as therapist or practitioners. Good *super vision* takes a 'wider view'[1] and in this sense is a meta-activity which cuts across not only theoretical orientations but also disciplines and professional activities, a view which is represented and elaborated in Part Three. In Chapter 12 Paul Hitchings discusses the advantages of supervision across theoretical orientations. He offers specific examples of concepts from other theories which, he argues, are helpful in the supervision of person-centred practitioners. He also offers ideas about how we may translate these concepts into language that is compatible with person-centred practice. In the next chapter Ian Townsend, a qualified homeopath, shows some of the connections between homeopathic theory and the person-centred approach. Ian traces the need for and development of supervision within homeopathy and shows how supervision according to person-centred principles is especially compatible with homeopathic practice. In the last chapter Rachel Freeth, a psychiatrist working within the National Health Service, writes about her experience of her work and the importance of supervision in managing some of the complex and difficult situations she faces. She examines the contributions and the challenges that lie at the interface between psychiatry and the person-centred approach, and recognises that both the contributions and the challenges go both ways.

As its name suggests, and as Wood (1996) confirms, the person-centred approach is an *approach*: 'it is neither a psychotherapy nor a psychology . . . It is merely, as its name implies, an approach, nothing more, nothing less. It is a psychological posture, if you like, from which thought or action may arise and experience be organized. It is a "way of being"' (pp. 168–9). Building on the exploration of the person-centred approach to supervision in Part One, and developments and dialogues within the person-centred practice of supervision in

---

1. The Latin word *super* carries the meaning of 'beyond', 'besides' and 'in addition' and not only 'above'. This is important in our attempt to widen the meaning of the word and the implications of the activity.

Part Two, the contributions in Part Three take us beyond counselling and psychotherapy and are an expression of our conviction that person-centred supervision is an aspect of the person-centred *approach*. In this sense person-centred supervision is relevant not only to person-centred therapists but also to others within and beyond the helping professions. As Townsend points out in his chapter, homeopaths have, in recent years, and largely influenced by the theory and practice of psychotherapy supervision, taken on and developed the practice of supervision. This trend is also reflected in other professions such as nursing (Butterworth and Faugier, 1992), psychology (Lunt and Pomerantz, 1993), health visiting (Swain, 1995), occupational therapy (College of Occupational Therapists, 1997), and in both statutory and voluntary organisations (see Pritchard, 1995), including the police (Towler, 1999).

In our shared frame of reference, good supervision encourages practitioners to reflect on their work and to think for themselves. In a book on the subject, *The Reflective Practitioner*, Schon (1983) suggests that 'practitioners themselves often reveal a capacity for reflection on their intuitive knowing in the midst of action and sometimes use this capacity to cope with the unique, uncertain, and conflicted situations of practice' (p. viii). We have taken the title of this volume from Rogers' (1969, 1983) work on education: *Freedom to Learn*. The theme of freedom is echoed on the cover which shows a view of Kinder Scout in Yorkshire, the site in 1932 of a mass trespass of working-class fell walkers whose direct action secured certain access rights for walkers and the 'freedom to roam'. Compare this freedom of range and enquiry with Casemore's (2001) approach to training students with regard to touching clients:

> At the start of the academic year, I say to all my students on the counselling courses I run: 'Watch my lips. Do not touch your client, even if they ask you to. The very most you should do is to shake their hand when they arrive and when they leave—and you will need to check out if that is acceptable to them.' I tell them that this also includes when they are working with each other as counsellor and client in the practice periods within the course. We then explore the reasons and the rationale behind this, on a number of occasions throughout the course. I also make a note of the date and time I do this and tell the students that I have done so, in order that if a complaint is ever taken out against them as a result of their touching their client, they will not be able to claim they were never taught not to do that. (p. 115)

Both us were genuinely shocked when we first read this passage. It seems to us one of the worst and most worrying examples of a defensive reaction to complex issues in the practice of therapy. It reveals an approach to training and, by implication, supervision, based on a mistrust of adult student therapists, on a hierarchical and patronising view of education and training ('I'll tell you what to do and then we'll explore the rationale within those parameters'), and a deterministic, defensive position in relation to clients and students. This is especially ironic, and disturbing, in that Casemore claims to be Rogerian and the course in question is a 'person-centred' course. By contrast, drawing on the work of Freire (1967/1976), *Education: The Practice of Freedom* and (1972) *Pedagogy of the Oppressed* and hooks (1994), *Teaching to Transgress*, as well as Rogers' (1969, 1983) work *Freedom to Learn*, we propose an *engaged* and *critical* pedagogy. We hope that the reader/practitioner will experience this book as an invitation to reflect, to think and to question; to roam, trespass and transgress; to be curious, critical and creative.

REFERENCES

Butterworth, J. and Faugier, J. (1992) (Eds.) *Clinical Supervision and Mentorship in Nursing*. London: Chapman and Hall

Carroll, M. (1996) *Counselling Supervision: Theory, Skills and Practice*. London: Cassell

Carroll, M. and Holloway, E. (1999) *Counselling Supervision in Context*. London: Sage

Casement, P. (1985) *On Learning from the Patient*. London: Tavistock

Casement, P. (1990) *Further Learning from the Patient: The Analytic Space and Process*. London: Routledge

Casemore, R. (2001) Managing boundaries: It's the little things that count. In R. Casemore (Ed.) *Surviving Complaints Against Counsellors and Psychotherapists* (pp.111–20). Ross-on-Wye: PCCS Books

College of Occupational Therapists. (1997) *Standards, Policies and Procedures Statement on Supervision in Occupational Therapy*. London: College of Occupational Therapists

Conradi, P. (1996) Person-centred therapy. In M. Jacobs (Ed.) *In Search of Supervision* (pp.53–74). Buckingham: Open University Press

Cornell, W.F. and Zalcman, M.J. (1984) Teaching transactional analysts to think theoretically. *Transactional Analysis Journal*, *14*(2), 105–13

Freire, P. (1972) *Pedagogy of the Oppressed*. Harmondsworth: Penguin

Freire, P. (1976) *Education: The Practice of Freedom*. London: Writers and Readers Publishing Cooperative. (Original work published 1967)

Hawkins, P. and Shohet, R. (1989) *Supervision in the Helping Professions*. Milton Keynes: Open University Press

Hawkins, P. and Shohet, R. (2000) *Supervision in the Helping Professions* (2nd edn.). Buckingham: Open University Press

Hess, A.K. (1980) (Ed.) *Psychotherapy Supervision: Theory, Research and Practice*. New York: John Wiley and Sons

Holloway, E. (1995) *Clinical Supervision: A Systems Approach*. London: Sage

hooks, b. (1994) *Teaching to Transgress*. London: Routledge

Jacobs, M. (1996) (Ed.) *In Search of Supervision*. Buckingham: Open University Press

Kadushin, A. (1976) *Supervision in Social Work*. New York: Columbia University Press

Lambers, E. (2000) Supervision in person-centred therapy: Facilitating congruence. In D. Mearns and B. Thorne *Person-Centred Therapy Today* (pp.196–211). London: Sage

Lunt, I. and Pomerantz, M. (1993) (Eds.) Supervision and psychologists' professional work [Special issue]. *Educational and Child Psychology, 10*(2)

Mearns, D. (1995)

Merry, T. (1999) *Learning and Being in Person-Centred Counselling*. Ross-on-Wye: PCCS Books

Merry, T. (2001) Congruence and the supervision of client-centred therapists. In G. Wyatt (Ed.) *Congruence* (pp. 174–83). Ross-on-Wye: PCCS Books

Page, S. and Wosket, V. (1994) *Supervising the Counsellor: A Cyclical Model*. London: Routledge

Patterson, C. H. (1964) Supervising students in the counseling practicum. *Journal of Counseling Psychology, 11*, 47–53

Patterson, C. H. (1983) A client-centered approach to supervision. *The Counseling Psychologist, 11*(1), 21–5

Patterson, C. H. (1997) Client-centered supervision. In C. E. Watkins (Ed.) *Handbook of Psychotherapy Supervision* (pp.134–46). New York: John Wiley

Pritchard, J. (1995) (Ed.) *Good Practice in Supervision: Statutory and Voluntary Organisations*. London: Jessica Kingsley Publishers

Proctor, B. (1988) Supervision: A co-operative exercise in accountability. In M. Marken and M. Payne (Eds.) *Enabling and Ensuring*. Leicester: Leicester National Youth Bureau/Council for Education and Training in Youth and Community Work

Rogers, C. R. (1951) *Client-Centered Therapy*. London: Constable

Rogers, C. R. (1958) A process conception pf psychotherapy. *American Psychologist, 13*, 142–9

Rogers, C. R. (1959) A theory of therapy, personality and interpersonal relationships, as developed in the client-centred framework. In S. Koch (Ed.) *Psychology: A Study of a Science, Vol. 3: Formulation of the Person and the Social Context* (pp.184–256). New York: McGraw-Hill

Rogers, C. R. (1969) *Freedom to Learn*. Columbus, OH: Charles E. Merrill

Rogers, C. R. (1983) *Freedom to Learn for the 80s*. Columbus, OH: Charles E. Merrill

Schon, D. A. (1983) *The Reflective Practitioner*. New York: Basic Books

Stoltenberg, C.D. and Delworth, U. (1987) *Supervising Counselors and Therapists*. San Francisco, CA: Jossey-Bass

Swain, G. (1995) *Clinical Supervision: The Principles and Process*. London: Health Visitors' Association

Towler, J. (1999) Supervision in uniformed settings. In M. Carroll and E. Holloway (Eds.) *Counselling Supervision in Context* (pp.177–200). London: Sage

Villas-Boas Bowen, M. (1986) Personality differences and person-centered supervision. *Person-Centered Review, 1*(3), 291–309

Wood, J. K. (1996) The person-centered approach: Towards an understanding of its implications. In R. Hutterer, G. Pawlowsky, P. F. Schmid and R. Stipsits (Eds.) *Client-Centered and Experiential Psychotherapy: A Paradigm in Motion* (pp. 163–81). Frankfurt am Main: Peter Lang

Worrall, M. (2001) Supervision and empathic understanding. In S. Haugh and T. Merry (Eds.) *Empathy* (pp.206–17). Ross-on-Wye: PCCS Books

Zalcman, M. J. and Cornell, W. F. (1983) A bilateral model for clinical supervision. *Transactional Analysis Journal, 13*(2), 112–23

PART ONE

PERSON-CENTRED PHILOSOPHY AND THEORY IN THE PRACTICE OF SUPERVISION

CHAPTER ONE

PERSON-CENTRED PHILOSOPHY AND THEORY IN THE PRACTICE OF SUPERVISION

KEITH TUDOR AND MIKE WORRALL

The approach that Rogers developed began as 'client-centred therapy' (CCT), became 'person-centred therapy' (PCT), and is now more commonly called 'the person-centred approach' (PCA). One of the useful consequences of this development is precisely that this third phrase identifies the person-centred as one possible *approach* to many aspects of life, including therapy, though not limited to it. Although person-centred theory began as and begins with a theory of *therapy* (Rogers, 1959), its principles have, since its earliest description, informed other areas of life. Rogers wrote, for instance, about education (Rogers, 1969, 1983), groups (Rogers, 1973), conflict resolution (Rogers, 1978), and organisations (Rogers and Roethlisberger, 1952/1988). In this tradition, we want to explore the philosophy and theory of the approach as it relates to the practice of supervision. What are the implications of basing the practice of supervision on person-centred philosophy? Does person-centred theory as it stands have anything useful to say about supervision? If it does, does it help us think about our work as supervisors? Are those conditions which Rogers calls necessary and sufficient for therapeutic personality change either necessary, sufficient or both for the process of supervision? These are all questions we'll address in this book.

Perhaps the bigger question, the one that embraces these other questions, is about the relationship between the activities, tasks, processes and outcomes of therapy on the one hand, and of supervision on the other. It is tempting to assume and then assert a *parallel*, or a precise similarity, between therapy and supervision. This is only partially helpful: parallel lines never meet except at infinity. Our experience suggests that the domains of therapy and supervision meet sooner than that, and that at moments the two are indistinguishable. Particular moments in supervision look like and may feel like therapeutic moments; they may even have similar effects and outcomes. What defines them as different is not their nature but where they occur, their context. In this sense we describe supervision and therapy as processes which are similar in some respects, *analogous* rather than *parallel*. We hold this distinction in mind throughout the first part of this book, and especially in this chapter, and use it to reflect on the relevance of particular elements of theory.

'No theory', says Rogers (1959), 'can be adequately understood without some knowledge of the cultural and personal soil from which it springs' (p. 185). Person-centred theory springs from the soil of Rogers' own personal and philosophical beliefs, and from his experiences as a therapist. We begin, therefore, by reviewing the philosophical assumptions of the approach. Taking Rogers' (1959) general structure of the theory of the approach as a starting point (Figure 1.1), we then suggest a rearranging of some of the elements of that theory, and look at some of those elements as they seem relevant in the domain of supervision. Out of this, we evolve a tentative theory of person-centred supervision.

PERSON-CENTRED PHILOSOPHY

Wittgenstein (1922/1961) argues that philosophy consists of a series of propositions, and describes a proposition as 'a picture of reality' (p. 21). We see the person-centred approach as holding two essential propositions or pictures of reality: the organism and its tendency to actualise:

1. At the heart of his thinking about life Rogers assumes a living, breathing, pulsing entity which he calls the organism. In this, he follows Goldstein (1934/1995) and other organismic psychologists. He uses the term to stand for any living being, and describes it as unselfconscious, fluid, responsive to its environment, social, creative, constructive and truth-seeking.

2. Person-centred practice in any sphere assumes and depends upon the organism's innate tendency to actualise. Drawing on work by Angyal (1941), Rogers (1959) describes this as 'the inherent tendency of the organism to develop all its capacities in ways which serve to maintain or enhance the organism' (p. 196). The whole approach assumes this tendency as a point of departure, and neither the theory nor the practice of the approach makes any sense without it.

In the context of supervision, this belief in an organism and its tendency to actualise reminds supervisors that both their supervisees, and the clients or patients with whom their supervisees work, are tending innately towards actualising their potential as fully as possible, given inner and outer circumstances. This helps free supervisors to hold a high level of trust in the work that their supervisees are doing, and in the capacity of their supervisees' clients to make the most of and take the best from that work. It follows from this that supervisors do not normally need to assess, monitor or police the work of their supervisees, and can instead devote their attention to helping supervisees explore their own thoughts and feelings about their work. Seen in isolation, this stance may seem naive or even negligent, and is open to criticism. Writing about the work of only one supervisor, and from within the legal framework of one particular State, Davenport (1992) asserts that person-centred supervision, 'appealing as it may be, fails to meet the rigorous ethical and legal guidelines now required of counselor supervisors' (p. 227). We take Davenport's concerns seriously. It's important that supervisors work within their legal and ethical responsibilities, or know, at least, when they risk working outside of them. We think, though, that the stance we're describing is an attitudinal and behavioural manifestation of a belief in the organism's innate tendency to actualise, and is more thoughtful, credible and defensible than she allows.

However, legal and ethical considerations, important though they are, are only two of a number of relevant domains. In Chapter 5 we identify and explore seven domains which we think are relevant to any practitioner. In our view the legal and ethical responsibilities of practitioners and supervisors are often misrepresented and misunderstood (see Chapter 5, Jenkins, 1997; Cristofoli, 2002). We think that philosophical considerations are, at least, equally important. The relationship between the philosophical assumptions and the principles of the person-centred approach, and the personal philosophy of individual practitioners is an interesting one and we look at this in Chapter 5.

PERSON-CENTRED THEORY

This review of person-centred theory begins with a recognition that Rogers didn't develop a theory of supervision. He began as a therapist, learned to be a therapist by being one, and developed the various elements of person-centred theory inferentially from his experiences as a therapist. He thought first about what seemed to work in therapy, and only then, retrospectively, as it were, about the conditions under which his clients had developed. That history helps explain the structure of the theory as Rogers presented it in his 1959 paper, which begins

13

with a theory of therapy and personality change, and then develops, in order, a theory of personality, a theory of the fully functioning person and a theory of interpersonal relationship. In his diagram of the structure of the theory (see Figure 1.1), Rogers puts the theory of therapy in the middle, and puts the other theories around it.

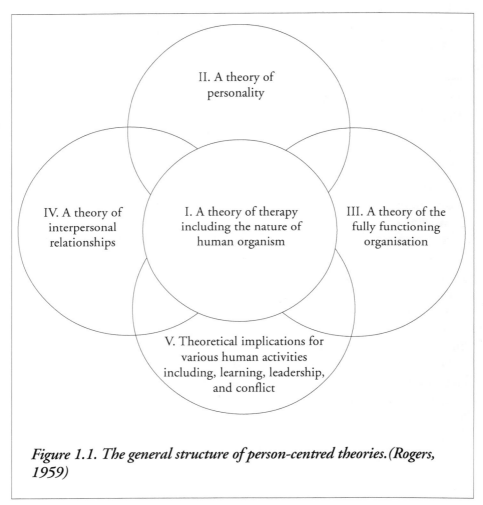

Figure 1.1. The general structure of person-centred theories.(Rogers, 1959)

Rogers (1959) reminds us that he's most sure of the theory of therapy, and that 'the possibility of magnification of error in the theory increases as one goes out from the center' (p. 193).

We suggest that it makes some sense now for us to reorder this formulation, and to put a theory of personality at the centre of our thinking, rather than a theory of therapy. Our reasons for suggesting this reordering are as follows:

• We've already identified the organism as the first of the two central propositions of person-centred philosophy. Personality theory starts from the integrity of the new-born organism, and then describes the conditions under which we develop limiting patterns of thought and behaviour, the awareness and discomfort of which prompt us to seek therapeutic help in the first place.

• The theory of therapy holds the approach's second proposition, the organism's tendency to actualise, as central, and offers some structures to help us think about what conditions might support it, how we might describe the processes that happen in therapy, and what we might expect by way of outcomes.

• This chronology mirrors life's: organismic integrity at conception; experiences in childhood and later which support our development or restrict our growth; and experiences in therapy or elsewhere which offer us opportunity to question and dissolve those restrictions.

So, for the purposes of this chapter, we'll begin with a theory of personality and then develop a theory of supervision based on Rogers' theory of therapy and personality change, including the conditions, process and outcomes of supervision (see Figure 1.2).

PERSONALITY THEORY

Rogers' (1951, 1959) personality theory suggests that we are born a congruent and unselfconscious organism. Gradually, each of us learns that we're more likely to be accepted consistently if we behave in certain ways and not in other ways. In response to this learning we develop over time a self-concept, a picture of ourselves informed largely by our experiences of others' responses to us. This self-concept limits what experiences we can safely acknowledge to ourselves and articulate to each other. This is the beginning of incongruence, of inconsistency between organism and self, and between experience and awareness.

In the context of supervision, this model seems relevant in a number of ways. In the first instance, it reminds us that we all, supervisors and supervisees, have the capacity, 'latent if not evident' (Rogers, 1954/1967, p. 35), to be congruent and unselfconscious. Equally, we have all developed ideas about how we ought to be in the world, and about how we believe we have to be as people in order to be accepted. We all come into this work limited to some degree by the sense we've made of other people's responses to us, and we all have areas of experience that we struggle to acknowledge or to articulate accurately: anger or boredom perhaps,

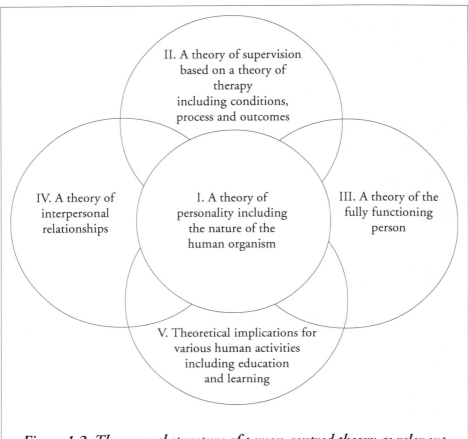

Figure 1.2. The general structure of person-centred theory as relevant to supervision (based on Rogers, 1959).

attraction or incompetence. One counsellor was brought up to do well academically, and experienced herself to be more acceptable when she was doing well at school. She struggled in supervision to expose what she thought of as her inadequacies and mistakes. Only when she felt safe enough to risk exposure was she free to explore those incidents and learn from them. Another practitioner was brought up always to be interested in what people were saying to him. To be bored was to risk being unacceptable. In the main, as an adult, he was genuinely interested in what his clients were saying. He was, however, so reluctant to acknowledge boredom that he didn't differentiate those times when he felt more engaged with his clients, from those when he felt less engaged, and so deprived himself and his clients of that aspect of his experience.

Personality theory is relevant in another way too. We suggest that the process of development that Rogers' personality theory describes, from unselfconscious organismic integrity through conditions of worth to a limiting self-concept, is a process that happens again and in miniature as we become therapists. In other words, if we have any therapeutic aptitude at all, we begin our training as naive, unselfconscious and probably quite effective therapists, untrained but not unskilled. We learn, through our training, that being a therapist requires of us that we be and do particular things in particular ways. We are subject to a new set of conditions of worth, out of which we develop a new strand to our self-concept, a strand that is particularly concerned with our practice as therapists. We might call this a professional self-concept, and say that it comprises our beliefs about what kind of practitioners we are, and about what we are and are not allowed to do and be as practitioners. Just as our self-concept limits our behaviour, so our professional self-concept will limit our behaviour as therapists.

This echoes Robinson's (1974) developmental model of competence: from unconscious incompetence, through conscious incompetence and conscious competence, to unconscious competence; and Stoltenberg and Delworth's (1987) model of supervisor development (see Chapter 3).

We're not saying that professional training courses intend to impose a new set of conditions of worth, although some clearly do. We *are* saying that each of us brings to our training an already formed and relatively stable self-concept, and a tendency to assimilate new experiences according to its shape and nature. If we have experienced our schooling as humiliating and punitive, then we will have made certain decisions and developed certain beliefs about ourselves: that we are untrustworthy, for instance, or stupid. We're likely to experience any subsequent training similarly and to feel confirmed in those decisions and beliefs. Just as a client in therapy reviews and dissolves his self-concept, so a practitioner in supervision may review and dissolve that aspect of his self-concept that concerns his being as a practitioner.

A THEORY OF SUPERVISION

In this part of the chapter we develop a theory of supervision growing out of Rogers' theory of therapy, taking as a template his structure of conditions, process and outcomes.

The necessary and sufficient conditions

Accepting the primacy and centrality of the organism's tendency to actualise, Rogers' theory of therapy develops by asking which conditions most fully support and enhance that tendency. On the basis of his experience with clients, and informed by necessarily limited and doggedly empirical research, Rogers hypothesises that there are six conditions which best serve the organism's tendency to actualise. He argues that these conditions are both necessary for therapeutic change to happen, and sufficient to initiate it. There is, we think, no substitute for reading Rogers' descriptions of these conditions (Rogers, 1959). However, given that we and others refer to them throughout this book, we will also describe each of the conditions ourselves shortly.

As we've said, Rogers developed this piece of theory out of his experience of therapeutic relationships. We think it's legitimate to ask whether the conditions he described are relevant also for supervision. Are they necessary, sufficient, or both for the growth of a supervisee in a supervisory relationship? In effect we're asking two questions here. We're asking of each condition individually whether it's necessary to the effective relationship between supervisor and supervisee. We're also asking whether the six conditions as a whole are sufficient for the task of supervision, or whether the particular demands of the supervisory relationship call for additional conditions.

The six conditions in the context of supervision

1. Psychological contact

Rogers (1959) defines psychological contact as 'the minimum essential of a relationship, when each makes a perceived or subceived difference in the experiential field of the other' (p. 207). This implies that supervisor and supervisee need to be minimally aware of each other's presence. On the face of it, it seems sensible to accept this as a necessary condition. However, implicit in Rogers' description is the idea that psychological contact depends upon an awareness that is both reciprocal and simultaneous: each is aware of the other. Most meetings between supervisor and supervisee meet this condition. That, though, is not the same as saying that it's a necessary condition, a condition without which supervision is impossible. Supervision by e-mail, for instance, which we think is possible, does not depend on psychological contact. Two people are in a relationship of sorts, and may be in a relationship that grew out of a more conventional relationship. However, when one reads the other's message the two people are not in the kind of contact Rogers describes as necessary for therapeutic change. Each is in contact with the other's message, maybe at some distance in time from when the message was sent, and maybe also at some considerable physical distance. When one is reading a message, the one who sent it may be in the shower, watching a movie or sleeping the sleep of the just. They need not be in contact with each other, and yet one can help the other explore his thoughts and feelings about his work. Supervision, therefore, is possible. E-mail is, of course, a recent development and a particular way of going about things. However, it seems not to require psychological contact, and this means that we cannot assert such contact as a necessary condition.

2. Client incongruence

Rogers (1959) argues that therapy is possible only when a client experiences some incongruence or discrepancy 'between the self as perceived, and the actual experience of the organism' (p. 203). Is the same true of supervision? Does a supervisee need to be incongruent in some way to benefit from supervision?

One of the immediately obvious differences between therapy and supervision is that most clients choose to be in therapy, while supervision, at least for counsellors and psychotherapists in the United Kingdom, is mandatory. Clients don't normally seek therapy unless they're aware, however dimly, of some incongruence. Counsellors and psychotherapists, however, need to see their supervisor whether they're aware of incongruence or not. This has implications which one of us (Worrall, 2001) has explored elsewhere.

We'd suggest that most of us are incongruent to some degree most of the time. If complete congruence, or integration, is a counsel of perfection, then incongruence is inevitable. There are, however, degrees of incongruence. Most of us get through much of our lives relatively smoothly, despite varying degrees of incongruence. Our incongruence has to reach a certain point, or we have to symbolise and articulate our experience of it to a certain degree, before we feel its effect. The same is true, we think, in supervision. Supervisees often are incongruent. They often experience a discrepancy between organismic experience and the demands of what we have called their professional self-concept. Whether this is a necessary condition, though, is open to question. Supervisees sometimes present with no apparent or marked incongruence. They might occasionally want simply to share the joys or the burdens of the work in one of the few places where they can legitimately do that.

3. Congruence

Rogers (1961/1967b) describes congruence as when 'the feelings the therapist is experiencing are available to him, available to his awareness, and he is able to live these feelings, be them, and able to communicate them if appropriate' (p. 61). He says that it is one of a therapist's necessary characteristics. Does a supervisor need to be similarly congruent? We think that a supervisee's use of supervision, and in particular his willingness to explore his work honestly and in depth, depends on his trust in his supervisor, and that this in turn depends on his perception of whether his supervisor is congruent or not. To the extent that our suggestion is accurate, it's important therefore that a supervisor be congruent, and be experienced as such. Returning to Rogers' description, we may say that congruence can embrace three elements: experience, awareness of that experience, and communication of that awareness. We take the view that it's the congruence between a supervisor's experience and awareness that matters primarily, rather than the congruence between her awareness and communication. That is to say that we see congruence as an internal affair, primarily to do with our own uncluttered awareness of whatever we're experiencing. Anything we say about our experience should, of course, reflect our experience accurately, but whether we speak of it, and what we say if we do speak of it, need not be primary concerns.

4. Unconditional Positive Regard

Rogers (1959) describes unconditional positive regard as 'one of the key constructs of the theory', and says that it involves valuing a person 'irrespective of the differential values which one might place on his specific behaviors' (p. 208). Writing about the therapeutic relationship, Bozarth (1996) argues that a client's perception of a therapist's unconditional positive regard is 'the fundamental change agent' (p. 50). We hold that the same is true in supervision, and that a supervisee's perception of his supervisor's unconditional acceptance is similarly central to the process of supervision and to the supervisory relationship. We recognise that the phrase 'unconditional positive regard' is, as Rogers (1957) says, 'an unfortunate one, since it sounds like an absolute, an all or nothing dispositional concept' (p. 98). Accepting, then, the impossibility of positive regard that is genuinely and completely unconditional, we hold nevertheless that a supervisee's willingness to explore those areas of his work about which he feels most unsure is in direct proportion to his perception of his supervisor's unconditional acceptance of him. In other words, the more unconditionally a supervisee feels accepted, the more likely he is to explore in supervision those areas of his work which he finds difficult, demanding or confusing. We modify our self-concept only when we symbolise without distortion experiences that are inconsistent with it. We risk that only when we feel unconditionally accepted, and therefore free from the threat of external evaluation. In the current context of increasing demands for counsellors and their supervisors to be assessed, qualified, accredited, registered, and accountable, this is an especially challenging condition to hold.

5. Empathic Understanding

'To sense the client's private world as if it were your own,' says Rogers (1959/1967), 'but without ever losing the "as if" quality—this is empathy, and this seems essential to therapy' (p. 284). In the context of therapy, Bozarth (1996) suggests that such empathic understanding 'is the vessel by which the therapist communicates unconditional positive regard in the most pure way' (p. 48). We think it's the same in supervision, and that a supervisor's accurate empathic understanding is crucial to a supervisee's continuing exploration of her work. We see at least two reasons for this. The first is that empathic understanding helps dissolve alienation. 'For the moment, at least,' says Rogers (1980), 'the recipient finds himself or herself a connected part of the human race' (p. 151). Although alienation seems a powerful word to use, a therapist's work necessarily leaves her relatively isolated. She works largely on her own, and ethical commitments require her to keep much of what she hears confidential. Supervision is perhaps the only space where she can legitimately talk in some detail about her experiences of her work. The second is that an accurate empathic understanding up to the edge of what's already symbolised encourages, or at least allows, exploration of what's not symbolised yet. In this sense, a supervisor's accurate and empathic understanding actively supports a supervisee's expanding congruence. We agree with Lambers (2000) that this is one of a supervisor's primary functions.

6. Perception
Rogers (1959) argues that therapy is finally effective only when a client perceives, 'at least to a minimal degree' (p. 213), the therapist's unconditional positive regard and empathic understanding. We think that it is necessary also for the process of supervision that a supervisee perceives her supervisor's unconditional positive regard and empathic understanding. We take the view that a supervisor's acceptance and understanding are effective not in and of themselves, but only insofar as a supervisee perceives them. In this sense, this condition is a hugely significant one and, paradoxically, one which we as supervisors can do little to guarantee. This reminds us of the need to stay humble about the limits of what we can achieve, and recognises the reality that a supervisee is in charge of her work, her experience of her work, and her experience of supervision.

To sum up, we argue that the first two conditions are not strictly necessary for the process of supervision; that the third, fourth and fifth conditions are necessary; and that the sixth condition is the one that ultimately determines the efficacy of the relationship and of the work. Working reflexively from supervision back to therapy, this line of argument may question the relative necessity of the individual conditions there also. For more on this, see Tudor and Worrall (in preparation, 2004).

Are these conditions sufficient?
We suspect that the conditions we've argued are necessary for supervision to begin are also sufficient. We think too that a supervisor can embody and offer certain other qualities which, while they may not be strictly necessary to the process of supervision, enhance it significantly.

Knowledge

We think it's helpful if a supervisor has a broad knowledge of person-centred history, theory and literature; and of more generic professional, clinical, ethical and relevant legal thinking. We're not saying that a supervisor needs to know more than a supervisee, and not sure how anyone would measure that anyway. We're saying simply that a supervisor probably needs to know about the approach, and about counselling matters more generically, and to feel confident in what she knows. Such knowledge and confidence may help a supervisor be a dependable resource to a counsellor seeking supervision.

The question of a supervisor's knowledge takes on a different significance in the discussion about supervision across disciplines or theoretical orientations. We wouldn't expect a person-centred therapist supervising a homeopath to know much about homeopathy. Nor would we expect any supervisor to have in-depth and up-to-date knowledge of theoretical orientations other than her own. And yet, as Hitchings argues in Chapter 12 of this volume, supervision across orientations is both possible and, in some circumstances, desirable. This supports our contention that knowledge is a desirable rather than a necessary condition for effective supervision.

Experience

A supervisor who's widely experienced in her own field, and who has considered her own experiences, is more likely to be open to hearing her supervisee's experiences without either over-reacting or under-reacting to them. This enhances the likelihood that her supervisee will experience herself as held and trusted, and the relationship as secure and safe. Again, we're not saying that a supervisor needs to be more experienced than her supervisee, although she often is. We're saying simply that she must be experienced in her own right.

Currency

By this we mean that a supervisor's knowledge and experience should be up to date. New dilemmas arise all the time, and the world within which clients, practitioners and supervisors live and work, changes continuously. (For more on this see Chapter 5.) A supervisor whose thinking about her work is bound by out-of-date assumptions is not as helpful as she could be. This thinking supports the idea that supervisors, whatever else they are, should also be currently practising in their field.

Generosity

By this we mean that a helpful supervisor is not only knowledgeable, experienced and up to date, but willing also to share what she knows and what she's experienced in the service of her supervisee's continuing growth and development as a practitioner.

We don't see these qualities as additional conditions but simply as specific manifestations of the four therapist conditions: contact, congruence, unconditional positive regard, and empathic understanding.

Process and outcomes

We start this discussion of the processes and outcomes of supervision with a clarification of terms. Rogers tried several times to describe the process of therapy. Before we attempt the same of supervision we want to highlight two ideas from that last sentence: the idea of *description* and the idea of *process*, both of which carry precise meanings that we want to clarify. When Rogers talks about *describing* a process he's using the word in its phenomenological sense, where it means to approach an event or a process with as few preconceptions as possible and to articulate simply what seems to be there rather than why or how it seems to be there or what it might mean. Writing about his struggle to capture the process of therapy, Rogers (1958/1967) says that he planned to take 'a naturalist's observational, descriptive approach' to things, and then 'draw forth those low-level inferences which seem most native to the material itself' (p. 128).

When Rogers talks about describing a *process* he's using the word to convey the sense of an organic, seamless and ongoing movement rather than a sequence of more or less discrete events.

A further clarification seems necessary. Outcomes are simply differentiated aspects of process. In other words, what we call outcomes are only apparent or convenient markers of process, particular pauses, points or plateaux to which we can give a name and by which we can distinguish the present from the past. Process is continuous, and it sometimes helps us to describe it and live with it if we can identify within it more or less clearly marked outcomes, which are always provisional. An outcome, therefore, is not an end-point. It's just a point in the process at which a change or a series of changes crystallises into something distinctive.

In this next part we draw on Rogers' process conception of psychotherapy (Rogers, 1958/1967, 1959), which he and others developed as a research instrument (see Rogers and Rablen, 1958; Rogers et al., 1967). We use it to describe the process of supervision with a particular focus on the person of the supervisee. Most writing and thinking about this part of Rogers' work focuses on the seven stages of the process he describes. We want to focus instead on the seven continua along which Rogers describes clients moving. He sums the process up by suggesting that a client in effective therapy will move from a position of 'fixity' and rigidity to one of 'fluidity': 'this seems to be the process that is set in motion when the individual experiences himself as being fully received' (Rogers, 1958/1967, p. 155). The idea of being 'received' is an important one, as Rogers elaborates:

> There is implied in this term the concept of being understood, empathically, and the concept of acceptance. It is also well to point out that it is the client's experience of this condition which makes it optimal, not merely the fact of its existence in the therapist. (p. 131)

This is consistent with what we've argued above: that a supervisee's experience of being empathically understood and unconditionally accepted is perhaps the single most important factor in effective supervision, and we retain in our thinking about supervision the idea that a supervisee will benefit to the degree that he experiences himself as fully received.

Assuming that a client feels received, Rogers identifies and describes seven elements to the ensuing process (see Box 1.1), each of which can be measured along a scale.

We think that some of Rogers' descriptions of process in psychotherapy map directly on to the process of supervision.

1. A loosening of feelings

Patterson (1968/2000) has argued that 'the greatest problem in counselor education . . . is getting counseling students to reduce the cognitive factor and attend to the affective aspects of the client, his problems, and the relationship' (p. 79). If this is so, then anything to enhance the loosening of a practitioner's feelings in relation to his clients will be helpful. We each have experience of working with therapists who have come to supervision describing themselves as 'stuck' in their work with particular clients. In many cases, resolution has come when the therapist has felt safe enough to acknowledge what he feels, about his client, about himself, about their relationship, or about the situation. It seems relatively easy for many therapists to think about their work with clients, and less easy for them to feel deeply. Our experience suggests that the act of acknowledging and articulating feelings in supervision is in itself helpful, whether or not a therapist ever then shares those feelings with his client.

2. A change in the manner of experiencing

Rogers (1958/1967) describes clients making friends with their experiencing, and finding that whatever they're experiencing becomes for them 'an inner referent' to which they can turn for 'increasingly accurate meanings' (p. 157). The same happens in supervision. Counsellors over time often develop a higher degree of self-acceptance, become more simply curious about what they're experiencing

FROM FIXITY . . .   . . . TO FLUIDITY

A loosening of *feelings*

From remote, unowned, not present . . . to a process of
experiencing a continually changing flow of feelings

A change in the manner of *experiencing*

From a fixity and remoteness of experiencing . . . to living
freely and acceptantly in a fluidity of experiencing

Congruence

From incongruence . . . to congruence

Communication

From unwillingness to communicate . . . to a willingness to
communicate a changing awareness of internal experiencing

Constructs

From construing experience in rigid ways . . . to developing
constructions which are modifiable by each new experience

The individual's relationship to their *problems*

From problems being unrecognised (and, therefore, the individual
having no desire to change) . . . to living problems subjectively,
and being responsible for their part in the development
of problems

The individual's manner of *relating*

From avoiding close relationships . . . to living openly and
freely in relation to others

**Box 1.1. The seven elements of process (developed from Rogers,
1958/1967)**

while they work, and can think about what it might signify. 'The facts are friendly', said Rogers (1961/1967a, p. 25), writing about scientific research into the therapy process. That sentence also sums up what we're talking about here. The facts of our own experience are friendly, and if we can stay open to the entirety of what we're experiencing we can know more clearly what we need to do next.

3. Congruence

Clients in effective therapy find it increasingly easy to acknowledge what they're experiencing ever more accurately, with increasingly subtle awareness of contradictions and inconsistencies, and ever closer to the moment of experiencing it. Again, this fits with our experience of supervision. As supervisees feel more free simply to acknowledge to themselves what they're experiencing in their work, they also experience it more fully, more clearly and more immediately. This allows them to be more fully present when they work, and more spontaneous.

4. Communication

So far, the processes Rogers has described have been largely internal to the person of the client, and have culminated in a fuller, more accurate and more immediate awareness of experience. He suggests that clients in effective therapy will also feel more willing to choose to speak truthfully out of the depths of their experience. We've indicated elsewhere our conviction that the accuracy of a practitioner's awareness of her experience is more important than what she might say about that to her clients. Nevertheless, we value her *willingness* to share her experience, and equate it with a willingness to be appropriately transparent in her relationships with her clients.

5. Constructs

Rogers (1958/1967) describes 'a loosening of the cognitive maps of experience' (p. 157) as one of the signs of effective therapy. By this he means that clients in therapy will come to hold what they think they know more lightly, and, rather than fit new experiences to old beliefs, will let new experiences alter what they believe about themselves and the world. We see this happening in supervision also. Practitioners will gradually let go of whatever theories they may hold about their clients in the abstract, or about depression or bereavement, and for as long as they are sitting with their clients will let their clients' experiences alter what they themselves believe. This is one of the specific ways in which practitioners are changed by their work they do with their clients.

6. The individual's relationship to their problems

Just as clients take gradually increasing levels of responsibility for their own part in the problems they experience in life, so supervisees look increasingly at their own contributions to their relationships with their clients, and especially to areas that are problematic. This is probably inevitable if supervision is effective, and helpful, in that the process of supervision can access only a practitioner's part in the relationship, and not a client's part in it. Person-centred counsellors, perhaps more than others, can feel hampered by the lack of taught techniques in the approach, and can tend to blame problems in their work on this paucity of techniques, or on their clients, or on their own inadequacies. A corollary of their increasing willingness to look at their own responsibility for the problems they experience in their relationships is their willingness to be discriminating about what they're responsible and not responsible for and to be humble about what they can reasonably expect of themselves and their clients.

7. The individual's manner of relating

Rogers (1958/1967) notices that clients who perceive close relationships as dangerous may over time come to live 'openly and freely in relation to the therapist and to others' (p. 158). We notice practitioners in supervision make similar movements in relation to both their clients and their supervisors. The movements are not of the same order, in that most practitioners don't find close professional relationships overly dangerous or actively threatening. But we notice practitioners come to relish close relationships more actively and to embrace more warmly the joys and challenges of such relationships.

In addition to the seven continua Rogers described, we notice two others that seem particularly relevant to the context of supervision.

The first of these concerns a practitioner's *locus of evaluation*, which Rogers (1959) describes as 'the source of evidence as to values' (p. 210). In other words, a person's locus of evaluation is the place to which he looks for assessments about what is good or bad, right or wrong, desirable or undesirable. It can be internal, in which case a person looks inside himself for answers to questions about the value of a particular item or course of action; or external, in which case he looks to others. We notice that effective supervision allows a significant shift in a practitioner's locus of evaluation from relatively external to relatively internal. We see practitioners typically move away from seeing their supervisor, training institute or professional body as the arbiter of good practice, and towards acknowledging and owning their own expertise and authority. This involves them recognising the validity of external opinion, and indeed seeking external opinion where appropriate, yet without compromising their own integrity or responsibility.

The second concerns a practitioner's *ability to make meaningful and appropriate relationships between philosophy, theory and practice*, a point we pick up at the end of Chapter 5. Beginning practitioners are often concerned to practise according to some newly-learned and cherished theory. Over time, however, many come to see that a theory, however good it is, and however useful, is simply a more or less adequate description and explanation of what seems to happen in practice. Writing about its relevance to practice, Rogers (1951) says that 'theory, to be profitable, must follow experience, not precede it' (p. 440). This move from theory-bound to experience-sensitive allows practitioners to take what's useful from whatever theories seem relevant to them, and also to stay open to times when what they experience as practitioners seems not to fit the theory as they understand it. If the facts are friendly, and if the facts don't fit the theory, the theory needs amending.

OTHER THEORETICAL CONSIDERATIONS

In this chapter we have elaborated two of the five areas of the general structure of person-centred theory as relevant to supervision (see Figure 1.2 above, p. 16). Other theories which we find relevant and useful include:

• A theory of the fully functioning person (Rogers, 1959), and his later descriptions of the 'emerging person' (Rogers, 1975), the 'political person' (Rogers, 1978), and the 'person of tomorrow' (Rogers, 1980). Rogers describes this person as being a sceptic, especially as regards traditional notions of science and technology, and as being anti-institutional. We view these as descriptive of and directly relevant to the development of the supervisor.

• A theory of interpersonal relationships (Rogers, 1959) which includes a description of the improving relationship. As a general theory of relationships, this is as relevant to the supervision relationship as to any other.

• Theories of education and learning (Rogers, 1959, 1969, 1983), the principles of which could usefully inform the education and training of supervisors.

REFERENCES

Angyal, A. (1941) *Foundations for a Science of Personality*. New York: Commonwealth Fund
Bozarth, J. D. (1996) A theoretical reconceptualization of the necessary and sufficient conditions for therapeutic personality change. *The Person-Centered Journal*, 3(1), 44–51
Cristofoli, G. (2002) Legal pitfalls in counselling and psychotherapy practice, and how to avoid them. In P. Jenkins (Ed) *Legal Issues in Counselling and Psychotherapy*

(pp. 24–33). London: Sage

Davenport, D. S. (1992) Ethical and legal problems with client-centered supervision. *Counselor Education and Supervision, 31*, 227–31

Goldstein, K. (1995) *The Organism.* (Original work published 1934)

Jenkins, P. (1997) *Counselling, Psychotherapy and the Law.* London: Sage

Lambers, E. (2000) Supervision in person-centred therapy: Facilitating congruence. In D. Mearns and B. Thorne *Person-Centred Therapy Today* (pp. 196–211). London: Sage

Patterson, C. H. (2000) Is cognition sufficient? In, *Understanding Psychotherapy: Fifty Years of Client-centred Theory and Practice.* Ross-on-Wye: PCCS Books (Original work published in 1968)

Robinson, W. L. (1974) Conscious competency: The mark of a competent instructor. *Personnel Journal, 53*, 538–9

Rogers, C. R. (1951) *Client-Centered Therapy.* London: Constable

Rogers, C. R. (1957) The necessary and sufficient conditions of therapeutic personality change. *Journal of Consulting Psychology, 21,* 95–103

Rogers, C. R. (1959) A theory of therapy, personality and interpersonal relationships, as developed in the client-centred framework. In S. Koch (Ed.) *Psychology: A Study of Science, Vol. 3: Formulation of the Person and the Social Context* (pp. 184–256). New York: McGraw-Hill

Rogers, C. R. (1967) Some hypotheses regarding the facilitation of personal growth. In C. R. Rogers *On Becoming a Person* (pp. 31–8). London: Constable. (Original work published 1954)

Rogers, C.R. (1967) A process conception of therapy. In C.R. Rogers *On Becoming a Person* (pp. 125–59). London: Constable. (Original work published 1958)

Rogers, C.R. (1967) Significant learning: In therapy and in education. In C.R. Rogers *On Becoming a Person* (pp. 279–96). London: Constable. (Original work published 1959)

Rogers, C. R. (1967a) 'This is me': The development of my professional thinking and personal philosophy. In C. R. Rogers *On Becoming a Person* (pp. 3–27). London: Constable. (Original work published 1961)

Rogers, C. R. (1967b) What we know about psychotherapy: Objectively and subjectively. In C. R. Rogers *On Becoming a Person* (pp. 59–69). London: Constable. (Original work published 1961)

Rogers, C. R. (1969) *Freedom to Learn.* Columbus, OH: Charles E. Merrill

Rogers, C. R. (1973) *Becoming Partners.* London: Constable

Rogers, C. R. (1975) The emerging person: A new revolution. In R. I. Evans *Carl Rogers: The Man and His Ideas* (pp. 147–75). New York: Dutton

Rogers, C. R. (1978) *Carl Rogers on Personal Power.* London: Constable

Rogers, C. R. (1980) *A Way of Being* . London: Constable

Rogers, C. R. (1983) *Freedom to Learn for the '80s.* Columbus, OH: Charles E. Merrill

Rogers, C. R., Gendlin, E. T., Kiesler, D. J. and Truax, C. B. (1967) (Eds.) *The Therapeutic Relationship and its Impact: A Study of Psychotherapy with Schizophrenics.* Madison, WI: University of Wisconsin Press

Rogers, C. R. and Rablen, R. A. (1958) *A Scale of Process in Psychotherapy.* Mimeographed manual. University of Wisconsin

Rogers, C. R. and Roethlisberger, F. J. (1988) Barriers and gateways to communication. *Harvard Business Review*, 19–25. (Original work published 1952)

Stoltenberg, C. D. and Delworth, U. (1987) *Supervising Counselors and Therapists*. San Francisco, CA: Jossey-Bass

Tudor, K. and Worrall, M. (2004, in preparation) *Clinical Philosophy: Advancing Theory in Person-Centred Therapy*. London: Brunner-Routledge

Wittgenstein, L. (1961) *Tractatus Logico-Philosophicus*. London: Routledge and Kegan Paul. (Original work published 1922)

Worrall, M. (2001) Supervision and empathic understanding. In S. Haugh and T. Merry (Eds.) *Empathy* (pp. 206–17). Ross-on-Wye: PCCS Books

CHAPTER TWO

ON BEING RECEIVED: A SUPERVISEE'S VIEW OF BEING SUPERVISED[1]

DEBORAH GIBSON

(OR THE ART OF TURNING JELLY INTO FRUIT LOAF)

SUPERVISORY RELATIONSHIPS

Let me begin by saying something of my general relationship with my current supervisor. I think of Joan[2] as my *main* supervisor. I have had other supervisors in the past; I have others now who supervise my own work as a supervisor and some aspects of my training work. Of course there is always an enormous amount of crossover and I find it impossible to separate my work neatly without feeling disjointed. As my main supervisor, I use Joan to bring my thinking about all of my work together. I use her as another perspective providing stereoscopic vision that helps me gain a full three-dimensional picture of all that I carry to supervision. She is also a sounding board, an advisor, teacher, mentor, colleague, therapist, and someone with whom I discuss relevant areas of my work and personal life.

---

1. I have necessarily picked out only a small number of my supervisory encounters for this chapter, and therefore mentioned only a few of my supervisors. I could have chosen many others to illustrate what it is to be received, so I offer my heartfelt thanks to all my supervisors over the years without whom I could not have written a word on this subject.
2. For the purposes of writing this chapter I have changed the names of all the supervisors to whom I refer.

Given that my professional life and my personal life affect one another equally, I take to her anything that I feel a need to take and even that for which I do not yet recognise a need. I share with her the myriad dimensions of all the professional and personal relationships I maintain: with clients, trainees, supervisees, colleagues, managers, and personal relationships with friends and family. I share, as well, the difficulties I experience and those things I find easy to accomplish, my failures and my successes.

Over the five years I have been with Joan, the quality of our relationship has been based on mutual respect for one another as people and as professionals. I chose her as a supervisor when I was looking for someone to supervise my training work in an organisation offering counselling to women survivors of childhood sexual abuse. I wanted someone who had an understanding of organisational issues, and I wanted too, to be able to bring aspects of my counselling, psychotherapy and art therapy in Primary Care and private practice. She has a working knowledge of industry, managerial skills, training skills, a background in co-counselling, and an eclectic approach to psychotherapy with some experience of the person-centred approach. I first encountered her on a person-centred training weekend on empathy and I appreciated the depth with which she spoke about her work and what felt to me her enthusiastic and considered contribution to the training group. I responded to her energy. I recognised a connection. I felt also that she had responded to mine, although not overtly. I would describe it more accurately as not-clashing.

I know, as I'm certain everyone does, when I 'click' with a person. I am less clear in the moment as to what exactly constitutes that positive connection. At our first meeting, as we discussed how we could work together as supervisor and supervisee, I began to feel a connection with her that was both gut reaction and intellectual processing. I feel a great deal in my belly and solar plexus: that area, rather than my heart, would seem to be the centre of my emotions. When all is well, I experience a visceral calm; when I am anxious or excited, an agitation and jumping; when I am afraid, a tension; and when sad, a dragging, sinking sensation and heaviness. This can translate into an external energy, and become accordingly a receptive or a protective field around me. At times I know that the other person sees this energy in my face, my posture or my movements; at other times I am sure they do not see with their eyes, rather that my energy appears to have a more subtle effect on them. They either tune in or they don't. When they do, they respond sometimes with awareness of my energy, and sometimes in a mode that is less consciously aware.

In the same way that the other person is processing their receiving of my energy, I am also experiencing, distilling and analysing something of their energy. It is a phenomenon of which I am acutely aware at initial meetings or at times of particular stress, or conversely at times of quiet, when I am apparently free of emotional or psychological weight. The symbolising of such organic experience occurs when I perceive a need to know what is happening within, around and to me. I must recognise and acknowledge the physical sensations in order to create a dynamic relationship between the cerebral and the visceral before that translates into something I can use with awareness in relation to the world, and, in terms of my work, in relation to my clients. The way I describe this may give the impression that it is a step-by-step mechanism; it is not. It is a more organic, organismic processing in the way Rogers describes in his propositions for a person-centred theory of personality and behaviour (Rogers, 1951). It is, however, purposeful, in that I wish to have my perceived needs satisfied. When I can communicate those needs and they are received, if not met, I experience satisfaction.

I say all of this as a prelude to a description of my first meeting with Joan. At our first meeting, I warmed to Joan's openness about her experiences and her limitations and to the fact that she was willing to experiment to a degree with the format of our sessions. I wanted to share some of our sessions with my work colleague, some I wanted to have individually for those aspects of my work that did not concern my colleague. We agreed that we would give it a go and if it didn't work out for any one of us, including my work colleague, we would make the necessary changes. At this juncture, we were both receiving one another, and—and this always helps the process of receiving—we were in agreement.

I have also had experience of not being in agreement with a supervisor, of not being received by her. It took some time before I could accept her perspective. I know she struggled to accept mine. My first main supervisor after graduating as an art therapist came from the psychodynamic tradition, which fitted the main orientation of my training. Felicity had a good and enduring reputation as a counsellor and supervisor and was interested in and willing to work with imagery. Although we moved in different social circles, I understood her politics to be close enough to mine, and she lived close enough for me to be able to travel easily on public transport. And she was a woman. (I discuss later in this chapter, in the section on trust, the significance of this aspect of my decision.) Not really knowing a great deal about supervision at the time, these criteria were the important ones. Looking back, they seem significant in a technical sense and somewhat superficial, too. This was borne out after 18 months of our relationship, in which I felt I had struggled to live up to her expectations of me.

I had some pretty strong ideas about my work and the boundaries I kept. I needed a certain amount of flexibility because I would frequently encounter clients socially, not necessarily closely, but in my community. Our main difference of opinion was that my supervisor thought that I should not put myself in the same circles as my clients at all, or at least that I should not take on any clients I was likely to see around. My need was to be able to talk about and explore how to work with these out-of-hours dynamics, and I felt criticised for even presenting these issues. Bearing in mind that at this point I was still quite inexperienced, and that I saw my supervisor as an elder practitioner due some respect, I forgot that I too was due some respect. It was only later that I began to recognise that I had not felt my views to be fully respected. Another dimension to this was having been used to supervision where the supervisor was responsible for making a placement report on me to the training course, and feeling it necessary to demonstrate to her what I already knew. All of these dynamics were at play in this relationship. I can see now how she would have found it very hard to hold a rookie therapist, who was defending herself to the hilt, when our therapeutic philosophies were so at odds. I recall it was my supervisor, not I, who first articulated the struggle in which we were engaged. I think she had referred to her own frustration, a countertransferential response, I think she would have named it, and from that identified my conflict. She pointed out that I seemed to be working in a way that did not entirely fit with her understanding of the psychodynamic model: had I considered that I might be more inclined to the humanistic therapies? This came as a blow to me, though not a surprise. I felt rejected and hurt. I had after all done my best to please my supervisor and have her be impressed with me.

Shortly after this, I took some time out of psychotherapeutic work in order to deal with personal issues arising in my life and my supervisor supported and held me in this. I began to realise that my supervisor was not just there to police my work. She really was on my side and wanted what was right for *me* in relation to my clients, and not only what was best for my clients. She *had* struggled to hold this in her work with me, to fully receive me in my inexperience. In my turn, I had not recognised the empathic dimension of her supervision of me, and had not admitted to my own awareness those times when she had been receiving me.

On my return to work I sought out a supervisor whom I thought would help me come to some decisions about my theoretical orientation. In Anna I found a supervisor with a working knowledge of psychodynamic theory who worked within the person-centred framework. I worked with her for the next four years, during which time I experienced what it is to be received in my wholeness as a person and a therapist, to see and be seen. During these four years I completed a person-centred counselling diploma, progressively consolidating the approach into the whole range of my work and life.

When I am seen, when I know that I am heard and I feel understood, I enter a space which French philosopher Gaston Bachelard (1958/64), looking at the process of creativity in the work of poets, describes as an 'intimate immensity'. To this I might add my own impression of an 'infinite intensity'. I am intensely aware of both my own personal edge and boundary, and also, paradoxically, that I have no edge. Through an open, accepting relationship with a supervisor by whom I feel received, I am connected to a world or universe more vast than my own immediate human frame, or than otherwise defined by that one relationship. It is but a momentary thing. Bachelard suggests that this state is most usually attained and sustained through daydream, a peculiarly individual, singular activity. That is my experience. However, I also refer to those times when, in being most specific about myself, when I have shared something that is particularly individual to me, I have been most deeply understood by others, because it touches both the specific and the universal in them. I would say, and am saying, that I achieve this state in that moment of being seen and received in an environment where I am held and with another, or others, whom I trust and who trust me.

TRUST

Trust is of profound importance to me. It matters to me that I trust my supervisor implicitly. If I feel judged by her, I feel myself tensing inside, not just physically, I mean, but emotionally and psychologically too. I am far less likely to tell her about the time I know I was clumsy with a client, or when I may have chosen to take a calculated risk with boundaries, for instance, or indeed when my courage failed in taking just such a risk. It is these very things I want, and need, to be able to discuss openly with a supervisor, so that I can examine what I have done, how I have been, and to process retrospectively my decision and the subsequent impact on both my client and myself, as person and therapist. If I think I have done something wrong, and I can trust my supervisor to hold me in my certainties and confusions without judging me, if she can offer me unconditional positive regard, I can readily and freely do my best to deal with the consequences.

In order for me to feel that trust, I need my supervisor to demonstrate her trust in me. I need her to believe in my ability to actualise, and to believe also that I know what I need to do, even when it is clear to me that I haven't a clue what I feel. I want to know that we both believe in me, that I will know what I feel sooner or later, and that until I do, we can both be with my not-knowing, as I hope to be with clients and supervisees in their not-knowing.

I realise that in using the feminine pronoun to describe my supervisors, I may give the impression that I use it for supervisors collectively. I do not intend to do so. All of my supervisors have been women. This has been, in part, a definite choice for me: a matter of trust. I have thought that, generally, I know women better than I do men. It has been easier to understand and agree with women, to create together more readily the conditions for receiving one another. My previous encounters with men and boys had been generally difficult, and rarely neutral, experiences. Men were stern and distant grown-ups, mostly negative authority figures. Others, although good fun and high in energy, I found lacking in empathy and therefore only to be associated with when I felt certain of myself and confident in my own energy; to be trusted only for the more superficial things in life. Though early on I was disabused of this impression when I encountered men in training groups who were fully themselves in their masculinity and with whom I felt comfortable in entirely unexpected ways. This was, perhaps, because I was able to receive the uniqueness of each of them rather than see them as a homogenous group. Now more trusting of men, more balanced in my awareness and more trusting of my self, I am keen to push my growing edge. I am not unwilling now to work with a man as a supervisor, although, apart from Steve, with whom I work in a small peer supervision group from our days as person-centred trainees, it is difficult to find one.

In thinking about this chapter, about what it is to be supervised, and by whom, I recognise that as I mature into an experienced practitioner, I am increasingly self-referencing. It occurs to me, however, that if I was wholly self-referencing, I would not need supervision. I am self-referencing in my knowing what I feel more often than I used to. I realise sooner rather than later the source of a sensation, emotion, thought or action. I *own* what I feel more readily, rather than blame someone else. I know, too, that I need supervision to help me maintain this ability, like exercising a muscle, to keep a path clear to my internal locus of evaluation.

SUPERVISION AND PSYCHOTHERAPY

In supervision I feel very grown up in a way that I do not in therapy. I think it has to do with being more consciously aware of my own internal locus of evaluation. I feel more responsible for myself in a supervision session than perhaps I would do in therapy. Even as I write this, I am not wholly convinced of the truth of it. Perhaps in the early days of being in supervision and being in therapy, the distinction may have been more marked. I could conceivably have pointed to my therapist as being like an all-embracing parent, benevolent and kind and hugely scary. I had all the power to displease or to placate her. I gave her all the power to mould me into a fully-functioning human being.

I could possibly have painted a picture of my supervisor as well-meaning, although with the potential to turn into an angry parent, disappointed in her child. Hugely scary. I had the power to prove to her that I knew what I was doing. I gave her the power to create in me a tip-top counsellor. So maybe there was little difference then and, although I am more sophisticated in the therapeutic milieu, and I have taken back much of my responsibility for myself in both relationships, there is little difference now between therapy and supervision. Today I describe my therapist as warm, caring, respectful and willing to understand me, and my supervisor's qualities look pretty much the same. Experientially, in the moment, I think there is little difference.

What does differentiate one from the other for me lies in their purpose and application. In my personal therapy, clients are more incidental to my world, in which I am central to my purpose. *I* am the point of therapy. In supervision, I am more acutely aware of the clients with whom I work; they are central to my reason for seeking supervisory help. The point of supervision is its professional focus, that I develop clarity in my own personal processes in order to be available to relate to my clients' worlds.

I want now to describe a particular experience.

I arrive for supervision carrying a melting jelly, runny, sticky. I try my best to hold it together. When I leave my supervisor's house, I have a warm, moist fruit loaf, rich, weighty and solid. No—I don't have an inequitable bartering arrangement with my supervisor! The image of the fruit loaf arises from talking to a group of colleagues about a recent supervision session, and seeing how supervision can be, among many other things, a recipe for, and a process of, firming up thoughts, feelings, ideas and a fragile sense of oneself and one's professional identity.

There are many layers of experience and meaning to the supervisory exchange described below, some of them apparently contradictory. I hope to get hold of some of its facets and depths enough to share them, and ground them coherently in person-centred philosophy and practice. I cannot hope to address all of them. I offer, too, some insights and learning from my work with imagery, to include my perspective as an art therapist. I hope to communicate some of my experience of what it is to be received, and what it is to *not* be received, in supervision.

My day has been a demanding one, indeed I have experienced the whole week as deeply challenging and I am almost in tears on my supervisor's doorstep. I feel like jelly. My working environment is deteriorating and I have no control over it. I could soon be out of a job. Each of the clients with whom I work seems in deep crisis and I feel increasingly challenged to hold each of them in a situation that isn't holding or nurturing me. As I tell my woes to my supervisor, Joan, I feel both sad and angry: sad about a colleague who has recently resigned, for clients and for the organisation I work in, whose future funding is so uncertain that closure looks likely; and angry that I am in this situation at all. I feel overwhelmed and about to go under. Joan sees my distress, and tells me I look wobbly. I am shaking and tearful. She points out that I have been in a stressful situation for some months (indeed, my father has been seriously ill and my partner's mother has recently died). Yes, I agree, I *am stressed*. Yes, you are she agrees *and* you have been in a stressful situation. Gradually as this dialogue goes back and forth, neither of us saying anything much different, it gradually dawns on me that what Joan is saying *is* different. *I* mean that I should not feel stressed, that I should be coping; I am giving myself a hard time for not coping. *She* is saying that she sees what I have shown her, and have been showing her for many months now, that I have more at present to cope with than I am consciously acknowledging, and that I have been coping magnificently with several heavy loads. She adds from her own agenda: perhaps isn't this the one final straw? Finally—Aha! Yes, absolutely! Insight and relief. The pressure drops away. Immediately I feel seen and validated and, as with most flashes of insight, I realise that I already know this, and haven't allowed myself to know that I knew for fear of feeling even more overwhelmed. I didn't dare to see myself as someone who might not be able to cope. We go on to discuss ways of dealing with the situation, but really it is not necessary for me to do so. I have already seen and named within me, in that moment of total recognition, what I need to do and how I want to be with it all. I know I have been seen, heard and understood. I can move on again.

Presenting fluidity as a desirable consequence, Rogers (1961) describes psychotherapy as a *process* on a continuum from a position of *stasis* or *fixity*, rigidity or inflexibility, to a place of greater 'changingness', *fluidity*, or flowing, where one's relationship with oneself, others and the world is 'in motion'. He posits this model as affecting *feelings*, ways of *experiencing*, states of *congruence* or otherwise, and internal and external *communication* and *relating*, including our willingness to *avoid* situations or *problems* or to move through life with open hearts and minds. The metaphor of processing runny jelly into a firm chunk of fruit loaf may seem to be at odds with this concept. However, I think my *experience* makes it otherwise.

Through this encounter, I was able to symbolise my felt experience. I had already found an image for the sensations, that of runny jelly. My supervisor held my image without chasing it down for a meaning, holding her own meaning, willing to share mine if and when it arrived. She allowed me to know fully the impossibility and in that, paradoxically, the possibilities of my situation, allowing me to find my own symbolic and actual transformation. Rogers puts forward the notion of the process of symbolisation in his Theory of Personality and Behaviour (1951, pp. 481 ff.). He refers to areas of consciously perceived experience within the whole of the organismic experience, the greater portion of which remains as background rather than the focus of conscious attention. As the organism perceives a need or a desire to recognise the unformed experience, it is symbolised; that is, the organism creates for it named feelings, images or words. To quote Rogers from an earlier chapter of the same book:

> The human being deals with much of his [*sic*] experience by means of the symbols attached to it. These symbols enable him to manipulate elements of his experience in relation to one another, to project himself into new situations, to make many predictions about his phenomenal world. In therapy one of the changes which occurs is that faulty and generalized symbols are replaced by more adequate and accurate and differentiated symbols. (Rogers, 1951, pp. 144–5)

Although Rogers is writing about therapy, I would say that the same process of finding increasingly adequate symbols can and does happen in supervision.

The way I see it, this process of symbol formation is for me a movement from utter chaos in which I can make no conscious sense, to increasingly recognisable, useable characteristics that are my unique properties as an individual. It is a deeply creative process, that I see happening anywhere on the organism's continuum of bringing experience to awareness, and returning material to the morass should the full awareness of experience carry too great a perceived risk, of pain for instance, or fear, or further confusion perhaps. The formation of symbols is occurring at every level of our organismic experiencing. Once the symbol is communicable, then there is potential for a shared recognition and understanding of the experience as a whole, especially within a therapeutic relationship where the therapist, or, in my case, supervisor, is willing and able to look at the world through my eyes. In the process of transforming jelly to fruit loaf, I found a series of symbols, many seemingly unrelated, and formulated and reformulated them until they made quite specific sense in relation to my self and my work.

Arising from his phenomenological observation of the process of therapeutic change, Rogers saw his theory of therapeutic change as representing what he saw and reasoned to be of value to a great many people. He recognised that others, individually or culturally, may choose their own solidity or stability, preferring to avoid any relationships that offer potential for change (Rogers, 1961, p. 155). I was seeking solidity, something substantial, reliable and known. And although my imagery presents a fluid mess becoming solid, importantly, the process represents an *internal* shift for me from a fixed state of panic to a more subtle, flowing one. I could actually make use of the substantial knowledge I carry within me that I hadn't been able to access because I felt, and was, stuck.

Within the six conditions that Rogers (1959) puts forward as necessary and sufficient for therapeutic change to occur, it is essential that the client 'is in a state of incongruence . . . being vulnerable and anxious'. That was me that day! The therapist, says Rogers, needs to be 'congruent in the relationship'. My supervisor demonstrated her congruence within our relationship by being acutely aware that I had not heard her. She had felt the quality of our relationship change and wanted to reconnect with me. I had simply felt confounded that she kept repeating herself: echoes of her assertiveness and co-counselling background. Joan replied that she had been puzzled about the shift in our contact, not especially aware of any other agenda, and had recognised that I had not received her. Her original intention having been to communicate her awareness of my long-held distress, her purpose became then to re-establish our more usual quality of psychological contact, the first of Rogers' conditions for change, requiring 'that two persons are in contact' (Rogers, 1959, p. 213), or '*psychological* contact' (Rogers, 1957, p. 96).

The idea of contact, or psychological contact, implies a mutual activity, in which both parties are engaged, if not to the same degree, at least *together*. I cannot separate the idea of being received, that is, that a client (or supervisee) experiences the therapist's (or supervisor's) 'empathic understanding of the client's internal frame of reference' (Rogers, 1959, p. 213), from that of being able to receive. The title of this chapter refers, in part, to the sixth of Rogers' hypothesised conditions for therapeutic personality change to occur: that of being received. To quote: 'that the client perceives at least to a minimal degree, conditions 4 and 5, the unconditional positive regard of the therapist for him [sic], and the empathic understanding of the therapist' (ibid., p. 215). In other words, that the client or supervisee can receive the communications of the therapist or supervisor. It would seem to be obvious that in situations other than the therapeutic relationship, the ability to receive another person's communication of self and feelings is a fundamental asset to social intercourse. However, it is within the therapeutic relationship that the ability to receive and be received becomes key. This final condition may well be argued, as indeed Tudor suggests (2000), to be the most fundamental of all the conditions, without which the otherwise 'core' conditions of therapist's congruence, unconditional positive regard and empathy are powerless to help, rendered useless.

From where I sit, as a client, a therapist, a supervisee, a supervisor, as a person in each of these situations, to *not* be received feels like a block, a wall. I feel obstructed, impeded. It is fertile ground in which many of my fantasies about the other person can take root and grow. It can be a lonely, painful place. It can also give me time to regroup my internal resources so that I can feel protected when I am under perceived threat.

To return to my original scenario, as my supervisor spoke of her sense of being out of contact, I knew that I had frozen around our connection, trying to preserve it, knowing that it had changed. I was holding our relationship tight against me rather than, as is usual between us, feeling relaxed, and open, anticipating the buzz of energy that frequently arises out of our encounters. In being in touch with my own feelings about my predicament, I was fixed in the viscous mess of it all, unable to see any way out of it and increasingly unwilling to change my situation because it appeared to be unchangeable. At this juncture, I was experiencing any challenge to my internal state, that is my supervisor's empathy, however well-intentioned, as threatening to my perceptions and beliefs about the circumstances and myself. Rogers (1951, pp. 481ff.) propounds a phenomenological perspective of personal congruence with the self and the world. I was behaving with perfect congruence in relation to the situation I perceived to be irresolvable in that moment. As well as understanding, my supervisor offered me an alternative perspective to add to my phenomenological experiencing and it was that, rather than her empathy, that I was able, eventually, to make use of and to modify my perception and thus my congruent responses. Discussing again the work of poets, Bachelard (1958/64. p. 59) suggests that:

> When two strange images meet . . . they apparently strengthen each other. In fact, this convergence of two exceptional images furnishes as it were a countercheck for phenomenological analysis. The image loses its gratuitousness. The free play of the imagination ceases to be a form of anarchy.

I think this insight can be easily transposed to the work of therapist and supervisor. There is a phenomenological and a creative process, and both are necessary to effective transformation. It is, however, difficult and exacting work allowing myself to receive and to be received to the degree offered by my supervisor when she is not only open to my experience, but grounded also in her own. I frequently carry this refreshed awareness away with me from supervision back to my work with clients and supervisees, for whom the quality of contact and empathic understanding presents a threat and is, at times, unbearable.

My supervisor knows when I do not receive her; equally, I know when she is not receiving me. I know because what I say seems to elicit a response that does not fit, does not feel right, does not settle. When I catch myself feeling puzzled, uncertain, irritated, or I experience a desire to tune her out of the relationship, I ask myself whether she has understood my intention. What is *her* intention? Is she trying to teach me something I don't want to learn? Sometimes I simply ignore her intention. Sometimes I acknowledge aloud the dissonance. Sometimes I go with her intention, either as a conscious choice on my part, because I think that perhaps she has something I really might want to learn; or sometimes because I have not consciously recognised that she has not received me. On those occasions when I accord with my supervisor's intention and I do acquire new knowledge, it takes time to talk through the ramifications of my learning. Whereas when I arrive at understanding myself, I seem to arrive there without effort, regardless of any exertion on my part before the moment of insight. When I learn my own lessons, I need no other input.

This experience has served to show that where there is runny jelly there is chaos and so also there is infinite potential for creative movement and transformation within me. The process of achieving concrete change for me requires time and space in which to reflect, in all the senses of this word. This necessarily involves another who will receive my reflection. Having concentrated on the relationship between supervisor and supervisee I have focused too on the significance of being received, that is, knowing that I have been accepted and understood. I have recognised, moreover, the importance of receiving my supervisor, which is a necessary aspect of the process enabling me to firm up my fragmented feelings into a useful whole. Fruit loaf is a thing to be shared.

REFERENCES

Bachelard, G. (1964) *La poétique de L'espace* [The Poetics of Space] (M. Jolas, Trans.).Boston, MA: Orion Press. (Original work published 1958)

Rogers, C.R. (1951) *Client-Centered Therapy*. London: Constable

Rogers, C.R. (1957) The necessary and sufficient conditions of therapeutic personality change. *Journal of Consulting Psychology, 21*, 95–103

Rogers, C.R. (1959) A theory of therapy, personality and interpersonal relationships, as developed in the client-centered framework. In S. Koch (Ed.), *Psychology: A Study of a Science, Vol. 3: Formulations of the Person and the Social Context* (pp. 184–256). New York: McGraw-Hill

Rogers, C.R. (1961) *On Becoming a Person*. London: Constable

Tudor, K. (2000) The case of the lost conditions. *Counselling, 11* (1), 33–7

CHAPTER THREE

PERSON-CENTRED PERSPECTIVES ON SUPERVISION

KEITH TUDOR AND MIKE WORRALL

In Chapter 1 we laid the groundwork for a person-centred theory of supervision. In this and the next chapter we apply this perspective to consideration of 'generic' aspects of supervision referred to in the Introduction (function, role, process, etc.) as developed by a number of authors. These are presented essentially in chronological order, a reading which gives a sense of the historical development of ideas and concerns in the field of supervision, beginning, appropriately enough, with different definitions of supervision itself. We consider two process models of supervision separately (in Chapter 4) as they are both sufficiently substantial and influential to warrant separate consideration.

DEFINITIONS OF SUPERVISION

There are many definitions of supervision, each of which carries a particular perspective or emphasis and certain underlying assumptions. Here we review some of them, also in chronological order.

• Supervision is 'a teaching process in which a more experienced practitioner, the supervisor, observes the work of the less experienced participant, the supervisee, with the aim of helping the supervisee acquire certain essential therapeutic skills through better understanding of the dynamics involved in mental illness and through resolution of personality factors that block performance of effective psychotherapy' (Wolberg, 1954).

Although the requirement for supervision as a part of the psychoanalytic training process dates back to 1925, this is the oldest definition we have come across in psychotherapeutic literature. It clearly equates supervision with teaching and advocates this by means of direct observation, presumably through a one-way mirror. Live observation by a supervisor of a therapist working with a client would generally be considered today to raise too many issues (of contracting, confidentiality, ethics and transferential attitudes, to name but a few) to make this viable or desirable. Moreover, the development of technology, from the phonograph to the minidisk, has given the supervisor increased access to the verbal interactions of the therapeutic encounter. Direct observation of therapists in training working with other trainees is, however, common and forms a large part of the practice component on training courses, certainly in counselling and psychotherapy. Other definitions which directly link supervision with training include Pepinsky and Patton (1971), Lambert (1980) and Efstation (1987). This definition views the 'resolution of personality factors' in the supervisee as a proper subject of and, indeed, a crucial function of supervision. In the light of debates about the differences between supervision, training and personal therapy, this would generally be viewed today as one of the functions of therapy. However, given its emphasis on trusting the supervisee's tendency to actualise through process and presentation, this perspective is broadly compatible with a person-centred approach to supervision.

• 'Our supervisory paradigm consists of . . . goals, processes, and relationships which interlock to define supervision and differentiate it from other interpersonal endeavours. The complementary goals of supervision—to learn to be therapeutic with clients and alternatively to assist a therapist in training to be therapeutic— are complex . . . The way in which the supervisor interacts with the therapist and assists him to cope with the conflict generated in each of those relationships [therapist-client, therapist-supervisor] as those conflicts unfold, merge, and interact defines the supervisory process' (Mueller and Kell, 1972, pp. 15–16).

This definition, in some ways ahead of its time, acknowledges both the complexity of supervision, especially of the training therapist, as well as the potential conflicts inherent in the supervisory process. Most significantly, it defines the supervisory process as one which is measured by the interactions of the two parties and the resolution of conflicts, again processes compatible with the person-centred approach.

• 'Supervision is a quintessential interpersonal interaction with the general goal that one person, the supervisor, meets with another, the supervisee, in an effort to make the latter more effective in helping people' (Hess, 1980, p. 25).

As a generic definition this describes the roles in and purpose of supervision, although from a person-centred perspective the notion of the supervisor 'making' a supervisee anything is an anathema. Betraying a behavioural bent, earlier in the same chapter Hess (1980) talks about supervision 'modifying the behaviour of the supervisee' (p. 16).

• '. . . the supervisory field . . . as a relationship between two people one of whom has the purpose of using it to improve his work with someone in his life . . . and the other of whom has the purpose of helping him to do so . . . I therefore see myself as an educator; that is, I am using myself in a relationship with my supervisee for the purpose of facilitating their efforts to live their lives more successfully. In other words, I am being an educator with the purpose of helping someone else be an educator' (Bromberg, 1982, pp. 94–5).

This is the first definition which refers to the supervisory relationship as a 'field', echoing Lewin's (1952) field theory which first focused attention on the total psychological environment and the dynamic interactions between different elements of the field such as the interplay between organism and environment. Bromberg's view of being an educator is different from the previous definitions concerning the supervisor as trainer, and hints at this as a process which is paralleled by the supervisee as practitioner/educator. It also widens the view of supervision to encompass the successful living of the supervisee, a perspective which is also compatible with an approach centred on the whole person of the practitioner.

• Supervision is 'an intensive, interpersonally-focused, one-to-one relationship in which one person is designated to facilitate the development of therapeutic competence in the other person' (Loganbill, Hardy and Delworth, 1982).

This classic definition articulates and emphasises the qualities (intensive), focus (interpersonal) and form (one-to-one) of the supervisory *relationship*; the *role* of the supervisor (facilitation); and the shared *task* (the development of a supervisee's therapeutic competence). In an article published a year earlier, Rattigan (1981) elaborated the different forms of supervision: individual, group and peer group.

• 'Supervision is regarded as an interpersonally based process where one experienced person (the supervisor) assists a less experienced person (supervisee) develop the personal integration of a counselling style and the acquisition of professional values, [and] attitudes concerning the values of the profession; and in undertaking this the supervisor bears more than equal responsibility for outcomes including minimising the danger of harm to clients' (Urbano, 1984).

This definition highlights both that supervision is a process and that it is interpersonal. Like other definitions, it also assumes a seniority on the part of the supervisor and implies a certain training function, neither of which allows of an equality of experience between supervisor and supervisee. The second part of the definition carries a number of assumptions and implications:

i. That the supervisor acts as a conduit for the supervisee's integration, especially in relation to the particular profession concerned;
ii. That the supervisor is (more) responsible for the supervisee's practice in terms of outcomes (although the greater degree of responsibility is not defined); and
iii. That having such greater responsibility minimises the danger of the practitioner causing harm to clients.

We take issue with these assumptions about the responsibilities of the supervisor in Chapter 5.

• 'The clinical supervisor has been described as an agent of social influence whose goal is to enhance the trainee's therapeutic competence within the context of an intensive interpersonal relationship' (Ward et al., 1985, p. 111).

This sense of influence compares (favourably in our view) with a number of definitions that talk in terms of bringing about behaviour change in the supervisee (see Pepinsky and Patton, 1971; Hess, 1980; Lambert, 1980).

• Supervision 'denotes a role, not a person. The supervisor's job is to show that the questions the worker has brought can be thought about, and maybe to show ways in which they can be thought about. Supervision is a process whereby one person enables another to think better' (Christian and Kitto, 1987).

This definition focuses clearly on the role of supervision as distinct from the person of the supervisor. This, in some ways, is a great leveller: it's a job specification, not a person specification and, as such, challenges notions of seniority and even experience. Secondly, this definition is the first to be explicit about the nature of reflective practice in supervision. The supervisor's role is not to answer the practitioner's questions but rather to help her think about them and to stimulate further thought and reflection. This is entirely congruent with the notion of facilitation within the person-centred approach.

• 'Counselling supervision/consultative support refers to a formal arrangement which enables counsellors to discuss their work regularly with one or more people who have an understanding of counselling and counselling supervision/ consultative support. Its purpose is to ensure the efficacy of the counsellor-client relationship. It is a confidential relationship' (British Association for Counselling, 1988, B.3.2).

The form and style of this definition echoes its content: formal, arranged and precise, with clear roles and purpose.

• 'Supervision ... [is] a cooperative, facilitating process with a twofold aim. The first is to enable the student or worker "being supervised" to develop as an effective working person. The second, related, aim is to offer a forum in which the worker renders an account of herself in order to assure herself, and anyone who may be requiring her to be accountable, that she is practising responsibly' (Proctor, 1988).

This definition echoes some others in that it refers to supervision as a process (see Urbano, 1984) which is cooperative or interpersonal (see Loganbill, Hardy and Delworth, 1982; Urbano, 1984) and facilitative (implicit in Christian and Kitto, 1987). Here the supervisee is seen as a whole working person, and their overall effectiveness the business of and for supervision. Finally, accountability is put on the map but, significantly, only in an 'if . . . , then . . . ' format, one which Rogers used a lot in his formulations of theory. This is significant in that it highlights the consensual and autonomous nature of accountability and responsibility, that is, that we opt in to taking responsibility rather than having it thrust upon us or assumed by another.

• 'Supervision . . . provides a container that holds the helping relationship within the "therapeutic triad"' (Hawkins and Shohet, 1989, p. 3).

Drawing explicitly on Winnicott's concept of the 'nursing triad', comprising baby, mother and father/partner or other supportive adult, Hawkins and Shohet emphasise the safe setting of the supervisory relationship which contains the therapeutic or helping relationship between practitioner and client, and in which, analogously, the supportive adult (supervisor) 'holds' the practitioner and, specifically, provides a container for him to express, survive and reflect upon issues, dilemmas, difficulties and emotional disturbance. Whilst we find the concept of a contained and containing supervisory environment useful, we avoid developmental analogies or metaphors which infantalise the client or the supervisee.

• 'Clinical supervision is . . . a formal process of professional support and learning which enables individual practitioners to develop knowledge and competence, assume responsibility for their own practice and enhance consumer protection and the safety of care . . . It is central to the process of learning and to the expansion of the scope of practice and should be seen as a means of encouraging self-assessment and analytical and reflective skills' (National Health Service Management Executive, 1993).

This definition is strong on self-development and learning. In contrast to Urbano (1994), it is strong on the practitioner's self-responsibility, and is expansive and encouraging. It clearly locates supervision in the context of its concern, that is, care, health and safety within the National Health Service. It also refers to *clinical* supervision, presumably to distinguish this activity from managerial supervision.

In our view, every supervisor—and supervisee—has a definition of supervision, however conscious, explicit or implicit, well or poorly articulated. We advocate that one of the early tasks of both parties in supervision, and probably best before agreeing to work together, is to make explicit their definitions, their implications, and to explore whether they are compatible. Such contact, which may be thought of as pre-supervision, sets the philosophical ground of mutuality, respect and understanding.

FUNCTIONS OF SUPERVISION

A view of what the functions of supervision are follows from an agreed or any given definition. The most common view of the functions of supervision is that it is 'educative, supportive and managerial' (Kadushin, 1976), a tripartite division popularised by Proctor (1988) as 'formative, restorative and normative'.

The formative or educative function of supervision is primarily concerned with developing skills and the understanding and ability of the supervisee by reflection on and understanding of the client's issues. Within this function of supervision, the supervisor may help the supervisee to understand the client better; to become aware of their own responses and reactions to the client; to look at their interventions, different options and their own effectiveness; and to explore other ways of working in this and similar client situations. This function is entirely compatible with the person-centred approach and indeed is informed by the person-centred focus on the facilitation of learning.

The restorative or supportive function of supervision is generally concerned with the anxiety, distress, pain and even fragmentation of the supervisee in response to their clients' situations and feelings, which may be quite evocative or provocative for the practitioner. In this regard the supervisor may help the practitioner to understand their own responses better by distinguishing between those responses which are empathic and those which are reactive, perhaps the result of some restimulation of their own issues or pain. This is commonly viewed as a necessary function of supervision, as all effective workers will be affected by their clients. Supervisees who do not get this kind of support from their supervision, or indeed do not have supervision, may become either overidentified with or defended against their clients, dynamics which often lead to stress, crisis and 'burnout'. Again this function is highly compatible with the person-centred approach with its emphasis on self-development and congruence (see Lambers, 2000).

Most supervisors take some or much responsibility to ensure that a supervisee's practice is appropriate, professional and ethical in the context of their work, whether this is in private practice or in an organisation or agency. Such responsibilities both derive from and form the normative or 'managerial' function of supervision. Further areas of focus within this function of supervision may include: an overview of a supervisee's 'caseload' or workload, including the balance of their work and the amount of supervision they are receiving; the supervisee's time management; their relationships with other workers and agencies; their knowledge of policy development and implementation; their training and development needs. (Depending on the attitude of the supervisor, their appreciation of training and development needs could also be experienced by the supervisee as part of the formative function of supervision.) As the person-centred approach values mutuality and self-responsibility, the issue of who's responsible for what is a point of discussion rather than assumption or imposition. This is particularly relevant in terms of the extent to which the supervisor is or is viewed as 'clinically responsible' for the supervisee's work. Generally the person-centred practitioner is viewed as responsible for her own work and, in this context, the person-centred supervisor is a co-interpreter of external, normative values, frameworks and codes, which, of course, apply equally to the supervisor (see over, Figures 3.1 and 3.2).

We place 'managerial' in inverted commas as it is rare, and in our view, undesirable, that a clinical supervisor is also the line manager of the practitioner. This is, in part, because it is hard for a line manager, with accountability and ultimately with authority for hiring and firing, to offer genuinely and unconditionally much of the formative or restorative functions to their supervisee/ worker, and for that supervisee to receive them.

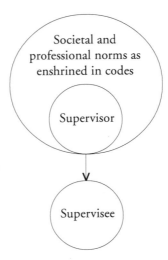

Figure 3.1. Supervisor holds normative/ 'managerial' function

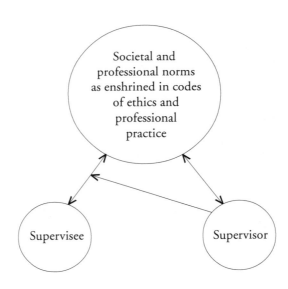

Figure 3.2. Supervisor facilities supervisees understanding of and relationship to norms

The *Roles* of Supervisor and Supervisee

In an early paper on supervision Zalcman and Cornell (1983) identify the activities and focus of attention (as well as functional modes) for *both* supervisor and supervisee/therapist. This is particularly useful in challenging unilateral models of supervision which tend to assume that there is only one activity (supervision) and focus of attention (the supervisee) in the supervisory process and that sole responsibility for such activity and focus rests with the supervisor. The bilateral activities identified by Zalcman and Cornell are:

For the Therapist	*For the Supervisor*
Theoretical and empirical knowledge	Assessment of the supervision problem
Clinical skills and expertise	Selection of supervisory interventions
Ethical and professional practice	Supervision planning
Personal skills and development	Evaluation of the supervisee
	Evaluation of the supervision

With the exception of the 'selection of supervisory interventions' (assuming, of course, that the supervisor conceptualises their interactions as 'interventions'), all the other activities identified separately could, and in our view *should*, be shared, both ways. Similarly, the focus of attention Zalcman and Cornell identify for the therapist—on the client, related others, the social system, the type of problem and on the therapist themselves—is an equally important role for the supervisor. However, in discussing 'the direction in which the supervisor intends to influence the trainee's behavior' (p. 119), the behavioural origins and influences of Zalcman and Cornell's model become explicit. Although influencing others, in the context of also being open to be influenced by others, is not problematic from a person-centred perspective, the kind of operant conditioning implied by Zalcman and Cornell is. This, along with 'modelling' behaviour, is as Wood (1995) points out (in the context of a discussion about groups) 'diametrically opposed to the person-centred approach which would be more interested in participants discovering their own way of being' (p. 3). Nevertheless, the concept of roles, of role relationships, and of shared responsibilities, is an important one for both supervisor and supervisee and, especially when there are third parties involved, such as an organisation funding the supervision, is one which needs to be made explicit and discussed at the initial stages of the relationship.

DEVELOPMENT IN SUPERVISION

A developmental approach to supervision implies (again more or less explicitly) that the supervisor pitches and indeed modifies their interactions or interventions according to their assessment of where the supervisee is on a pre-theorised and sequential stage model of development. This approach to supervision is popular. It may be traced back to Hogan's (1964) paper on four stages of the development of the psychotherapist. Within 25 years, as many different developmental models had been published (Borders, 1989). The developmental approach is also influential: Hawkins and Shohet (2000) report this is the main model of supervision in the USA, and a number of authors uncritically assert its relevance (e.g. Page and Wosket, 1994). One of the most common and popular is Stoltenberg and Delworth's (1987) model which presents a four-level developmental approach to supervision, and draws on both the analogy of stages of human development (childhood, adolescence, early adulthood and maturity), and the metaphor of the medieval European craft guilds (novice/apprentice, journeyman, independent craftsman, and master craftsman). Hawkins and Shohet (1989, 2000) conceptualise the different concerns of the supervisee at these different levels of development as:

1. 'Self-centred'—which may be summarised as 'Can I make it in this work?'
2. 'Client-centred'—'Can I help this client make it?'
3. 'Process-centred'—'How are we relating together?'
4. 'Process-in-context-centred'—'How do processes relate to each other?'

Although Hawkins and Shohet caution against the rigid use of this model, in re-presenting it (for a second time in the second edition of their book), they too appear generally uncritical of this and of developmental models *per se*.

In his approach, Casement (1985) presents a view of the development of the internal supervisor: from thinking which is borrowed from an external supervisor; through the development of a capacity of spontaneous reflection; to autonomous functioning through dialogue between external supervisor and internal supervisor; and to continuous 'becoming' which may include further growth gained through supervising others. In this, Casement specifically avoids a 'stage theory' approach, viewing this sequence as a spiral and, echoing T.S. Eliot's lines about arriving where we started and knowing the place for the first time, suggests that the therapist is back where they have been before but yet where they have never been before.

From a person-centred perspective, developmental approaches based on stage theories present a number of problems:

1. As most developmental models are based on a model of child development, they are inherently infantilising (as they are when similarly applied as an approach to the training of therapists).

2. In effect they propose an end stage of mastery (the master therapist). Compare this with an emphasis on *becoming*, found in theorists as diverse as Rogers (1961) and Bion (1975). Citing Bion, Casement (1985) suggests that 'at the time of qualifying, a more autonomous internal supervisor may be forming in the therapist' (p. 33). He goes on to say that he hopes that 'there will never be a time when therapists cease from this "becoming" or imagine that they have "arrived"' (ibid., p. 33).

3. They do not account for the fact that someone becoming a supervisor will already be an experienced practitioner and may well be, for instance (and accepting Hawkins and Shohet's summarising schema), 'process-centred'. In our view and experience it is more likely that this focus is transferred to the new field of supervision, rather than that the new supervisor regresses to an 'earlier' concern with and focus on self.

4. They are culturally specific. As Carroll (1996) points out, developmental models have been almost entirely developed in the North American context; the analogies and metaphors are not necessarily relevant or applicable elsewhere, let alone necessary or sufficient.

5. They are both simplistic (in their determined and invariant stages) and overly complex. A stage model of development must also apply to supervisors, as indeed Stoltenberg and Delworth (1987) suggest. It follows that in any interaction between supervisee and supervisor, the interaction of developmental stages must also be considered. Thus, a 'self-centred' novice (Level 1) supervisor says something to a 'process-centred' independent (Level 2) therapist. When the four possible stages or levels of the supervisor's development are combined with the same for the supervisee, the result is a matrix of 16 possible combinations of levels of interactions or interventions!

6. They do not account for more recent developmental theories (such as Stern, 1985), which generally suggest an unfolding and ongoing *process* of human development (as distinct from stage theories), or for the processes of development in supervision described by Casement (1985).

Rejecting stage theories in favour of *process* theories, person-centred practitioners, supervisors and educators nevertheless account for the development of the *adult* learner in a learning relationship and, in doing so, may draw on a number of models which are consistent with a person-centred philosophy of education and learning (see Chapter 1).

ORGANISATION AND TASKS OF SUPERVISION

A number of models of supervision have emerged in the last ten years which focus on how to organise supervision and specific tasks of supervision, in some models identified by means of a checklist.

Page and Wosket (1994) present a cyclical model of supervision which aims to encompass process, function, aims and methodology. Their stage model comprises five stages: contract, focus, space, bridge and review. Each stage, in turn, has five steps which are summarised and presented in tabulated form in Box 3.1.

Stage	Step 1	Step 2	Step 3	Step 4	Step 5
Contract	Ground-rules	Boundaries	Accountability	Expectations	Relationship
Focus	Issue	Objectives	Presentation	Approach	Priorities
Space	Collaboration	Investigation	Challenge	Containment	Affirmation
Bridge	Consolidation	Information-giving	Goal-setting	Action planning	Client's perspective
Review	Feedback	Grounding	Evaluation	Assessment	Recontracting

Box 3.1. A cyclical model of supervision (from Page and Wosket, 1994)

In its form and language, this model is reminiscent of Egan's (1997) approach to effective helping, and, perhaps unsurprisingly, one of the authors declares in the preface that her work has been closely informed by Egan's work. As such, this model essentially draws on a cognitive behavioural model of helping and facilitation and, as a prescriptive 'stage' or 'step' theory, sits uncomfortably with the process-orientated approach of person-centred supervision.

From a task-oriented perspective, Carroll (1996) identifies seven generic tasks of supervision:

1. To create or 'set up' the learning relationship
2. To teach

3. To counsel
4. To monitor professional/ethical issues
5. To evaluate
6. To consult
7. To monitor administrative aspects of practice in both counselling and supervision.

The language of this model is quite hierarchical and promotes the image and figure of the expert supervisor 'doing' to the supervisee. In this it draws more on the 'banking' concept of education, critiqued by Freire (1967/1976, 1972). This model was the subject of Carroll's previous research (1994) and was originally tested on 23 supervisors recognised by the British Association for Counselling. This group, of course, by definition, guarantees a certain consensus about certain issues such as the purpose and tasks of supervision. For instance, within the teaching task, Carroll's research concluded that modelling is seen as an important teaching method. This is antithetical to the person-centred approach (see Wood, 1995).

Page and Wosket (1994) view their model as (all) encompassing: of process, function, aims and methodology. However, as with Holloway's (1995) seven-dimensional systems model, with each system having a number of elements, 29 in all, we find this too complicated. Clarkson (1992) proposes a 'brief supervision checklist' (the 'brief' referring to the checklist rather than to the supervision), which comprises:

☑ Contract—fulfilled

◯ Key issues—identified

⬇ Possibility of harm (to client)—reduced

⬆ Developmental direction (of supervisee)—increased

▭ Process—modelled (by supervisor)

= Relationship—equal

55

to which we would add:

Context

and

ή   Ethics

Clarkson (1992) states that the purpose of the checklist is 'for pinpointing the category or "band" of key issues in a particular supervision session or at a particular stage in a trainee's development. The choice of such a "band" enables the supervisor to focus the supervision in the area which he/she considers crucial and most relevant' (p. 273). In this passage we can see Clarkson's subscription to a stage development model of supervisees' development, and to a prioritising of the *supervisor's* choice and assessment of what's crucial and 'most relevant' in a supervision session. Herein lie the difficulties with checklists. Most models which focus on organisation and task have their merits, specifically in terms of providing an organising framework for discussion of and training in supervision and, in the case of Clarkson's checklist, a manageable model for supervisory practice. However, they all organise supervision from the supervisor's perspective, encourage a one-sided view of responsibility and focus, and, in effect, promote the manualisation of supervision and therapy. One example of this is in the examination of Supervising Transactional Analysts, within the European Association for Transactional Analysis, the scoring scales for the oral examination of which are based directly on Clarkson's (1992) checklist.

CONTEXT OF SUPERVISION

Like therapy, supervision exists in a wider context. From an organismic perspective in which the organism cannot be understood outside of its interaction and exchange with the environment, supervision not only takes place in a context or a number of contexts, but also 'context' takes a place in supervision. Without the context of culture, organisation and time, we cannot understand supervision, supervisory processes or supervisory relationships.

Culture
Writing in 1951 Rogers identifies experiential knowledge of cultural setting and influence as important preparation for the training therapist. In his exploration

of the impact of multicultural issues on the supervision process, Igwe (1997/98) argues similarly for an experiential awareness of cultural/racial differences and prejudices. In its *Standards for Counselling Supervisors* the Association for Counselor Education and Supervision (1989) advocates that the counselling supervisor 'demonstrates knowledge of individual differences with respect to gender, race, ethnicity, culture and age, and understands the importance of these characteristics in supervisory relationships' (Section 4.1). The British Association for Counselling and Psychotherapy (BACP) requires that supervisors seeking accreditation work within its *Ethical Framework* which includes the statement that: 'the practitioner is responsible for learning about and taking account of the different protocols, conventions and customs that can pertain to different working contexts and cultures' (BACP, 2002). Very little has been written about the impact of gender in supervision; rare exceptions include Nelson and Holloway's (1990) research on the connection between gender and issues of power and involvement in supervision, and Granello, Beamish and Davis' (1997) article on the empowerment of supervisees. In addition to further work by Nelson and Holloway (1999) on supervision and gender issues, Carroll and Holloway's (1999) edited volume on *Counselling Supervision in Context* includes chapters on supervision and disability (Spy and Oyston, 1999) and sexual orientation (Hitchings, 1999). For us, there is a significant gap in the literature to do with the impact of class on therapists and supervisors.

Slightly more has been written about culture and, specifically, race. Focusing on the triangular relationship, client-therapist-supervisor, and communication process between cross-racial or cross-cultural pairings, such as a white supervisor and a black therapist, Lago and Thompson (1997) talk in terms of a 'front' or 'proxy-self', which the person from the minority group may project. This 'ensures their survival in, and acceptability to, white society, in order to protect their real self' (p. 124). The implication of this for supervision is 'the possibility that the supervisor also develops a false view of the client and the client's difficulties. This view will be generated, in part only, by their receipt of information from the therapist's proxy-self' (p. 126). Whilst we find Lago and Thompson's focus on communication in the supervisory relationship useful, they are, in our view, overly concerned with the supervisor's focus on the client, rather than the therapist. Grant (1999) writes about supervision and racial issues and raises issues of the effect of race on supervision, and the preparation of supervisors to work on racial issues. However, she writes from the perspective that the responsibility for ensuring that issues of race are addressed and obtaining information about racial groups in their area, rests solely with the supervisor. In the second edition of their book Hawkins and Shohet (2000) devote a chapter to 'Working with difference: Transcultural supervision'. This is a thorough and stimulating review which encompasses different understandings of culture, power and anti-oppressive practice, and considers 'differences' in terms of their seven modes of supervision.

In terms of the 'persons and relationship' perspective which the person-centred approach represents, we find process models of personal development and relationship development more useful than prescriptive, 'how to do it' models. Helms' (1984) model of the development of white consciousness (involving contact, disintegration, reintegration, pseudo-independence and autonomy) and Atkinson, Morton and Sue's (1989) model of minority identity development (conformity, dissonance, resistance and immersion, introspection and synergetic articulation and awareness) represent both sides of a particular majority culture-minority culture dynamic. In a contribution on intergroup relations, one of us (KT) proposed a number of processes which reflect the interaction between people and groups involved in these developmental processes (see Box 3.2).

It seems to us that the processes identified as intergroup relations in Box 3.2 describe the interactions across many cultures as experienced and expressed in supervision. In this volume Seneviratne addresses issues of race and culture in supervision (Chapter 6).

Organisation

Just as supervision takes place in a cultural context, so too do therapist and supervisee meet in an organisational context. Even if both parties are freelance, in independent practice, they are usually members of an association or network and, as such, work within an organisational frame of reference which usually includes codes or frameworks of ethics and professional practice. The impact and significance of organisational context on supervision is discussed by, amongst others, Hawkins and Shohet (1989, 2000), Borland (1995), Holloway (1995), and a number of contributors in Carroll and Holloway's (1999) book who discuss supervision in various settings: education (Tholstrup, 1999), medical (Henderson, 1999), religious (Mann, 1999) and workplace (Carroll, 1999). As we discuss with regard to Hawkins and Shohet's model (see Chapter 4), it is important to know the organisational context and culture, not least because of the implications of employment law (see Chapter 5). The impact of organisation may be defined by means of three-handed or multiple contracts, involving the therapist, supervisor and the organisation (agency, placement, training organisation), and clarify issues such as the roles, responsibilities, duties, expectations and authority of all parties. A key issue in supervising within, or for, or when paid by an organisation concerns responsibility and accountability for the work and lines of communication between all parties, and the role of the (external) supervisor in a consultative capacity, for instance, if the supervisor is hearing things in supervision that give her cause for organisational concerns.

White racial consciousness (Helms, 1984)	Intergroup relations	Minority identity development (Atkinson, Morton and Sue, 1989)
Contact		Conformity
	Unconscious coexistence Usually no explicit tensions in supervision	
Disintegration		Dissonance
	Conscious unease Some differences, tensions and anxieties expressed, perhaps focused on different and disputed use of language	
Reintegration		Resistance and immersion
	Polarisation Often explicit disagreements about micro and macro issues, and feelings associated with misunderstandings	
Pseudo-independent		Introspection
	Re-evaluation and encounter Increasing ownership of language, issues, personal and cultural history, together with often tentative rapprochement	
Autonomy		Synergetic articulation
	Mutual respect Positive personal and intergroup relations based on contact, congruence (including respectful criticism, positive regard and understanding, and both parties experiencing this.	

Box 3.2. Intergroup relations applied to cross-cultural supervision (based on Tudor, 1999)

Time

The third and final context for us is that of time. We live in interesting times in which time is of the essence, and brief or short-term therapy determines a lot of therapeutic practice, especially in the public sector. As Thorne (1999) puts it:

> . . . certainly the Zeitgeist exerts its own pervasive influence. We live in an era of management values where the articles of faith are short-term effectiveness, value for money, performance indicators, return on investment, accountability. It is good to remember that this is a modern and upstart faith with few moral roots, with no power to nourish souls and every capacity to destroy them. (p. 8)

Time is deeply cultural and highly political (see Tudor, 2002). Person-centred therapy is often viewed as effective in the long term only. Assumptions abound and personal prejudices and organisational exigencies exclude some person-centred practitioners from work in the public sector. For us, the question of effectiveness and so-called 'brief therapy' misses the point: we do what we can with what we've got. As Taft (1933) points out:

> Time represents more vividly than any other category the necessity of accepting limitation as well as the inability to do so, and symbolizes therefore the whole problem of living. The reaction of each individual to limited or unlimited time betrays his deepest and fundamental life pattern, his relation to the growth process itself, to beginnings and endings, to being born and to dying. (p. 12)

Furthermore, from a phenomenological perspective, the present session with a client or supervisee is the only one we know we've got.

For us, the only question regarding time and supervision is whether practitioners are sufficiently supervised (see Mearns, 1994). Rules and guidelines determine and advise about numbers of hours, say, per month, and ratios of hours of supervision to hours of practice. However, if therapists are working briefly then they may complete their work with a particular client before seeing their supervisor again. In such circumstances the supervisee may need more frequent and more immediate access to her supervisor.

In the next chapter we continue this review and critique generic process models of supervision.

REFERENCES

Association for Counselor Education and Supervision (1989) *Standards for Counselling Supervisors*. Alexandria, VA: ACES

Atkinson, D., Morton, G. and Sue, D. W. (1989) *Counseling American Minorities: A Cross-Cultural Perspective*. Dubuque, IA: William C. Brown

Bion, W. (1975) *Brazilian Lectures 2*. Rio de Janeiro: Imago Editora

Borders, L. D. (1989) A pragmatic agenda for developmental supervision research. *Counselor Education and Supervision*, 29(1), 16–24

Borland, P. (1995) Supervision in a statutory agency. In J. Pritchard (Ed.) *Good Practice in Supervision: Statutory and Voluntary Organisations* (pp. 31–8). London: Jessica Kingsley Publishers

British Association for Counselling (1988) *Code of Ethics and Practice for Counsellors*. Rugby: BAC

British Association for Counselling and Psychotherapy. (2002) *Ethical Framework for Good Practice in Counselling and Psychotherapy*. Rugby: BACP

Bromberg, P. (1982) The supervisory process and parallel process in psychoanalysis. *Contemporary Psychoanalysis*, 18, 92–111

Carroll, M. (1994) The Generic Tasks of Supervision: An Analysis of Supervisee Expectations, Supervisor Interviews and Supervisory Audio-taped Sessions. Unpublished PhD thesis, University of Surrey, Guildford

Carroll, M. (1996) *Counselling Supervision: Theory, Skills and Practice*. London: Cassell

Carroll, M. (1999) Supervision in workplace settings. In M. Carroll and E. Holloway (Eds.) *Counselling Supervision in Context* (pp. 140–58). London: Sage

Carroll, M. and Holloway, E. (1999) *Counselling Supervision in Context*. London: Sage

Casement, P. (1985) *On Learning from the Patient*. London: Tavistock

Christian, C. and Kitto, J. (1987) *The Theory and Practice of Supervision*. London: YMCA National College

Clarkson, P. (1992) *Transactional Analysis Psychotherapy: An Integrated Approach*. London: Routledge

Efstation, J. F. (1987) Construction of a measure of the working alliance in counsellor supervision and the prediction of training outcome.

Egan, G. (1997) *The Skilled Helper: A Systematic Approach to Effective Helping*, fourth edition. Pacific Grove, CA: Brooks/Cole

Freire, P. (1972) *Pedagogy of the Oppressed*. Harmondsworth: Penguin

Freire, P. (1976) *Education: The Practice of Freedom*. London: Writers and Readers Publishing Cooperative. (Original work published 1967)

Granello, D. H., Beamish, P. M. and Davis, T. E. (1997) Supervisee empowerment: Does gender make a difference? *Counselor Education and Supervision*, 36, 305–17

Grant, P. (1999) Supervision and racial issues. In M. Carroll and E. Holloway (Eds.) *Counselling Supervision in Context* (pp. 7–22). London: Sage

Hawkins, P. and Shohet, R. (1989) *Supervision in the Helping Professions*. Milton Keynes: Open University Press

Hawkins, P. and Shohet, R. (2000) *Supervision in the Helping Professions* (2nd edn.). Buckingham: Open University Press

Helms, J.E. (1984) Towards a theoretical model of the effects of race on counseling: A black and white model. *The Counseling Psychologist, 12,* 153–65

Henderson, P. (1999) Supervision in medical settings. In M. Carroll and E. Holloway (Eds.) *Counselling Supervision in Context* (pp. 85–103). London: Sage

Hess, A.K. (1980) Training models and the nature of psychotherapy supervision. In A.K. Hess (Ed.) *Psychotherapy Supervision: Theory, Research and Practice.* New York: John Wiley and Sons

Hitchings, P. (1999) Supervision and sexual orientation. In M. Carroll and E. Holloway (Eds.) *Counselling Supervision in Context* (pp. 54–82). London: Sage

Hogan, R. A. (1964) Issues and approaches in supervision. *Psychotherapy: Research and Practice, 18,* 209–16

Holloway, E. (1995) *Clinical Supervision: A Systems Approach.* London: Sage

Igwe, A. (1997/98) An exploration of the impact of multi-cultural issues on the supervision process. *RACE Journal,* No.15, 30–2

Kadushin, A. (1976) *Supervision in Social Work.* New York: Columbia University Press

Lago, C. and Thompson, J. (1997) The triangle with curved sides: Sensitivity to issues of race and culture in supervision. In G. Shipton (Ed.) *Supervision of Psychotherapy and Counselling: Making a Place to Think* (pp. 119–30). Buckingham: Open University Press

Lambers, E. (2000) Supervision in person-centred therapy: Facilitating congruence. In D. Mearns and B. Thorne *Person-Centred Therapy Today* (pp. 196–211). London: Sage

Lambert, M.J. (1980) Research and the supervisory process. In A.K. Hess (Ed.) *Psychotherapy Supervision: Theory, Research and Practice* (pp. 23–50). New York: Wiley

Lewin, K. (1952) *Field Theory in Social Science.* London: Tavistock

Loganbill, C., Hardy, E. and Delworth, U. (1982) Supervision: A conceptual model. *The Counselling Psychologist, 10,* 3–42.

Mann, E. (1999) Supervision in religious settings. In M. Carroll and E. Holloway (Eds.) *Counselling Supervision in Context* (pp. 159–176). London: Sage

Mearns, D. (1994) *Developing Person-Centred Counselling.* London: Sage

Mueller, W. J. and Kell, B. L. (1972) *Coping with Conflict: Supervising Counselors and Psychotherapists.* New York: Appleton-Century-Crofts

National Health Service Management Executive (1993) *A Vision for the Future: The Nursing, Midwifery and Health Visiting Contributions to Health Care.* London: HMSO

Nelson, M. L. and Holloway, E. (1990) Relation of gender to power and involvement in supervision. *Journal of Counseling Psychology, 37,* 473–81

Nelson, M. L. and Holloway, E. (1999) Supervision and gender issues. In M. Carroll and E. Holloway (Eds.) *Counselling Supervision in Context* (pp. 23–35). London: Sage

Page, S. and Wosket, V. (1994) *Supervising the Counsellor: A Cyclical Model.* London: Routledge

Pepinsky, H.B. and Patton, M.J. (1971) *The Psychological Experiment.* New York: Pergamon Press

Proctor, B. (1988) Supervision: A co-operative exercise in accountability. In M. Marken and M. Payne (Eds.) *Enabling and Ensuring*. Leicester: Leicester National Youth Bureau/Council for Education and Training in Youth and Community Work

Rattigan, B. (1981) *Counselling*, No.36, pp. 6–8

Rogers, C. R. (1967) *On Becoming a Person*. London: Constable. (Original work published 1961)

Spy, T. and Oyston, C. (1999) Supervision and working with disability. In M. Carroll and E. Holloway (Eds.) *Counselling Supervision in Context* (pp. 36–53). London: Sage

Stern, D.N. (1985) *The Interpersonal World of the Infant*. New York: Basic Books

Stoltenberg, C.D. and Delworth, U. (1987) *Supervising Counselors and Therapists*. San Francisco, CA: Jossey-Bass

Taft, J. (1933) *The Dynamics of Therapy in a Controlled Relationship*. New York: Macmillan

Tholstrup, M. (1999) Supervision in educational settings. In M. Carroll and E. Holloway (Eds.) *Counselling Supervision in Context* (pp. 104–22). London: Sage

Thorne, B. (1999) The move towards brief therapy: Its dangers and challenges. Counselling, *10*(1), 7–11

Tudor, K. (1999) *Group Counselling*. London: Sage

Tudor, K. (2002) Introduction. In K. Tudor (Ed.) *Transactional Approaches to Brief Therapy* (pp. 1–18). London: Sage

Urbano, J.M. (1984) Supervision of counsellors: Ingredients for effectiveness. *Counselling, 50*, 7–16

Ward, L. G., Friedlander, M. L., Schoen, L. G. and Klein, J.C. (1985) Strategic self-presentation in supervision. *Journal of Counselling Psychology*, *32*(1), 111–18

Wolberg, L.R. (1954) *The Technique of Psychotherapy*. New York: Grune and Stratton

Wood, J. K. (1995) The Person-Centered Approach to Small Groups: More than psychotherapy. Unpublished manuscript

Zalcman, M.J. and Cornell, W.F. (1983) A bilateral model for clinical supervision. *Transactional Analysis Journal*, *13*(2), 112–23

CHAPTER FOUR

PROCESS IN SUPERVISION:
A PERSON-CENTRED CRITIQUE

KEITH TUDOR AND MIKE WORRALL

Two principal works describe process in the generic literature on supervision. One focuses primarily on the supervisor's own internal process and development, and the other focuses on the various choices open to the supervisor in her interaction with a supervisee.

THE INTERNAL SUPERVISOR (CASEMENT)

In his seminal work based on his own 'learning from the patient', and reflecting on the dynamics of the therapeutic relationship from an independent psychoanalytic perspective, Casement (1985, 1990) develops the concept of the 'internal supervisor'. Significantly, he came to this through noticing that:

> . . . trainees in supervision often lean too heavily upon the advice or comments of the supervisor, which creates a barrier between the social worker or therapist and the client or patient. The effect of this becomes evident in the trainee's subsequent clinical work. I therefore came to see that formal supervision alone does not adequately prepare the student to deal with the immediacy of the therapeutic present. (p. 30)

He goes on to discuss a number of reflective processes which are developed in personal analysis or therapy, through being supervised, through working without formal supervision (a counterintuitive notion in these codified times), and through supervising others.

He suggests, for instance, that in therapy the patient is encouraged to observe with the analyst what he (the patient) is experiencing, thus developing an 'observing ego' alongside an 'experiencing ego': 'it is here, in their own experience of being a patient, that therapists establish the first roots of what later becomes the internal supervisor' (Casement, 1985, p. 31). Such separation of experience and of self-structure appears at odds with a person-centred approach to personality integration (see Rogers, 1951). However, encouraging clients and practitioners to be reflective is highly compatible with the person-centred approach. Furthermore, considering this from an experiential perspective, the process described by Casement is similar to 'evocative reflection': a method developed by Rice (1974), which aims 'to open up . . . experience and provide the client with a process whereby he can form successively more accurate constructions of his own experience' (p. 290). The transfer of experience and observation from being a patient or client to becoming a practitioner is not emphasised in person-centred psychology. Most person-centred therapists will have some experience of personal therapy, not least those who, seeking accreditation with the British Association for Counselling and Psychotherapy, must have completed a minimum of 40 hours. However, making this a *requirement* of training, entry to training, accreditation or registration is problematic from the point of view of an approach which trusts a person's tendency to actualise, does not direct her experience, and values autonomy. Traditionally, the person-centred approach has placed much more emphasis on personal development, usually taking place in group/s on the training course itself; indeed, as Mearns (1994) puts it, 'personal development for professional working is so crucial to the person-centred approach that it cannot be left to the vagaries of individual therapy' (p. 35).

A PROCESS MODEL (HAWKINS AND SHOHET)

Although Casement (1985) put (internal) process in supervision on the map, the most well-known 'process model' of supervision is Hawkins and Shohet's (1989) double matrix model which, following Inskipp and Proctor (1995), in the second edition of their book (Hawkins and Shohet, 2000), they refer to as the seven-eyed supervisor model (see Figure 4.1).

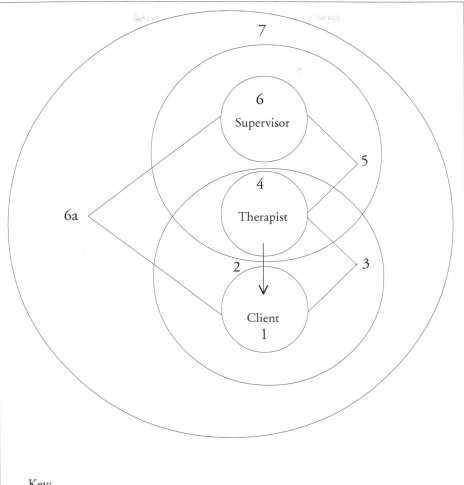

Key:
Mode 1   The content of the therapy session
Mode 2   Focusing on strategies and interventions
Mode 3   Focusing on the therapy relationship
Mode 4   Focusing on the therapist's process
Mode 5   Focusing on the supervisory relationship
Mode 6   Focusing on the supervisor's own process
Mode 6a   The (fantasy) supervisor-client relationship
Mode 7   Focusing on the wider context (organisational, professional, economic, social)

Figure 4.1. The seven-eyed model of supervision (adapted from Hawkins and Shohet, 2000)

This model was originally referred to as the double matrix model as it is based on the overlapping of two matrices:

i) The 'therapy' matrix (assuming the primary activity is that of therapy) which involves the client and practitioner (in this case, a therapist); and
ii) The supervisory matrix, comprising the practitioner and her supervisor.

This visual representation acknowledges that the client is, with rare exceptions, not present 'in supervision'; and that the first three modes of supervision (concerning the content of the therapy session, the strategies and interventions used by the therapist, and the therapeutic relationship) are only accessible insofar as the therapist and her supervisor reflect upon them.

The process model of supervision—a brief summary

Mode 1 The content of the therapy session

This refers to the client's presentation: what they say and do, their 'presenting problem' or issue, as well as their continuing presentation throughout therapy. With regard to the supervisee, in this mode of supervision, he may be invited simply to describe the client in as much detail as possible. Social workers, for example, used to be trained to complete what were referred to as 'process recordings' immediately after meeting with a client. This was a written record of everything that the social worker could remember of the meeting or session. In this mode the supervisee may also reflect on his first impressions of, thoughts about and responses to a client.

From a person-centred perspective this focus on description and on the development of fine observational skills is useful in developing the 'as if' quality of empathic understanding. However, there is at times a fine line between description and prescription, understanding and interpretation: that a certain presentation necessarily means something specific, a view based on a particular theory of the person. Also, descriptions are not neutral, either in values or context. Hawkins and Shohet (2000) themselves comment on the importance of the supervisor challenging the therapist's assumptions about the client, and watching for what they refer to as the therapist's 'ideological editor'. When both authors worked for the probation service, social enquiry reports on people awaiting sentencing would often begin in a standard fashion: 'Mr Jones is unemployed and lives with his family of five in council property on Willow Farm estate'. Whilst factually accurate, this way of introducing the 'guilty party' to a Magistrates bench, predominantly comprising middle-class people, reveals certain assumptions based on class. Similarly, it is important to recognise that our first impressions, thoughts and responses are *ours* and do not belong to or reside in the client (we discuss this later with regard to parallel process (pp. 72–3). A further caution with regard to this mode of supervision is an undue focus on the client (see Mearns, 1995).

Mode 2 Focusing on strategies and interventions

This is often referred to as focusing on what's in the therapist's 'tool box': their skills, techniques, thinking, strategies, options, and creativity. It can be enormously restorative for a supervisor to facilitate and stimulate creative thinking and activity, particularly when a therapist feels 'stuck' with a client. Focusing on strategies and interventions, the supervisor may ask questions such as:

- 'If you weren't stuck what would you do?'
- 'What would you like to have done?'
- 'What other options do you have?'

These can be freeing questions to contemplate and answer. This mode of supervision may also be formative in that the supervisor may teach her supervisee/s a particular technique. This mode is often the one in which she is most obviously or explicitly active.

Of course, from a person-centred perspective, both 'strategies' and 'interventions' are problematic, as for that matter are 'techniques'. This is because, essentially, they all imply that they are something that the therapist does to the client, often without their cognisance or consent. As Warner (1998, personal correspondence) points out: 'anytime anyone makes a decision on behalf of someone else, he is being patronising'. Warner (2000) has developed a five-level framework of 'interventiveness' of therapist responses and styles, which she describes as 'the degree to which a therapist brings in material from outside the client's frame of reference and the degree to which this is done from a stance of authority or expertise' (p. 31):

- Level 1 The therapist's contact is purely intuitive (a largely hypothetical level).
- Level 2 The therapist conveys solely her understanding of her client's internal frame of reference.
- Level 3 The therapist brings material into the therapeutic relationship in ways which foster client choice.
- Level 4 The therapist brings material into the therapeutic relationship from her own frame of reference, from a position of authority or expertise.
- Level 5 The therapist brings into the therapeutic relationship material that is outside the client's frame of reference, and in such a way that the client is unaware of both the intervention/s and the therapist's purpose or motivation.

These levels may be applied to all therapies and help to define and distinguish the person-centred practitioner from more directive and interpretive therapists, with regard to which Warner suggests that there is a fundamental dividing line between Levels 3 and 4. We think that this framework may equally be applied to supervisors' responses and styles and that person-centred supervision may be characterised as 'interventiveness' or (we prefer) engagement at Levels 2 and 3. (Using this framework in a way which parallels therapy with supervision, we regard Level 1 as the practitioner's self-supervision.)

Mode 3 Focusing on the therapy relationship

In this mode the focus in supervision is on the nature of the therapeutic relationship: on the system the two (or more) parties create, and the conscious and unconscious interactions between therapist and client. This may be considered in a variety of ways depending on the practitioner's theoretical orientation. Hawkins and Shohet (2000) suggest that the supervisor asks the practitioner questions such as:

- How did you meet?
- How and why did this client choose you?
- What did you first notice about the nature of your contact with this client?
- Tell me the story of the history of your relationship. (p. 75)

In their description of this mode, Hawkins and Shohet (2000) rely heavily on the psychodynamic concept of transference to understand the therapeutic relationship (as they do on countertransference in modes 4 and 6). Person-centred therapy shares with psychodynamic therapy (and other approaches) the view that the therapy *is* the relationship and, indeed, client-centred therapy was first referred to by Rogers (1942) as 'relationship therapy' (for a brief history of which, see Embleton Tudor et al., in press 2004). Where the two approaches part company is on the centrality (in psychodynamic therapy) of the notion of the unconscious and on the role of interpretation (see Warner, 2000 and above). That supervision focuses on the process and relationship dimensions of therapy, including the attitudes and behaviour of the supervisee as therapist, has been acknowledged in the person-centred literature on supervision (see Rice, 1980; Villas-Boas Bowen, 1986).

The role of the supervisor in this mode has been seen as akin to that of the couples' counsellor in as much as she focuses on the relationship as distinct from one or other person. However, this analogy breaks down in that, with rare exceptions, only one party to the therapeutic relationship is present in supervision.

In the spirit of creativity and toying with concepts and elements of practice, the supervisor may ask the supervisee other questions with the purpose of stimulating reflection, ideas and discussion:

- 'What's the worst/nastiest/meanest thing you could say to your client?'
- 'What mistake do you most fear making with this client?'
- 'If you were a friend of your client's, what would you say to them?'

Up to this point, the modes of supervision in the process model have focused reflections on what lies outside the supervision, that is, in the therapy matrix, in and between therapist and client. From the fourth mode onwards, the material under consideration is all directly accessible within the supervision matrix by both therapist and supervisor. Insofar as the material concerns one or both parties and is accessible by one or both parties present in the supervisory relationship, all modes within this supervision matrix are more compatible with approaches to supervision based on person-centred principles.

Mode 4 Focusing on the therapist's process
In this mode Hawkins and Shohet (2000) draw exclusively on the psychodynamic concept of countertransference, distinguishing between four types of countertransference: the transference feelings of the therapist; the therapist's feelings and thoughts evoked by the role/s transferred onto them; the therapist's feelings, thoughts and actions used to counter the client's transference; and the projected material which the therapist takes in, often referred to as projective identification. In essence, 'countertransference' describes the therapist's unconscious reactions to the client. From a psychodynamic perspective, exploring and understanding countertransference is essential for the therapist to be able to respond rather than react to the client. Whilst we agree that greater self-knowledge is a good thing, there are two principal problems with the notion of countertransference:

- The first is the therapist's passivity. At worst, countertransference renders the therapist a passive victim of her client's feelings and projections. They are transferred as if by magic across the therapeutic space and 'enter' the therapist.

- Following on from this, the second concerns responsibility. If the therapist is feeling the client's feelings, and it is conceptualised in this way, then the client is responsible for having transferred them. What often follows may be summarised as:
  Passive therapist + Responsible client = Blamed client.

Unfortunately, notions of transference and countertransference have been adopted uncritically by many humanistic practitioners who, by definition, have not had a thorough immersion in their theory and practice, with the result that some therapists respond to subtle processes in an inappropriate way: 'I'm feeling scared, and I'm wondering whose scare it is'. This kind of fatuous intervention only serves to blame the client and, ironically, to confirm them as the victim of their own powerful and uncontrollable feelings.

Following Rogers' (1951) response to the 'problem' of transference, we summarise a person-centred perspective to the concepts of transference and countertransference:

1. 'Transference' is more accurately viewed as 'transference attitudes'. Warner (1991) suggests that when a client is intentionally trying to evoke negative feelings in their therapist, these are better understood as 'interpersonal strategies', secondary to their fragile process, rather than as an unconscious defence.
2. Given the focus in person-centred therapy and practice on acceptance and understanding, the response of the person-centred practitioner is the same as to any other attitude of the client.
3. Shlien's (1984) countertheory of transference may equally be applied to countertransference.
4. The notion, derived from self-psychology and intersubjectivity theory, of co-transference or, extending this, 'co-transference attitudes' is more consistent with a person-centred approach to this phenomenon. Interestingly, Shohet (personal communication, December 2003) agrees with this notion, viewing countertransference as a co-creation of both the client and the therapist, and suggests that 'the therapist is responsible for what he or she "picks up"' .

Mode 5 Focusing on the supervisory relationship
This and the next mode echo modes 3 and 4. The supervisory process and relationship is reflective of, and *in this sense* parallel to, the therapeutic process and relationship. The concept of a 'reflection process' in supervision was first identified by Searles (1955). A few years later, Ekstein and Wallerstein (1958) developed the notion of the process between client and therapist *influencing* the supervisory relationship. Later still, Doerhman (1976) demonstrated that themes can pass from supervision to therapy as well as from therapy to supervision. The phenomenon of 'influence' is disputed (see, for instance, Feltham and Dryden, 1994). Nevertheless, the paralleling in supervision of the therapeutic process, and similarly (although, we hope, less frequently) in therapy of the supervisory process, is a common and powerful narrative theme in supervision. Some supervision training courses promote and focus much of their assessment of students on whether they can identify the parallel process. In concluding his

excellent article on the subject, Mothersole (1999) suggests the following 'broad encompassing definition' of parallel process. It is:

> the reflection of aspects of the client/psychotherapist dyad and the supervisee/ supervisor dyad in each other. As such, parallels will always have some implication, however tentative, for all individuals in these dyads. It involves reciprocal and/or complementary roles and may involve shifts in these roles. Such roles are based on the involvement of aspects of the internal world of participants acting in a way that is currently out of awareness. In this sense, [parallel process] is an interpersonal process with major intrapsychic aspects. (p. 119)

In our view, this definition avoids the 'magical thinking' and grandiosity inherent in some views of parallel process, together with their consequent and problematic diagnostic assumptions.

Mode 6 Focusing on the supervisor's own process
Just as this is parallel to mode 4, so too are our comments. Hawkins and Shohet (1989, 2000) refer to a number of aspects of the internal experience of the supervisor: certain changes which 'come over us'; unrelated images spontaneously erupting in our consciousness; feelings such as excitement or fear. Hawkins and Shohet attribute all these 'interruptions' to 'the unconscious material of the therapist . . . being received by the unconscious receptor of the supervisor' (p. 83). From a person-centred perspective, we understand the same phenomena in terms of empathy: empathic resonation (Barrett-Lennard, 1981; Stern, 1985); idiosyncratic empathy (Bozarth, 1984); different kinds of empathy based on evolutionary consciousness (Neville, 1996); and empathic responding (Greenberg and Elliot, 1997).

One aspect of the supervisor's own process which Hawkins and Shohet identify in both editions of their work is the fantasy relationship between supervisor and client, in that both have a conscious 'fantasy' (as distinct from unconscious phantasy) about the other. Hawkins and Shohet suggest that the thoughts and feelings a supervisor may have about the client may be useful to the therapist. Again this relies on the importance given to the unconscious and triangular processes. In professional circles, where the client may also be a therapist, and the supervisor is known, either directly or by reputation, such fantasies become even more complex.

Mode 7 Focusing on the wider context
In the first edition of their book Hawkins and Shohet acknowledged two additions

which would make the model 'fuller': the inclusion of the client's wider social context or milieu, and a focus on the organisational, social and political context in which the supervised work (and, indeed, the supervision) is taking place. In the second edition of their book, they make these additions, and include a chapter on transcultural supervision. Hawkins and Shohet (2000) describe this focus on the wider context as a move 'from the specific client relationships that are figural in the session to the contextual field in which both the therapy work and the supervision work are taking place' (p. 84). This is entirely compatible with the emphasis in the person-centred approach on the active interchange between the organism and environment. Just as 'there's no such thing as a baby', but rather the baby and the mother (the immediate environment) in active interchange, so there's no such thing as an individual, rather an individual in context. Similarly, there's no such thing as an independent practitioner or supervisor, rather two people engaging, actively or otherwise, with their professional, organisational, institutional, social, political, cultural context/s.

THE PROCESS MODEL OF SUPERVISION—PURPOSE, USE AND CRITIQUE

Hawkins and Shohet (1989) developed their model of the process of the supervisory relationship

> when we were trying to understand the significant differences in the way each member of our own peer group supervised and the different styles of supervision that we had encountered elsewhere . . . From further exploration came the realization that the differences were connected to the constant choices we were making, as supervisors, as to what we focused on. (p. 55)

The declared purpose of the model is 'to provide a framework for new levels of depth and new ways of creatively intervening in a supervision session' (Hawkins and Shohet, 2000, p. 87). They go on to state that 'we have become increasingly convinced that to carry out effective supervision of any deep therapeutic work it is necessary for the supervisor to be able to use all seven modes of supervision' (ibid., p. 87). In this sense the model may be used in the training and assessment of supervisors.

In the above summary and review of Hawkins and Shohet's model we have made comments from a person-centred perspective on each of the seven modes, some more compatible with the person-centred approach to supervision than others. In conclusion, we offer two critiques of the overall model, regarding its hierarchical nature and its theoretical bias.

1. Its hierarchical nature

   The significance and impact of non-verbal communication is well documented. Some studies claim that up to 90% of the meaning of a message is transmitted non-verbally (e.g. Fromkin and Rodman, 1983). This is true also with regard to the visual construction and presentation of theoretical models. Thus, in Hawkins and Shohet's model, the fact that, of the three related circles signifying people, the supervisor is at the top, signifies a certain hierarchy and authority given to the person of the supervisor. At one point in the second edition of their book Hawkins and Shohet (2000) refer to the model as the 'seven-eyed *supervisor* model' (p. 87, our emphasis). There is an implied reporting of issues and dynamics going up which, of course, also indicates something of the authors' model of therapy or helping. Imagine if the sequence was (from the top) client, therapist, supervisor, or if the model was presented horizontally. Ultimately, this model promotes the view of supervision as an 'overview', rather than a *wider* view.

2. Its theoretical bias

   In both editions of their book, Hawkins and Shohet appear somewhat ambivalent about theory or, more precisely, about theoretical orientation, which they refer to, obliquely, as 'style' and 'type of training'. They do suggest that 'both supervisor and supervisee need to have enough of a common language and belief system to be able to learn and work together' (Hawkins and Shohet, 1989, p. 48). They suggest that 'it is also possible to integrate several different therapeutic approaches into one's own supervision style' (ibid., p. 48), but without elaborating how they propose this is done. In the first edition of the book Hawkins and Shohet (1989) use the term 'countertransference' to describe modes 4 and 6. In the second edition they change this to 'focusing on the therapist's process' and 'focusing on the supervisor's own process', respectively. Together with their use of and reliance on notions of the unconscious and of transference, this locates the model, or at least those particular levels or modes (3, 4, 5 and 6), as clearly influenced by the psychodynamic tradition. This, in itself, is not a problem. It only becomes a problem if and when the model is presented as theoretically neutral or generic—which it often is. In the preface to the second edition, Hawkins and Shohet (2000) report that their model has been described as humanistic, but acknowledge their own thinking that it is 'more of a holistic and integrative model which draws upon psychodynamic, humanistic, cognitive, behavioural and systemic approaches to therapeutic work . . . [it] is also very rooted in an intersubjective approach' (p. xviii). Given the emphasis on psychodynamic theory in its description and elaboration—Hawkins and Shohet (2000), for

75

instance, refer to 'the client's psychodynamics' (p. 80)—we view this as more psychodynamic than anything else and, therefore, as an orientation-specific model than as a generic or integrative model of supervision.

Having completed our review and critique of a number of themes in generic approaches to supervision, in the next chapter we turn our attention to discussing issues, questions and dilemmas which emerge in the practice of supervision.

REFERENCES

Barrett-Lennard, G.T. (1981) The empathy cycle. *Journal of Counselling Psychology, 28,* 91–100

Bozarth, J.D. (1984) Beyond empathy: Emergent modes of empathy. In R. Levant and J. Shlien (Eds.) *Client-Centered Therapy and the Person-Centered Approach: New Directions in Theory, Research and Practice* (pp. 59–75). New York: Praeger.

Casement, P. (1985) *On Learning from the Patient.* London: Tavistock

Casement, P. (1990) *Further Learning from the Patient: The Analytic Space and Process.* London: Routledge

Doerhman, M. J. G. (1976) Parallel process in supervision and psychotherapy. *Bulletin of the Menninger Clinic, 10(1),* 9–105

Ekstein, R and Wallerstein, R. S. (1958) *The Teaching and Learning of Psychotherapy.* New York: International Universities Press

Embleton Tudor, L., Keemar, K., Tudor, K., Valentine, J. and Worrall, M. (in press 2004) *The Person-Centred Approach: A Contemporary Introduction.* Basingstoke: Palgrave

Feltham, C. and Dryden, W. (1994) *Developing Counsellor Supervision.* London: Sage.

Fromkin, V. and J. Rodman (1983) *An Introduction to Language.* New York: CBS College Publishing

Greenberg, L. S. and Elliot, R. (1997) Varieties of empathic responding. In A. C. Bohart and L. S. Greenberg (Eds.) *Empathy Reconsidered: New Directions in Psychotherapy* (pp. 167–86). Washington, DC: American Psychological Association

Hawkins, P. and Shohet, R. (1989) *Supervision in the Helping Professions.* Milton Keynes: Open University Press

Hawkins, P. and Shohet, R. (2000) *Supervision in the Helping Professions* (2nd edn.). Buckingham: Open University Press

Inskipp, F. and Proctor. B. (1995) *Making the Most of Supervision. Part 2: Becoming a Supervisor.* Twickenham: Cascade Publications

Mearns, D. (1994) *Developing Person-Centred Counselling.* London: Sage

Mearns, D. (1995) Supervision: a tale of the missing client. *British Journal of Guidance and Counselling, 23,* (3), 421–7

Mothersole, G. (1999) Parallel process: A review. *The Clinical Supervisor, 18*(2), 107–21

Neville, B. (1996) Five kinds of empathy. In R. Hutterer, G. Pawlowsky. P. F. Schmid and R. Stipsits (Eds.) *Client-centered and Experiential Psychotherapy: A Paradigm in Motion* (pp. 439–53). Frankfurt am Main: Peter Lang

Rice, L.N. (1974). The evocative function of the therapist. In D. A. Wexler and L. N. Rice (Eds.) *Innovations in Client-Centered Therapy* (pp. 289–311). New York: Wiley

Rice, L. N. (1980) A client-centered approach to the supervision of psychotherapy. In A.K. Hess (Ed.) *Psychotherapy Supervision: Theory, Research and Practice* (pp. 136–47). New York: Wiley

Rogers, C.R. (1942) *Counseling and Psychotherapy: Newer Concepts in Practice.* Boston: Houghton Mifflin

Rogers, C.R. (1951) *Client-Centered Therapy.* London: Constable

Searles, H.F. (1955) The informational value of the supervisor's emotional experience. In H.F. Searles *Collected Papers on Schizophrenia and Related Subjects* (pp. 135–46). London: Hogarth Press

Shlien, J. (1984) A countertheory of transference. In R. Levant and J. Shlien (Eds.) *Client-Centered Therapy and the Person-Centered Approach: New Directions in Theory, Research and Practice* (pp. 153–81) New York: Praeger

Stern, D.N. (1985) *The Interpersonal World of the Infant.* New York: Basic Books

Villas-Boas Bowen, M. (1986) Personality differences and person-centered supervision. *Person-Centered Review,* 1(3), 291–309

Warner, M. S. (1991) Fragile process. In L. Fusek (Ed.) *New Directions in Client-Centered Therapy: Practice with Difficult Client Populations (Monograph Series 1)* (pp. 41–58). Chicago, IL: Chicago Counseling and Psychotherapy Center

Warner, M. S. (1998) Personal correspondence, workshop, The Metanoia Institute

Warner, M. S. (2000) Person-centered psychotherapy: One nation, many tribes. *The Person-Centered Journal,* 7(1), 28–39

CHAPTER FIVE

ISSUES, QUESTIONS, DILEMMAS AND DOMAINS IN SUPERVISION

KEITH TUDOR AND MIKE WORRALL

We've considered the philosophy and theory of a person-centred approach to supervision in Chapter 1, and person-centred approaches to the generic literature on supervision in Chapters 3 and 4. In this chapter we consider issues, questions, and dilemmas in supervision, again from a person-centred perspective. We want first to distinguish between issues, questions and dilemmas, in the belief that clarity in this area will lead to clearer, more differentiated thinking and therefore to more considered practice. We then look at some of the domains within which issues, questions, and dilemmas arise. Different domains are subject to different guiding frameworks including legislation, and we think it's helpful to clarify which domain we're working in so as to identify more accurately the most pertinent sources of guidance. We follow this with two discussions concerning authority and responsibility in supervision, and conclude with a brief discussion of the importance of congruence between personal philosophy, chosen theoretical orientation and practice with clients and supervisees.

ISSUES

One way of describing supervision is to say that it's a space within which we can look at some of the issues which arise for us as we work. These issues often begin as relatively vague enquiries without any necessary resolution. We may, for instance, wonder in supervision about the origins of a particular client's conditions of worth, or about the depth of our own emotional response to some aspect of a client's story. We may be curious about our own lack of empathy for one client, and puzzle over our attraction for another. These issues deserve and repay attention. If they are questions at all, though, they're rhetorical questions and they don't require specific or detailed answers. Issues of this sort tend not to carry or provoke any great emotional tension for supervisor or supervisee. They're characterised more by relaxed, engaged and free-ranging exploration.

QUESTIONS

Occasionally, issues resolve into more precise questions to do with how we behave towards our clients or our colleagues, how we conceptualise our work, how we balance our work with the rest of our lives, and so on. These questions are often more pressing and require more precise answers. At this point supervision becomes a space to look at options and to decide which options are most suitable, appropriate or desirable: Shall I do this or that? Of all the options I can see, which is the most consistent with who I am and with how I want to practise? Supervision offers an opportunity to ask these questions, and to seek provisional answers with which we can experiment and which we can review, return to and revise in the light of subsequent experience. As such, and at its best, it's an invaluable resource and one which supports critical thinking and a disciplined freedom of practice. Questions of this sort may carry a greater emotional charge or urgency than the issues we described above, particularly if practitioners need to make decisions about what to do in a particular situation. One example of this is the kind of questions which focus on ethical issues and what to do in certain problematic situations. There are a number of models which address such questions through a staged approach to ethical problem-solving (see Paradise and Siegelwaks, 1982; Austin, Moline and Williams, 1990; Bond, 1993).

We suspect that many supervisees use much of their supervision time to explore the kinds of issues and questions we've described here. Some questions are simply questions. They may not have definitive or satisfying answers, and the asking of them may have implications for the way we work as practitioners. In essence, though, they are simply questions that we can ask, explore, come back to and make eventual peace with. A dilemma, however, is more than a simple question.

Dilemmas

It may be helpful to think of a dilemma more as a series of questions, the answer to any one of which is at odds with the answer to any one other. According to *Chambers English Dictionary* (Schwartz et al., 1901/1988), a dilemma is 'a form of argument in which the maintainer of a certain proposition is committed to accept one of two propositions each of which contradicts his original contention' (p. 396). The form of argument was originally, in Ancient Greece, called a 'horned syllogism', and the victim compared to a man certain to be impaled on one of the horns of a bull (and hence the reference to the 'horns' of a dilemma). This definition is useful in that it articulates the *tripartite* nature of a dilemma: the original proposition, and two possible subsequent propositions either of which is undesirable in that it compromises the original proposition.

In our view, it is especially helpful to articulate and explore the original or underlying proposition, which we think is often missing from what practitioners present in supervision. An example might help. A therapist has been working for a long time with a particular client and feels moved to offer him a hug at the end of what seems like an especially significant session. She believes that it would be therapeutic and thinks that he would appreciate it. At the same time she doesn't feel confident about it. She is worried about how her client might experience it, and also about what her colleagues, her supervisor and her peers might think of her. She remembers her tutor at college telling his students that on no account, nor in any circumstances, should they touch their clients (see, for instance, Casemore, 2001). She feels in conflict. She decides not to offer a hug there and then, and takes the issue to supervision.

In supervision, she describes her conflict as a straight choice: to hug or not to hug. Her supervisor is sensitive to and suspicious of the implied polarity of this. He sees that she has given herself the choice to hug *or* to be ethical. They explore for a while the conflict as initially presented and both gradually recognise the limitations of this approach, one of which is that it encourages either approval or disapproval, and leaves little room for any more moderate, subtle or complex response. As a result of this polarity the supervisee feels sometimes defensive: *It's my therapy and I'll hug if I want to*; and sometimes self-critical: *I shouldn't have wanted to hug my client anyway*. For his part, and for as long as he too is stuck with this polarity, the supervisor feels both *concerned* to support his supervisee's internal locus of evaluation and *anxious* about the possibility that her client may complain. After some reflection he feels more keenly the limitations of this polarised discussion. He reminds himself that his supervisee has always been competent and trustworthy and, therefore, that there is probably, in her conflict, something important which neither he nor she has yet articulated. As a way of moving out of this polarity, he asks her to think about the consequences of first hugging and then not hugging. This allows her to see that if she hugs her client she fears being unethical, and that if she doesn't she risks being, seeming or feeling herself to be withholding or even negligent. She finds these realisations, in themselves, helpful. Furthermore, they both point to her underlying wish to be a good therapist. Now we have a dilemma, which, as we've seen, comprises an original proposition and two subsequent choices, either of which will compromise it. This dilemma is represented in Figure 5.1.

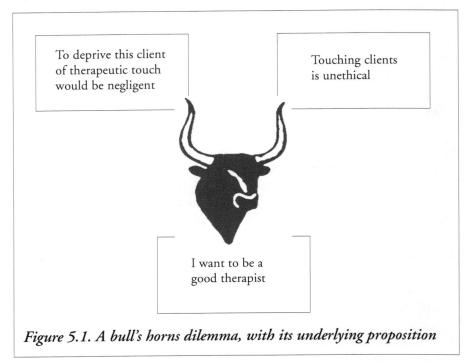

Figure 5.1. A bull's horns dilemma, with its underlying proposition

This therapist's original proposition is that she wants to be a good therapist. If she hugs her client, she feels at risk of crossing ethical boundaries, and would therefore not be a good therapist. If she doesn't hug her client, she feels as if she risks depriving her client of something therapeutic, and this would also compromise her wish to be a good therapist. Since, in simple behavioural terms, she can only hug, or not hug, she compromises her original proposition, her wish to be a good therapist, whichever she does.

There are broadly two ways out of the tension inherent in such a dilemma. We might choose one of the two subsequent propositions as preferable to the other, or we might examine and revise the original proposition. In this example the supervisee has three choices:

- She can decide to risk being unethical rather than negligent, offer her client a hug, and live with both the unease and the consequences;

- She can decide to risk withholding rather than being unethical, not offer her client a hug, and live with both the unease and the consequences of that; or

- She can change her construction of what being a good therapist entails, such that it becomes ethically allowable to hug a client sometimes and possible also not to hug a client without that constituting negligence.

This vignette shows how helpful it can be to identify the original proposition in a dilemma. It allows practitioners to step out of an initially limited and limiting mindset, and to develop additional, more creative choices. It also frames questions in terms of significant personal and philosophical positions, rather than simply pragmatic or behavioural ones.

DOMAINS

Issues, questions and dilemmas arise in and belong to particular domains. The ways in which we approach a particular issue, question or dilemma, and the freedom or latitude we have to move around within it, are at least influenced and sometimes governed by the rules or principles of the particular domain or domains to which it belongs. We think it's important to identify which domain we're operating in on any one occasion, so that we can appeal for guidance to the most relevant and appropriate guidelines. For the purposes of this discussion we identify the following domains: clinical; professional; ethical; personal; legal; social; and cultural. Each domain carries its own particular concerns and we think it's helpful to address those concerns within the guidelines relevant to the particular domain. It's not helpful, for instance, to appeal to *clinical* guidelines to help resolve a *legal* issue, nor to accuse someone of *unethical* practice just because he hasn't addressed the transference issue, which we would see as a concern from the *clinical* domain.

Clinical

Within this domain we see questions to do with a practitioner's practice of her particular discipline. Such questions will obviously differ from discipline to discipline, and, within broad disciplines, from one school to another. An acupuncturist, for instance, might ask questions to do with diagnosis, and would ask different questions from a homeopath or a psychiatrist who might also be interested in diagnosis. Within the practice of acupuncture a five-element acupuncturist would also ask different questions from an acupuncturist trained in Traditional Chinese Medicine. A psychodynamic counsellor might address questions of transference, countertransference and resistance, while a person-centred therapist might think about the depth of his empathic understanding or the quality of his unconditional positive regard for a particular client.

In all of these instances, guidance comes most immediately from each relevant discipline's body of theory, literature, research and accumulated experience. A supervisor trained in the same discipline as her supervisee can offer a valuable way into some of that material, especially if she is both *knowledgeable* and *generous*, as we've described in Chapter 1.

Professional

The professional domain covers questions to do with an individual practitioner's relationship with his colleagues and with the professional body to which he belongs, however formally or informally that is defined. It also covers questions to do with the setting within which the therapeutic work takes place, by which we mean questions of fees, contracts and boundaries. Again, practitioners from different disciplines will have different understandings of some of these issues. A person-centred therapist and a transactional analyst, for instance, may well agree that boundaries matter and yet have different ideas about what boundaries are appropriate.

Guidelines in this domain come formally in the shape of the codes of conduct which various professional bodies draw up, and informally in the shape of tacitly agreed and understood professional norms. Again, a supervisor from the same profession will be in a position to help induct her supervisee into their profession's *modus operandi*. This encouragement of acquiring certain professional values is explicit in some definitions of supervision, as we discussed in Chapter 3 (see, for instance, Urbano, 1984).

Ethical

Ethics, as the science of morals, concerns rules of conduct of human life. Within this domain we see questions to do with a professional body's agreed and established values as they are articulated in codes of ethical practice or ethical frameworks. Such codes or frameworks address questions of confidentiality, boundaries, contracting, advertising and so on. The difference between the ethical domain and the clinical domain, which also addresses some of these questions, is that the ethical domain addresses them from the perspective of moral values rather than the theoretical integrity of a particular discipline. The British Association for Counselling and Psychotherapy's (BACP) *Ethical Framework*, for instance, speaks to all who subscribe to it whatever their theoretical allegiance. Similarly, the British

Acupuncture Council's (1997) *Code of Ethics and Practice* covers the work of acupuncturists from several different traditions. As such, these codes and frameworks both define the bounds of the domain and usually constitute the most relevant source of guidance for issues, questions and dilemmas which arise therein.

Personal

Whatever theoretical discipline we trained in, whatever professional body we belong to and whatever ethical code or framework we subscribe to, we all have personal or inner values, which sit more or less comfortably with those outer structures. Most theoretical maps, professional codes and ethical frameworks acknowledge this, at least implicitly, and allow individual practitioners some degree of latitude to think for themselves within them and to act according to their own values. The BACP's *Ethical Framework*, for instance, does not prescribe in detail how a counsellor who subscribes to it should respond to a suicidal client. Within certain parameters, a counsellor's response in this situation will be a function of her personal beliefs and values about human nature and the sanctity of human life and the right of an individual client to take his own life, or not.

Morals, concerned with meaning, custom, manners, character, requirement, i.e. the nature of the distinction between right and wrong, virtue and conduct, are greater than specific ethics and ethical codes, and inform our views about issues, questions and dilemmas in life. Bond (1996) discusses two aspects or dimensions of morality:

- The *deontic* (after the Greek for duty)—which concerns the moral requirement to do certain things and not to do other things. Judgements in this dimension concern acts as prohibited, obligatory or permissible, and gives rise to ethical principles such as non-maleficence and beneficence. This aspect of morality is first found in the philosophical ethics of the German idealist philosopher, Immanuel Kant (1724–1804).

- The *aretaic* (after the Greek for virtue or excellence)—which concerns states or dispositions of character that are desirable or undesirable. Judgements in this dimension concern people and character as being virtuous or not. This aspect of morality may be traced back to the Greek philosopher Plato (c.430–347 BCE), his pupil Aristotle (384–322 BCE) and the Scottish philosopher David Hume (1711–1777).

Guidelines in this area are, necessarily, personal, although they will take into account other, outer codes and frameworks. We see an argument here for practitioners, in their training, on their own, and in their supervision to ask themselves what they really think and feel about any moral issue around which there is room for different people to take different views, both in terms of acts and character: on suicide, euthanasia, monogamy, abortion, and so on. This highlights the importance of personal philosophy (see pp. 94–5 below).

Legal

Whatever else we're subject to, we're all subject to the force of law. Most practitioners in the United Kingdom will probably go through most of their professional lives without coming into contact with the legal system on account of anything to do with their work. This, of course, may change. The law, however, has something to say about such issues as confidentiality, professional abuse, suicide, and duty of care. It also has different things to say to practitioners of different disciplines. There is, for instance, no legal requirement for counsellors to make or keep notes of their work. There are specific professional and ethical requirements, but not legal ones. For public health reasons, though, acupuncturists are legally required to keep accurate records of who they see and when they see them. The law also has different things to say depending on the age of the client or patient, and the context within which the work is taking place.

As with ethical codes and frameworks, the law both defines the parameters of the domain and is the most complete and relevant guide to issues, questions and dilemmas which arise within it. Lawyers train for many years to work competently within their own speciality, and it's unlikely that counsellors or therapists will acquire for themselves the skills and knowledge they'd need to find their own way around the law to that same degree of competence. That doesn't absolve us, however, of the need to take the law into account. The BACP *Framework*, for instance, (p. 6) says that those who subscribe to it must 'be aware of and understand any legal requirements concerning their work, consider these conscientiously and be legally accountable for their practice'. This, we think, makes sense, on two counts. The first is that ignorance is no defence: if we don't know in broad terms how the law is or might be relevant to our work, then we're exposing ourselves unnecessarily to the risk of breaking it. The second is that if we know, rather than imagine, what the law says we must and must not do, we might find that we have more options than we thought we had. In any case, we put ourselves in a better position to make informed and considered choices about what we do.

Social

Therapy and supervision of all sorts take place within a society and are subject to changing social mores and conventions. Although they may not impinge on our work as directly as some, these conventions nevertheless provide the backdrop against which we work. We may want to take them into account in our thinking and practice. Take, for instance, the question of fees. We can look at how much we charge from a number of perspectives. There may be *clinical* consequences, for particular clients or patients, at least, if we decide to charge one fee as opposed to another. There are, for some of us, *professional* and *ethical* requirements for us to be clear about what we charge, but not to do with how much we charge. Similarly, the *law* has little to say about how much we can charge or should charge. That leaves us answering the question of how much to charge based on *personal* values, to do with how much we feel comfortable charging, and *social* conventions, based on how much others around us are charging for a similar service, and on how much we think is a socially acceptable amount to ask for.

Cultural

Similarly, therapy and supervision take place within different cultural contexts and are also subject to different cultural norms and expectations. In Chapter 3 we reviewed some of the literature on the context and impact of culture in supervision. Culture informs different views of supervision itself as well as of the content and process of supervision (see also Chapter 6).

We find this articulation of domains useful for a number of reasons:

- It articulates the precise nature of a particular issue, question or dilemma.
- It helps us identify and consult the most relevant sources of help or guidance.
- It rules out some guidelines which are irrelevant.
- It identifies which courses of action are proscribed, which are allowed, and what penalties we risk if we choose to act against the rules or frameworks of the relevant domain.
- It clarifies our options in any given situation.

These domains are represented in Figure 5.2 overleaf.

We've arranged the domains in this way as we see them as nested, one on the other. Thus, the clinical is a specific domain within the professional domain which, in turn, contains considerations wider than the clinical, and so on. In terms of domains we see an argument for the cultural and the social being interchangeable. In some circumstances, cultural considerations may be 'sub-cultural' to the wider, social environment and domain; in others 'culture' is broader than the immediate social environment. Viewing these domains as different environments reminds us of Barrett-Lennard's (1998) point about the organism being 'a purposeful, open system, in particularly active interchange with its environment' (Barrett-Lennard, 1998, p. 75). We live in interesting times and in

87

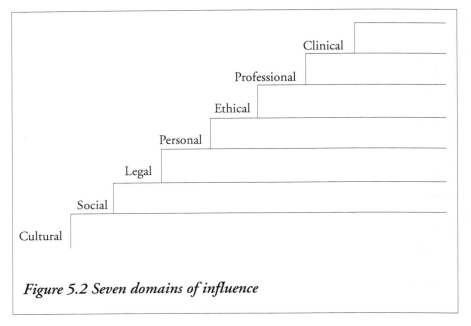

Figure 5.2 Seven domains of influence

a complex, changing world. As active, motivated, pro-social organisms, we are inevitably in relationship with our environment or environments. The issues, questions and dilemmas we face concern the nature of that activity and the extent of our analysis.

Clearly much of our work as practitioners and supervisors falls under the influence of several domains, rather than within one exclusively. That means that we may need to attend to several different domains when we want to explore an issue, answer a question or resolve a dilemma. That in itself can constitute something else to explore, answer or resolve, and may involve us having to act within the guidelines of one domain rather than another. Practitioners working within certain statutory or voluntary agencies, for instance, may be *legally* constrained and *so*cially encouraged to report instances of suspected sexual abuse to the Social Services authority, even if their ethical framework, professional allegiances, personal and cultural values allow them to take a different course of action, and even if they suspect that the clinical consequences would be unhelpful. This analysis of domains again helps us clarify the nature of the difficulty, identify possible options, and gives greater freedom to practise.

In the last parts of this chapter we consider two aspects of practice which pose issues, questions and dilemmas for practitioners and supervisors alike, concerning authority and responsibility. We discuss these drawing on examples from practice and offer a framework for understanding and practice which has echoes of Rogers' (1958/1967) process conception of psychotherapy (see Chapter 1).

Authority: internal or external?

Where does the authority for deciding how to practise lie? Does it lie with the practitioner, with some external body or bodies, or is it sometimes internal and personal and sometimes external and impersonal? Page and Wosket (1994), for instance, assert that 'a supervisor needs to be prepared to carry a more readily identifiable authority . . . which includes monitoring the practice of the supervisee' (p. 22).

Current trends towards accreditation, regulation and professionalisation are, perhaps necessarily, driven and monitored by external bodies, based on externally articulated criteria, and policed by external authority. Some training organisations, professional bodies and supervisors, in effect, tell students and practitioners what to think and what to do. The codification of behaviour into what is and what is not 'professional' and 'ethical' encourages, we think, overadaptation to certain given, fixed and external mores; passivity and inactivity in the face of complexity and uncertainty; and a marked dullness of intellect.

One recent example of this comes from the work of Casemore (2001), to which we've referred in the Introduction and above. He describes telling counselling students that they must not ever touch their clients, and then makes for himself a record of when he told them. Given such *ex cathedra* pronouncements, at such an early stage of their professional development, we understand how and why many practitioners learn not to trust themselves or their clients, and adopt a defensive way of working that is predicated on anxiety and motivated primarily by a desire to avoid harm, abuse or controversy rather than to do good. In our view, Casemore's behaviour may arise from and almost certainly provokes or perpetuates a level of fear or anxiety which in itself leads to fixed thinking and rigid practice: something is either right or wrong, ethical or unethical, and that's that. We agree with Shohet (1997) that 'any action or thought that springs from fear is ultimately unproductive' (p. 45). Writing from the perspective of a client, and writing about touch metaphorically rather than literally, Heyward (1993) argues that abuse is 'not simply a matter of touching people wrongly' but more 'a refusal to touch people rightly'. She goes on to say (ibid., p.10) that we 'are as likely to destroy one another and ourselves by holding tightly to prescribed role definitions as we are by active intrusion and violation'. We object to Casemore's practice because it encourages practitioners not only to hold tightly to 'prescribed role definitions', but to hold tightly to role definitions that have been prescribed from the outside and with the weight of external authority. This is in itself, we think, potentially abusive and at the very least inadequate in that it does not equip practitioners with the subtle, supple and grounded thinking necessary to meet, live with and talk about complex professional situations.

Another example is assessment. Assessment and evaluation are both concerned with 'setting' or ascribing value. The problem with assessment from a person-centred perspective is the locus of this evaluation. A number of models of supervision are quite detailed about both formative (ongoing) and summative (final) assessment (see Page and Wosket, 1994; and Carroll, 1996), but do so from an external, authoritative perspective. This perspective is paralleled in practice. Many trainee or student therapists in practice placements are not allowed to conduct the initial assessment session with the client; instead a more experienced therapist does the assessments and then allocates the client to the trainee. Sometimes this is done on the basis of some assumptions about the relative efficacy of different theoretical orientations. There are several problems with this:

- It concretises the initial assessment and sets up the assessor as the external expert.
- It artificially separates assessment and the client from the process of therapy.
- It discounts the fact that all practitioners, and clients, make their own assessments, however informally.
- It prevents the trainee developing his own assessment skills.
- It discounts the reality that assessment is an ongoing process.
- It also compromises the therapist's ethical, professional and personal responsibilities to assess his own competence to work with any and every client.

Mearns (1997) is particularly strident in his critique of the 'ridiculous' question of assessment, favouring the transfer of resources from employing 'expert' assessors to increased support for counsellors through training and, when necessary, intensive supervision.

The person-centred approach values personal, inner authority. Rogers (1961/1967) said that his own experience was for him the highest authority, above even the Bible, Freud or the findings of research studies! His theory of therapy predicts for clients a move away from reliance on external authorities and towards an internal authority instead. This valuing of personal authority is perhaps the most radical and subversive aspect of person-centred practice. Supervisors whose work is consistent with the philosophical values of the approach will reflect this recognition of individual authority. They will, therefore, not only allow but actively encourage the practitioners who come to them for supervision to explore their own experiences, find their own meanings and make their own decisions about their work. The result is to free ourselves and to help those we supervise from what Rogers (1958/1990) refers to as 'the *threat* of external evaluation' (p.123, our emphasis). In this, creativity and creative practice (Rogers, 1954/1967; N.

Rogers, 1993/2000) is the antithesis of defensive therapy (for a critique of which see Heyward, 1993), paranoid practice (for a critique of an example of which see Furedi, 2001), and restrictive regulations (for a critique of which see Mowbray, 1995).

We don't want to give the impression that person-centred supervision encourages practitioners to become thoughtlessly maverick or exclusively self-centred. Rogers describes the human organism as having social and constructive leanings. This aspect of an organism's tendency to actualise suggests that given the right relational conditions practitioners will naturally want to take external frameworks appropriately into account. Our experience supports this. The problem is not that professional, ethical or legal frameworks are external to the individual practitioner. It's inevitable that that's where they start, at least for the majority of practitioners who were not involved in drawing them up. The problem arises when they stay external. This is more likely to happen when practitioners subscribe to these ethical codes uncritically, and primarily in order to join or to stay within professional bodies. We have found that as we become familiar with the ethical and professional frameworks to which we subscribe, as we make them our own, they come to feel less like threatening or punitive authorities and more like sources of support to which we can turn and, crucially, with which we can dialogue. This process entails a commitment to get to know what the frameworks actually say, and to think critically, diligently and in detail about how they relate to our practice. For one of us (MW) it entails a commitment to read the BACP's *Ethical Framework* once every month or six weeks, as a way of becoming and remaining familiar with what it says.

RESPONSIBILITY: INTERNAL OR EXTERNAL?

There is a strong theme in the generic literature on supervision (see Chapter 2) concerning responsibility (see Ward et al., 1985; British Association for Counselling, 1988; Proctor, 1988; Page and Wosket, 1994). This can be traced back (at least) to Bordin's (1983) comment that 'supervisors are part of a professional gatekeeping apparatus designed to protect the public and the profession' (p. 38), an argument which is uncritically reiterated by Feltham and Dryden (1994). This 'protection' argument has been effectively demolished by Mowbray (1995) with regard to the registration of psychotherapists, and we consider much of his critique as transferable to the field of supervision. However, responsibility is a 'hot potato' in that one case in the States (reported by Stone, 1976) established the principle of vicarious responsibility by which the supervisor of a therapist was deemed negligent and liable for the action or inaction of the supervisee. However, as Jenkins (1997) observes, the term 'supervisor' has a specific connotation in the field of counselling and psychotherapy. In this field a supervisor is usually 'not required to be a supervisor in any formal managerial or organisational sense'. It would follow, therefore, that such supervisors do not necessarily hold vicarious liability in the sense that an employer would' (pp. 68–9) (see also Cristofoli, 2002). King and Wheeler (1999) report on a study in which they interviewed supervisors in private practice, none of whom considered themselves legally or clinically responsible for their supervisee's work.

Page and Wosket (1994), for instance, identify a number of responsibilities that the supervisor holds, including:

- Ensuring that the needs of clients are addressed; time is managed; boundaries are maintained; and the work is focused and balanced.
- Informing the supervisee about the methods, approaches and supervisory style.
- Addressing the issue of how the supervisee prepares for supervision.
- Providing a facilitative relationship; constructive, balanced and regular feedback; and formative reviews.
- Letting the supervisee know about his or her own responsibilities.

From a person-centred perspective this is far too external. It is monologic, not dialogic. Similarly, the now redundant *Code of Ethics and Practice for Supervisors of Counsellors* (British Association for Counselling, 1996) identified 16 issues or areas of responsibility for the supervisor—and none for the supervisee! A rare exception to this bias of responsibility is the perspective on clinical supervision from the National Health Service Management Executive (1993), quoted in Chapter 3, which advocates supervision as 'encouraging supervisees to assume responsibility for their own practice and [thereby] enhance consumer protection and the safety of care'. Horton (1993) reverses the traditional logic, arguing that, as supervision is a consultative arrangement, supervisors are primarily accountable to their supervisees.

Nowhere is the responsibility issue more true and more played out than in relation to trainee or student counsellors and psychotherapists. Vandecreek and Harrar (1988) assert that trainee counsellors are, with the help of their supervisors, obliged not to provide substandard care. They go on to state that the supervisor is also obliged to ensure that the client's needs are held as paramount. The language is revealing: 'obligation is matched only by the impossible task of ensuring another person's practice, and one set of needs, the client's, are simply asserted as of importance above all others'. What is more insidious is that this argument *appears* to have the authority of law as it is entitled 'The legal liability of supervisors'. However, in the context of United Kingdom law they were (in 1988)—and still are—wrong. Jenkins (1997) summarises the position clearly, with regard to proceedings under civil law and, in England and Wales, the question of *tort* (from the French meaning 'wrong'), *delict* in Scotland. Proving a case based on tort requires the fulfilment of three specific conditions (the existence of a duty of care to the client, breach of that duty, and resultant harm as a consequence of that breach), none of which especially applies to supervisors of trainees. Vandecreek and Harrar's (1988) empty assertions are revealed as little more than scaremongering. Jenkins (1997) concludes that 'the legal liability of supervisors in the UK for their supervisees is an untested area, where the likelihood of liability is probably rather limited' (p. 68).

If, as trainers and supervisors, we frighten trainees and practitioners, we only encourage them to be scared and defensive. If we discourage free-thinking and independence, we encourage overadaptation and dependence. If we don't trust them, they won't trust themselves—or us. If we do not encourage reflective practice or reflective practitioners, we encourage students and supervisees to look to external authority. If we take away responsibility, we encourage dependence, and, ultimately, perpetuate a blaming culture. If we're not creative and co-creative, we block the creative connection in others. If we infantalise adult learners, we encourage regression and transferential attitudes of dependence. Infantalising trainees and supervisees discounts the fact that they are, by and large, mature, adult learners who bring rich and diverse experiences to their training and practice as therapists, including the experience of responsibility in their lives. In our experience, the issue of responsibility, if there is one, is that students take too much responsibility for their work and the lives of their clients.

Such views, whether propounded by trainers and supervisors or by inexperienced therapists, may be understood as another example of fixity and rigidity, probably along all seven of Rogers' (1958/1967) continua of process in terms of:

- Unowned feelings—on the part of the supervisor, of, say, anxiety about what a client, trainee or supervisee may say or do, or not do.
- Remoteness of experiencing—whereby a supervisor may not engage with her supervisee.
- Incongruence—between the philosophy of the approach on the one hand and the practice of the supervisor on the other.
- An unwillingness to communicate—for instance, her anxiety.
- Rigid constructs—about authority and responsibility.
- Unrecognised problems—regarding authority and dependency.
- The avoidance of close relationships—for instance with people who may disagree.

Such views about responsibility and authority are not only to do with psychological processes. They also reflect and represent particular assumptions about the nature of knowledge and the nature of society, for further analysis and discussion of which see Tudor and Worrall (in press 2004).

PERSONAL PHILOSOPHY, THEORETICAL ORIENTATION AND PRACTICE

It will be clear from what we have written in this part of the book that we value a high level of congruence between:

i) An individual practitioner's personal philosophy;
ii) The philosophical values and principles of the theoretical approach within which that practitioner elects to study and work; and
iii) That practioner's clinical work—and supervision practice.

There are several reasons for this. The first is based on our belief on the inevitability of philosophy: what we do, how we are in our lives with partners, friends, children, people we meet, colleagues and clients is based on certain beliefs about ourselves, others and the world. Listening, modelling and giving advice are all based on different theories and, ultimately, different views of human nature and communication. We're not prescribing a particular view of the world. We are saying that practitioners will be better therapists and supervisors if they choose a theory whose philosophical principles are compatible with their own personal philosophy, not least because they will experience less discrepancy between themselves and their experience of life and of training. This underscores the importance of discovering, exploring and articulating our own personal philosophy.

Given this grounding in personal philosophy, practitioners are more able to examine, explore and challenge the principles of any theoretical approach; without it they are lost, and may be inclined to accept and adapt to received 'wisdom' (which is, of course, a contradiction in terms). To take one example, and whatever we think of it, some students may find Casemore's injunction not to touch clients helpful. It is, however, clearly and flagrantly at odds with person-centred principles of trust, mutuality, relationship and immediacy, and with person-centred ideas about learning. The point here is not about whether we touch or don't touch clients. The point is about whether what we do, and how we do it, is consistent with the principles we espouse—or not! As supervisors and trainers, we are committed to creating the conditions within which practitioners and students can dialogue freely between their personal philosophy and the philosophical assumptions which underlie their chosen theoretical orientation. It is in this spirit that we have edited and present this book.

REFERENCES

Austen, K. M., Moline, M. E. and Williams, G. T. (1990) *Confronting Malpractice: Legal and Ethical Dilemmas in Psychotherapy*. Newbury Park, CA: Sage

Barrett-Lennard, G. T. (1998) *Carl Rogers' Helping System: Journey and Substance*. London: Sage

Bond, E. J. (1996) *Ethics and Human Well-Being*. Oxford: Blackwell

Bond, T. (1993) *Standards and Ethics for Counselling in Action*. London: Sage

Bordin, E. S. (1983) A working alliance based model of supervision. *The Counselling Psychologist, 11*(1), 35–42

British Acupuncture Council. (1997) *Code of Ethics and Practice*. London: BacC

British Association for Counselling. (1988) *Code of Ethics and Practice for Counsellors*. Rugby: BAC

British Association for Counselling. (1996) *Code of Ethics and Practice for Supervisors of Counsellors*. Rugby: BAC

British Association for Counselling and Psychotherapy (2002) *Ethical Framework for Good Practice in Counselling and Psychotherapy*. Rugby: BAC

Carroll, M. (1996) *Counselling Supervision: Theory, Skills and Practice*. London: Cassell

Casemore, R. (2001) Managing boundaries: It's the little things that count. In R. Casemore (Ed.) *Surviving Complaints Against Counsellors and Psychotherapists* (pp.111–20). Ross-on-Wye: PCCS Books

Cristofoli, G. (2002) Legal pitfalls in counselling and psychotherapy practice, and how to avoid them. In P. Jenkins (Ed.) *Legal Issues in Counselling and Psychotherapy* (pp. 24–33). London: Sage

Feltham, C. and Dryden, W. (1994) *Developing Counsellor Supervision*. London: Sage

Furedi, F. (2001) *Paranoid Parenting: Abandon Your Anxieties and be a Good Parent*. London: Allen Lane

Heyward, C. (1993) *When Boundaries Betray Us*. San Francisco, CA: Harper

Horton, I. (1993) Supervision. In R. Bayne and P. Nicholson (Eds.) *Counselling and Psychology for Health Professionals*. London: Chapman and Hall

Jenkins, P. (1997) *Counselling, Psychotherapy and the Law*. London: Sage

King, D. and Wheeler, S. (1999) The responsibilities of supervisors. *British Journal of Guidance and Counselling, 27*(2), 215–29

Mearns, D. (1997) *Person-Centred Counselling Training*. London: Sage

Mowbray, R. (1995) *The Case Against Psychotherapy Registration: A Conservation Issue for the Human Potential Movement*. London: Trans Marginal Press

National Health Service Management Executive. (1993) *A Vision for the Future: The Nursing, Midwifery and Health Visiting Contributions to Health Care*. London: HMSO

Page, S. and Woskett, V. (1994) *Supervising the Counsellor: A Cyclical Model*. London: Routledge

Paradise, L.V and Siegelwaks, B. (1982) Ethical training for group leaders. *Journal for Specialists in Groupwork*, 7(3), 162–6

Proctor, B. (1988) Supervision: A co-operative exercise in accountability. In M. Marken and M. Payne (Eds.) *Enabling and Ensuring*. Leicester: Leicester National Youth Bureau/Council for Education and Training in Youth and Community Work

Rogers, C.R. (1958/1990) The characteristics of a helping relationship. In H. Kirschenbaum and V.L. Henderson (Eds.) *The Carl Rogers Reader* (pp.108–26). London: Constable

Rogers, C.R. (1967) Toward a theory of creativity. In C.R. Rogers *On Becoming a Person* (pp.347–59). London: Constable. (original work published 1954)

Rogers, C.R. (1967) A process conception of psychotherapy. In C.R. Rogers *On Becoming a Person* (pp.125–59). London: Constable. (original work published 1958)

Rogers, C.R. (1967) 'This is me': The development of my professional thinking and personal philosophy. In C.R. Rogers *On Becoming a Person* (pp.3–27). London: Constable. (original work published 1961)

Rogers, N. (2000) *The Creative Connection: Expressive Arts as Healing*. Ross-on-Wye: PCCS Books. (Original work published 1993)

Schwartz, C., Davidson. G., Seaton, A. and Tebbit, V. (1988) *Chambers English Dictionary W & R Chambers*. Cambridge:Edinburgh and Cambridge University Press

Shohet, R. (1997) Reflections on fear and love in accreditation. In R. House and N. Totton (Eds.) *Implausible Professions: Arguments for Pluralism and Autonomy in Psychotherapy and Counselling* (pp.45–50). Ross-on-Wye: PCCS Books

Stone, A. A. (1976) The Tarasoff decisions: Suing psychotherapists to safeguard society. *Harvard Law Review*, 90, 358–78

Tudor, K. and Worrall, M. (in preparation) *Clinical Philosophy: Advancing Theory in Person-Centred Therapy*. London: Brunner-Routledge

Urbano, J.M. (1984) Supervision of counsellors: Ingredients for effectiveness. *Counselling*, 50, 7–16

Vandecreek, L. and Harrar, W. (1988) The legal liability of supervisors. *The Psychotherapy Bulletin*, 23(3), 13–16

Ward, L. G., Friedlander, M. L., Schoen, L. G. and Klein, J. C. (1985) Strategic self-presentation in supervision. *Journal of Counselling Psychology*, 32(1), 111–18

PART TWO

DEVELOPMENTS AND DIALOGUES

CHAPTER SIX

RACE, CULTURE AND SUPERVISION

SENI SENEVIRATNE

INTRODUCTION

Recent discourse in therapeutic literature uses a number of terms to describe work across difference: inter-cultural, transcultural, multi-cultural, cross-cultural. Much of the work acknowledges that potential differences can be based on a variety of factors including race, gender, sexual orientation, class, or disability. While agreeing with Wolfe and Vitebsky (2003, p. 66) that 'every therapeutic encounter is at least potentially an inter-cultural one' and that 'in virtually every encounter between persons there is an inter-cultural dimension' (ibid., p. 67), I have chosen to focus in this chapter on racial difference and its impact on the supervision process.

In doing this I do not wish to separate racial difference from the impact of and interaction with other areas of difference. Nor do I want to deny the full range of connecting and disconnecting points between people. I do, however, wish to acknowledge specific issues in relation to race and the particular relationship that has developed between the concepts of race and culture such that in many environments they have become interchangeable with regard to understanding practice across difference. My belief is that by focusing very clearly on race and its implied symbiotic relationship with culture, I will be better able to explore the complexity of all the issues surrounding it, and therefore come to some understanding of how it impacts the supervision process.

RACE AND CULTURE

In a lecture on Race, Language and Counselling, Lago (1996) refers to Raymond Williams' book on keywords of the twentieth century, in which he notes that 'race' and 'culture' are two of the most complex words in the English language. Lago adds: 'They are both words rooted in complex systems of historic development carrying a whole range of meanings and connotations'. It would seem to be a useful starting point for this chapter to look at the origins of both these words before considering the development of the relationship between them.

What is race?
One dictionary (Chambers, 1992) defines 'race' as 'the descendants of a common ancestor especially those who inherit a common set of characteristics' and 'a class or group defined otherwise than by descent'. Moorhouse (2000, p. 90) points out that the term has 'largely been discredited in biological science' owing to the recognition that there are 'many more biological differences within races than between them' (ibid., p. 90). d'Ardenne and Mahtani (1989, pp. 4–5) have also considered the difficulty of relying on a biological definition of race:

> In everyday speech 'race' almost always refers to differences of skin colour and is often used in a derogatory manner. In anthropological circles 'race' refers to a wide range of genetic characteristics, for example skin colour, blood group and hair texture . . . The whole biological issue is fraught with complexity and contradiction.

Despite this and despite its connection with the negative aspects of colonial arguments about racial superiority, 'race' has 'been retained by some communities and theorists as a sociological term' (Moorhouse, 2000, p. 90) and continues to be used in a political context to describe individuals and groups in relation to racism. However, as McDermott (1999, p. 1) points out, 'most definitions of race fall back on geography, nationality, religion and culture, in which case race becomes almost interchangeable with culture'.

What is culture?
The dictionary definition of the noun 'culture' (Chambers, 1992) indicates its origins in the verb 'to cultivate' and suggests that it means 'something that is specifically grown or improved; the state of being cultivated or refined; the attitudes and values that inform a society'. d'Ardenne and Mahtani (1989, p. 4) define culture as the 'shared history, practices, beliefs and values of a racial, regional or religious group of people'. Pinker (1994, p. 411) defines culture as

100

'the process whereby particular kinds of learning contagiously spread from person to person in the community and minds become coordinated into shared patterns'.

For me, the notion of growth and refinement that is implicit in the etymological root has to be included in any definition of culture. Littlewood (Kareem and Littlewood, 1992, p. 8) does this when he refers to culture as 'a dynamic re-creation by each generation, a complex and shifting set of accommodations, identifications, explicit resistances and reworkings'. It is only when we perceive culture in this way that we can avoid the danger of regarding it as a static, unyielding influence on the lives of individuals. It is my belief that the cultures to which each individual is exposed are not only varied and diverse but are also refined by the constant interplay between each culture and between the individuals who are within each culture. As Littlewood again points out (1992, p. 8): 'Culture cannot be thought of as a bag of memories and survival techniques which individuals carry about with them and of which they have forgotten to divest themselves'.

Benedict (1968, p. 138) suggests that it is not useful to focus on 'the antagonism between culture and the individual' but to consider 'their mutual reinforcement' and to remember 'that it is not possible to discuss patterns of culture without considering specifically their relations to individual psychology'.

The implication of this for supervision or client work across cultures is that it removes the possibility of making simplistic judgements or assumptions about an individual's relationship to a culture based on 'digging around for gratuitous cultural information' (McDermott, 1999, p. 3). So, as well as considering the particular biases based on where the information comes from, one has to consider also how much of the information is based on a static interpretation of the culture rather than on an understanding of the ways in which the culture has the potential for what Littlewood (1992, p. 8) calls 'dynamic re-creation' through interaction between individuals within it and with external forces.

The relationship between race and culture

In my view, the relationship between race and culture has been shaped by racism. The white hegemony has either exoticised or denigrated black cultures as a way of marginalising black people along with their cultures. Cultural stereotypes have been created and black people have been reduced to fit these stereotypes.

Even the most well-intentioned white people can fall into the trap of romanticising and idealising black cultures. By doing so, they fail to acknowledge the real effects that colonialism and racism have had and continue to have on these cultures and the people who belong to them. This attitude also leaves no room for a consideration of the diversity that exists within cultures and has had the effect of limiting the definition of culture.

Black cultures have often been defined by white society as a series of static, unchanging beliefs and values that need to be learned in order to understand the people who practise them. Little value or credence has been given to the manifestations of change within those cultures. Black people, on the other hand, have often been driven to 'hide' in their cultures as a place of safety and security in the face of hostility and misunderstanding from white society. This has had the effect of limiting their possibilities for change and growth with and within their cultures.

One example of the fog that shrouds any analysis of race and culture and the relationship between them is the careless way in which the terms 'ethnic' and 'ethnic minority' are used as a way of referring to black people without reference to the history of power and oppression. The poet Merle Collins reflects the feelings of many black people in her poem 'What Ting is Dat?' (Collins, 1992, p. 58): 'It sound like something/that doesn't quite make the grade'. In the poem she locates the term in the context of racism and colonialism drawing attention to the fact that the term is never used to describe the white minorities in the Caribbean and South Africa. Thus she expresses very powerfully the link between language, history, power and oppression. Many institutions have adopted the term 'ethnic' as an alternative to 'black' and similarly the term 'multi-cultural' as an alternative to 'anti-racist'. The new terminology is intended to make the issue safe by making it colour-blind and removing any notion of power and oppression. It stems from an analysis that leads organisations to models of anti-discriminatory practice rather than anti-oppressive practice.

Browne and Bourne (1996, p. 37) have discussed the issue of effective transcultural work in a framework of anti-oppressive practice, drawing on the work of Julia Phillipson (1992, p. 13):

> Phillipson suggests that whereas anti-discriminatory practice relies on the model of challenging unfairness and is essentially reformist in orientation, anti-oppressive practice works to the model of empowerment and liberation and requires a fundamental rethinking of values, institutions and relationships.

With anti-discriminatory practice, the main issue becomes learning about other cultures. There is no challenge to the status quo and solutions are based on providing checklists of mix-and-match cultural facts, which Singh and Tudor (1997, p. 37) refer to as 'prescriptions about . . . "meeting, greeting and seating"'. As Patterson (1996, p. 228) points out:

There are numerous publications attempting to remedy the lack of knowledge about ethnic, racial and cultural groups and how to treat or not treat them . . .

He quotes a disturbing example of this from the US in a review by Pederson (1976):

When counseling Native American Indian youth, the counselor is likely to be confronted by passively non-verbal clients who listen and absorb knowledge selectively . . . The Native American is very conscious of having to make his own decisions and is likely to resent being pushed in a particular direction by persons seeking to motivate him or her. (p. 30)

The response of the client in question here seems like a wise one if faced with a counsellor who makes such sweeping generalisations.

Studies such as this are common in the US and have led to a worrying trend towards counselling professionals being recommended to 'use techniques that "fit" the presumed characteristics of clients' (Patterson, 1996, p. 228). Unfortunately for many years this trend has permeated much of the thinking in this country too and has 'overshadowed attention to the nature of the relationship between counselor and client' (Patterson, 1996 p. 229) as well as minimising the existence or the significance of the oppressive system within which that relationship is conducted.

If the existence of oppression is acknowledged the focus can shift to ways of working which challenge oppression and are much more demanding of the practitioners. Phillipson (1992, p. 13) puts it this way:

Oppression is a complex term which relates to structural differences in power as well as the personal experiences of oppressing and being oppressed. It relates to race, gender, sexual orientation, age and disability as separate domains and as overlapping experiences.

Taking this further, Hawkins and Shohet (2000, p. 97) have this to say:

To be anti-oppressive entails attending to the experiences of oppression in both the supervisees and the clients, and also attending to becoming aware of our own cultural biases and to becoming more adaptive to difference.

Unfortunately, the predominance of the anti-discriminatory approach is the context in which therapeutic practitioners operate and this cannot fail to have its effects. Like many other 'worlds', the world of therapy is dominated by a white hegemony which views difference only in relation to itself as the norm and assumes it has discovered, invented, or created the process called counselling. As Lawrence (2003, p. 134) points out:

> Counselling may be a western phrase, but the idea of a personal development process that may be experienced through a relationship with a 'central person/other people' (e.g. sage, guru, teacher, elder, mentor, clergy, parent) has been around from the beginning of time and within all cultures. *No one person or any one particular school of thought owns this experience.* If one wonders why counselling and psychotherapy training has not been too quick to embrace the clear benefits of better integration of racial and cultural issues one has only to look at the rest of the world for answers. The quest for power it seems is generally accepted as the root of most exclusion, oppression, war, greed, murder, exploitation and the like. For those promoting and perpetuating the idea that 'counselling' as a relationship concept comes from a limited area, a limited time and from certain individuals of the world keep certain schools of thinking as 'absolute truths' and the 'great and the good' in lofty positions where they are often afforded all respect, all value, all consideration or power.

RACISM AND ITS EFFECTS

In order to fully understand the relationship that exists between race and culture one has to consider racism and its effects. Lago and Thompson (1996, p. 20) define racism as a 'serious, punitive and extensive range of attitudes, behaviours and practices that were formed over several centuries to justify inhuman, disrespectful and colonial domination of black peoples'. 'Counsellors', they say (ibid., p. 20), 'must take note of the impact such historical relations may have on any therapy relationships they develop in the present.' The term 'black' has arisen out of the history of racism, to emphasise what Dupont-Joshua (1996, p. 220) calls 'a commonality of experience in relation to the European former colonial powers, rather than the diversity of cultural heritages'. Those of us who face racism have claimed the term 'black' as part of a reclaiming of a positive identity that goes beyond cultural origins and challenges negative stereotypes given to us by a system of racist oppression. Our cultural and racial identities are thus formed by our constant interaction with others in a racist world. Historically and culturally black people have always been placed as 'other' in relation to white people and this has affected the construction of black identity. Because black is seen as 'other' and white is not, white identity is secured as superior in relation to black identity.

Hall (1997, p. 127) sees black identities as being created through the politics of difference:

> Cultural identity . . . is a matter of 'becoming' as well as 'being' . . . it is not something which already exists . . . cultural identities come from somewhere, have histories. But like everything which is historical, they undergo constant transformation. Far from being eternally fixed in some essentialised past, they are subject to the continuous 'play' of history, culture and power.

Kareem (Kareem and Littlewood, 1992, p. 16) maintains that 'a psychotherapeutic process that does not take into account the person's whole life experience, or that denies consideration of their race, culture, gender or social values can only fragment that person'. It follows then that in a supervisory relationship it is important to take into account the context in which a black person's identity and concept of self have been formed. This is a context which includes 'socio-political and economic factors over which the individual may have little or no control, and which affect the inner world of all of us' (ibid., p. 15).

My concept of self has been shaped not only by my relationship to cultures and histories that are 'in constant transformation' (Hall, 1997, p. 127) but by my relationship to racism and my strategies for survival in a racist system. Traditional person-centred models of the self have, according to Holdstock (1993, p. 230), implied an isolated autonomous being:

> The point of departure of the person-centred approach has remained firmly embedded in the centrality of the self and the autonomy of the individual . . . The origin of control resided inside the person rather than within the larger system or field . . . Even in the social outreach of the theory, empowering the individual remained the focus through which societal change was thought to be brought about.

My understanding of my own concept of self does not easily fit with this and finds more resonance with the alternative models that Holdstock outlines. He talks (ibid., p. 230) of the:

> . . . possibility of a concept of the person which challenges the monocultural notion of the self as a demarcated entity, set off against the world. In this newer view, the self is considered to be inextricably

intertwined with other people. The extended concept of the self may even include the deceased as well as the larger universe of animals, plants and inanimate objects. Power and control are not considered to rest predominantly with the individual but within the field of forces within which the individual exists.

He also suggests (ibid., p. 236) that:

> Identity emerges from the groups in which one is embedded. It is the soil in which identity grows. The self is part of the social world and the social world is part of the self.

My concept of self includes locating myself as part of something bigger, a commonality of experience, and in particular the experience of racism which is 'inextricably intertwined' (ibid., p. 230) with the lives and experiences not only of the living but also of my ancestors and the ancestors of other black people who have experienced racism and colonialism. I experience myself striving to connect with others rather than to separate from them. The process of finding my identity has involved a conscious and constant consideration of who I am, where I come from, and what has shaped me in the context of a powerful and pervasive system of racism that has given me only negative definitions of myself. This process has opened me up to new ways of seeing myself and others. It has enabled me to see the endless possibilities for change and diversity. It has meant that I am not threatened by or afraid of difference because I have embraced difference as part of my self-concept in order to survive.

In my relationships with white people I am aware of my desire for them to see me as I really am with all these complexities and with all this history and experience embedded in my identity. I want them to 'walk alongside' me in my world without being blocked by their own fears. It often feels like they're afraid of being in my private world with me because of what it will raise for them. It seems like they don't want to face their own deeply internalised racist conditioning. The question is whether these experiences are inevitable and whether they make it impossible for successful supervision relationships across racial difference.

Lago and Thompson (1996, p. 27) note the 'potential complexity of any relationship between black and white people' given that it may well be 'overloaded, burdened and profoundly affected by the past … and by the past lives of two people engaging in the counselling relationship'. They suggest (ibid., p. 14) that counsellors need to acknowledge 'the profound and often unconscious impact our own cultural heritage has upon our attitudes and perceptions towards others, especially those who are racially and culturally different to ourselves'. Having acknowledged this, counsellors must then be willing and able to 'explore their cultural and social origins in order to try to understand better their own cultural identity, beliefs and value systems' (ibid., p. 14). They also need (ibid., p. 14) to 'become more aware of their attitudes towards other groups and cultures, to become more aware of their stereotypes and assumptions'. For me this would include an awareness of their stereotypes and assumptions about what culture is and in particular about what a black culture is. All of this is equally relevant for supervisors to consider in their work with counsellors.

The counter-argument to this is cited by Lago and Thompson (1996, p. 14) when they consider the belief that 'all counselling is cross-cultural in that it embodies two persons who … have already had differing backgrounds and thus … have their own unique identities [culture]'. I would agree that culture and identity are very closely connected concepts but argue that the added impact of the effects of racism come into play when there is a meeting between a black and white person. Those supervisors who say that they work in the same way with all supervisees, whatever colour they are, are missing the point. The issue is not whether black and white supervisees need different kinds of supervision. The issue is that racism will have had its effects on the supervisor, the supervisee, and the clients of the supervisee. The supervision needs to take account of this, in terms of the dynamic between supervisor and supervisee as well as in the therapeutic work the supervisee is bringing. As Igwe (2003, p. 216) puts it:

> It could be said that the primary task of the supervisor is to ensure
> that certain beliefs and understandings which may be, or appear to be,
> unconscious are brought to consciousness.

My belief is that an acknowledgement of difference can be a sounder basis for meaningful communication and understanding than a pretence of sameness. This needs to be combined with a knowledge of what Lago and Thompson (1996, p. 17) call 'the history between differing racial groups' and 'an understanding of the political processes in society that contribute to perpetuate racist and discriminatory processes' (ibid., p. 14). This will avoid the tendency to pathologise black individuals who are responding to racism and will enable us to recognise that 'racism … functions as a pathology of and in society (ibid., p. 16). In the same way other forms of institutionalised oppression such as sexism and homophobia need to be identified as pathologies of society rather than of the individual, while at the same time acknowledging the profound effects these can have on the individual's identity and concept of self.

ME IN CONTEXT AND THE DYNAMIC OF RACE

I come to this debate with my own experiences as a woman of mixed racial heritage and with the history of a personal journey that has involved a claiming of the totality of my cultural and racial heritage. By this I mean a claiming of the dynamic interplay between all the cultures and histories that have shaped me in the context of a racist system of power and oppression.

That process has involved learning to live with the paradox of labels. By this I mean learning to live with the contradiction of wanting them and not wanting them, all at once. I have embraced them in my journey to find places to belong and a base to organise from and I have denied them because they fragment me, limit me, define me in a way that I am often not in control of. That process has involved me finding ways to survive in a dominant world culture that forced me to whisper my differences and squeeze myself into definitions that were too narrow for the breadth of my experience and being. It has also involved me in a search for the voices and journeys of my ancestors and an exploration of the colonial history that dominated their lives and shaped mine.

My experience leads me to the view that encounters across racial difference often touch a place in us that is branded with the fear and hostility that characterised the history and development of racism in the world. It is often a place that is inaccessible and therefore uncomfortable. It is a place where people are sometimes silenced through fear of saying the wrong thing or being vilified. It is a place where walls of misunderstanding can block genuine meeting.

In trying to formulate the dynamics of race and its unique place in the consideration of difference, I search for meanings to make sense of my experience. How does the particular history of global racism impact psychologically on black people and on white people? What is it that makes the encounter with racial difference feel like such an uncomfortable and hidden place? It is shrouded in a fog of misinformation, and the misinterpretation of words. There is little written on the subject that expresses the complexity of it and describes the detail of those moments of meeting and being in relationship across difference. The following quotations are from interviews I conducted with black therapists:

- They don't know anything about your family, they don't know where you're from, they can't know anything about your sexuality but they can make all sorts of presumptions about you and feel that they know who you are and what you are about and all sorts just on the basis of the colour of your skin.

The hardest thing as a black therapist is often coming to terms with the fact that there are some things I may never know about the assumptions my clients may be holding about me:

- . . . you've no idea on the receiving end of that, you've no idea what you're evoking in that person and there might be all sorts of things.

- With race you get a lot of power, if you're not careful, taken off you, just because you haven't got access to what's in other people's heads and the dynamics of relationships are affected by all that stuff that's going on.

There are always questions about how I am being received and how much that is being affected by racism, which can be undermining as a practitioner and which necessitates finding a supervisor who can hold the processing of this with me in supervision:

- I might have to sit down and have a first session with a client who is completely regressing and backtracking all the time, while they are there because they don't want to talk to a black person about whatever it is and that may never be explicitly said and I wouldn't challenge a client on that unless they said something that gave me something to go on . . . I'll take that to supervision— work with my feelings and the impact that clients are having on me.

I'm interested in exploring particular responses I have that are bound up with my relationship to racism. As I write this chapter there is a war taking place in Iraq. If I look at my responses to the war beyond my political opposition to it, I find that I am locating myself as one of the 'other' who is under attack at the moment, being wiped out by the force of a new imperialist order, a new colonialism that is still white and is still targeting black people, black heritage, black culture. At the same time I am aware that as a black person living in the UK I have a privilege that means I am not *literally* being wiped out or slaughtered. I wonder how different that is to a white person's response? Where does this strong identification with black people who are under attack and dying at the hands of a new form of white imperialism take me? Is it a healthy place for me to find myself: hating Bush and Blair as much for their whiteness as for their power because they are playing out a part in the history of white power and dominance? And how does it feel to acknowledge that when I see Saddam Hussein, though I am opposed to his politics and his regime, I don't have the same response, the same hatred?

As I interact with others in the world, I carry with me a history of experiences, not all actually lived by me but held through a connection with a collective, historical experience of racism. In some situations all my past experiences as a minority facing the negative responses of the majority can get in the way of me being open to connecting with individuals. I am wary of their assumptions. I am protective of my vulnerabilities. I construct familiar defences. When I spoke to other black therapists they echoed my experience of this:

- 'At one of the places I work, all my colleagues are white and, however nice they are, I feel there is this unbridgeable divide between us so that I feel like I can't trust anybody.'

- I'm not open, I'm very suspicious and I'm very false because I don't present my suspicion or guardedness or grumpiness. Not only do I experience them as false but I'm also doing to them exactly what I feel they are doing to me. My expectation in that situation is to be used and not seen. That's what I'm defending myself against so I can't allow myself to trust anyone.

- There's also something about what I owe to other black people not to allow myself to be used or to be appropriated, or collude. It's about wanting to hang on to my otherness. Look after it, nurture it because it is really precious.

IMPLICATIONS FOR SUPERVISION

What then are the implications of all this for the supervisory relationship? Much of the theory about working across racial difference concerns itself with the notion of moving to a point of knowing in order to increase understanding. The knowing usually involves learning a series of cultural norms and matching them to the clients and supervisees with whom we work. Notions of Eastern and Western conceptual systems provide simplistic models into which individuals are placed. Writing about transcultural supervision, Hawkins and Shohet (2000, pp. 88–105) illustrate a model developed by Judy Ryde (1997) which defines two dimensions along which cultural norms can be distinguished. She describes one continuum between valuing of the experience of individuals and the valuing of the group, and another between emotional expressiveness and emotional restraint. Hawkins and Shohet note (2000, p. 91) that:

> the dominant British and most northern European cultures can be plotted in the individual/emotional restraint box. While the diagram does not cover all possible cultural differences, it does help us to orientate ourselves more easily to two important variables and therefore to think in a more culturally sensitive way.

They suggest (ibid., p. 91) that 'the more we can understand the ways in which the world looks different through different cultural lenses, the more able we are to work well across cultures'.

The problem with models like this is that they fall prey to the over-simplification of cultural identity and fail to address the impact of globalisation on notions of East and West. They are also based on the premise that if we know then we will understand and if we understand then we will make contact across difference. The reality is that what matters is the ability to be comfortable about not knowing and to be sufficiently at ease in the relationship to explore the difficult places that race and racism force us to encounter.

The simplistic view is that if we learn about different cultures then it will all fall into place. We need to challenge that approach not by a dismissal of culture but through a willingness and ability to put culture in context. We need to develop an awareness and a knowledge that is broader than our own world, from a starting place that is rooted in an acknowledgement, exploration and understanding of our own cultural and racial identity. We need to be open to mixing with people and with difference in all its variety, and never to assume sameness:

> It's that anthropological approach to race and culture that I find really irritating. Within the context of counseling, where you are looking at relationships and feelings, you are not going to know any more about a person or their family by what they eat or even what their religious beliefs are. You can learn a little bit but you still can't know them through their practices. You can't know an English family through what they eat, or what religion they are. It doesn't tell you anything. (From an interview with a black therapist)

As a supervisee it's more important to me to be working with someone I know has thought through all these issues for themselves and knows where they are in relation to them. It's not important that they know where I am or have some prior knowledge that helps them to understand me because that is not possible. Where I am is neither static nor packageable.

There are many variables that affect how racism impacts on me. My responses to the effects of racism can change according to what else is going on for me. There are often situations in which I experience hostility and I don't let it reach my vulnerable places, don't take it on as my problem. In another context I might feel really hurt and, because of all the different variables, there's no knowing when or why that will happen. It's not to do with the particular effects of certain comments or actions rather than others. It's more complex and unpredictable than that. One way I can describe it is as a process of learning to live with not always knowing. I experience many interactions where I sense negativity without knowing the motivations of the perpetrators or the origins of the negativity they display. I am sometimes unsure whether I am misinterpreting motives, or even expressions, because of my own past experiences. I have come to accept that in most situations there will be no opportunity to check it out. I will experience something, a look, a comment, a gesture, and wonder if racism is at the root of it, wonder if the perpetrator has any awareness of their motivations. I have come to accept the possibility that neither of us will ever know though the effects remain with me because of a history of my own and others' experiences. This would be a difficult place to find myself without an acceptance of the not-knowing part of it. That acceptance has freed me to focus on the moment-by-moment living with it and dealing with it and doing what I need to do for myself around it. I change. My responses to things change. My feelings about things change. I'm working on having a greater awareness of what my reactions are and where they come from. I'm learning more about my defences and how they limit me. I'm noticing my triggers and being open to what I can learn from them.

The quality of any supervisory relationship across racial difference will depend on how much each person has knowledge of themselves and how comfortable they are about not knowing everything about the other. It will depend on how possible it is to explore even the most uncomfortable, challenging and paradoxical of issues. I spoke to several black therapists and asked them what they look for in a supervisor. None of them expressed the need necessarily to find a supervisor who is of the same racial origin as they are. Their responses, however, reflected a concern for many of the issues I have raised in this chapter:

The importance of being accepted in all our complexity:

- to be heard and seen and the pro-active acknowledgement of difference.
- they feel comfortable and you feel comfortable so you can deal with the uncomfortable bits between you.

The need for supervisors and supervisees to be able to cut through the anxieties and expectations that surround issues of race:

- the ability to be still and attend fully without the need to prove themselves, or for reassurance or approval.
- solid enough not to need to prove anything, particularly in relation to race.
- not out to prove how anti-racist they are or how much they are up to the job of supervising a black supervisee.

The need for supervisors to have a confidence in themselves and an openness in their responses to difference:

- an awareness about their own identity.
- rootedness and confidence in their own instincts and opinions, and not be intimidated on issues of difference.
- really relaxed about knowing what are the issues and what might come up and open to learning.

The strength to hold the challenges:

- an ability to hold my insecurities without dismissing them or getting into reassuring.
- honesty and undefensiveness, experience and wisdom.
- sorted out about who they are whatever that is.
- openness to working with the possible difficulties and tensions.

And a knowledge, understanding and thoughtfulness about the broader context within which the relationships are taking place:

- their politics in terms of anti-discriminatory practice, respect for other cultures, for difference, for valuing difference would have to be part of the way they see the world and operate in the world.

There are no easy formulae for such a relationship. Like all relationships it requires a commitment to the creativity and uniqueness of the process as well as the honesty to engage with all the 'hidden agendas' where necessary. It is something which is ongoing and is hard work. It involves constantly learning about and challenging oneself. Dupont-Joshua (1996, p. 222) says that 'counselling and psychotherapy are social institutions and will reflect what is happening in society. To disentangle oneself from this requires conscious effort and difficult work'. It involves a constant awareness that 'we cannot be neutral, we are people and we bring our social status, our gender, our race, our life stage, attitudes and biases to the relationship, and these are very useful factors to work with' (ibid., p. 221).

It is the acceptance of this complexity that is the key to creating meaningful supervisory relationships across racial difference and to providing effective support to counsellors working with racially different clients. There is also certainly the need for supervisors to work constantly to acknowledge and explore their own cultural and racial identity and to encourage their supervisees to do the same. In addition they need to develop an understanding of the current manifestations of institutionalised racism and its roots in history. But beyond that, and most crucially, they have to be willing to engage with difficult and uncomfortable processes, and have the courage to hold the fluidity and genuineness of the relationship within the contradictions that are the products of racism.

References

Chambers (1992) *Maxi Paperback Dictionary*

Collins, M. (1992) *Rotten Pomerack.* London: Virago Press

d'Ardenne, P. and Mahtani, A. (1989) *Transcultural Counselling in Action.* London: Sage

Benedict, R. (1968) *Patterns of Culture.* London: Routledge Kegan Paul

Brown, A. and Bourne, I. (1996) *The Social Work Supervisor.* Buckingham: Open University Press

Dupont-Joshua, A. (1996) Race, Culture and the Therapeutic Relationship: Working with difference creatively. *Counselling,* August.

Hall, S. (1997) Cultural identity and Diaspora. In S. H. Mirza (Ed.) *Black British Feminism: A Reader* (222–37). London: Routledge

Hawkins, P. and Shohet, R. (2000) *Supervision in the Helping Professions.* Buckingham: Open University Press

Holdstock, L. (1993) Can we afford not to revision the person-centred concept of self? In D. Brazier, (Ed.) *Beyond Carl Rogers* (pp. 229–52). London: Constable

Igwe, A. (2003) The impact of multi-cultural issues on the supervision process. In *Working Interculturally in Counselling Settings* (pp. 210–31). Hove: Brunner-Routledge

Kareem, J. and Littlewood, R. (1992) *Intercultural Therapy: Themes, interpretations and practice.* Oxford: Blackwell Science

Lago, C. (1996) Race, language and counselling: A lecture for RACE AGM. November

Lago, C. and Thompson, J. (1989) Counselling and race. In W. Dryden, D. Charles-Edwards and R.Woolf (Eds.) *Handbook of Counselling in Britain* (pp. 207–22). London: Routledge

Lago, C. and Thompson, J. (1996) *Race, Culture and Counselling.* Buckingham: Open University Press

Lawrence, D. (2003) Racial and cultural issues in counselling training. *Working Interculturally in Counselling Settings* (pp. 120–41). Hove: Brunner-Routledge

McDermott, J. (1999) A conversation with myself. (Unpublished article)

Moorhouse, S. (2000) Quantitative research in intercultural therapy: some methodological considerations. In J. Kareem and R. Littlewood, *Intercultural Therapy* (pp. 88–110) Oxford: Blackwell Science Ltd.

Patterson, C. (1996) Multicultural counselling: From diversity to universality. *Journal of Counselling and Development, 74,* Jan/Feb, 227–31

Pederson, P. (1976) The field of intercultural counseling. In P. Pederson, W. J. Lonner and J.G. Draguns (Eds.) *Counselling across Cultures* (pp. 17–41). Honolulu HI: University Press of Hawaii

Phillipson, J. (1992) *Practising Equality: Women, men and social work.* London: CCETSW

Pinker, S. (1994) *The Language Instinct.* London: Penguin

Ryde, J. (1997) A step towards understanding culture in relation to psychotherapy. Working paper. Bath: Bath Centre for Psychotherapy and Counselling

Singh, J. and Tudor, K. (1997) Cultural conditions of therapy. *The Person-Centred Journal,* 4(2), 32–46

Wolfe, S. and Vitebsky, P. (2003) Assumptions and Expectations. In *Working Inter-Culturally in Counselling Settings,* (pp.66 and 67). Hove: Brunner-Routledge

CHAPTER SEVEN

PERSONAL AND ORGANISATIONAL POWER: MANAGEMENT AND PROFESSIONAL SUPERVISION

JOANNA VALENTINE

INTRODUCTION

As an Organisational and Leadership Development consultant within the National Health Service, I have spent much of the last eight years working with clinicians and their managers, both individually and in teams. I have also worked with service users and their carers, voluntary and statutory partners within the health and care community. I have offered both managerial and professional supervision, the latter to clinical team leaders, and to counsellors who were working with organisational teams. My interest is therefore to look at how practitioners are enabled to provide or prevented from providing a service to clients within an organisational context.

My particular interest in the person-centred approach is its application to organisations and leadership, and it is within this context that I will explore the relationship between managerial and professional supervision, the practice of person-centred supervision, and, in particular, the distribution of power in these relationships.

MANAGEMENT VS PROFESSIONAL SUPERVISION—A NECESSARY CONFLICT?

In most organisations, both within and outside the clinical and care fields, the term 'supervision' is synonymous with management and leadership. ACAS (the

Advisory, Conciliation and Arbitration Service—a publicly funded body specialising in employee relations whose core business is the prevention and resolution of workplace conflict) define a supervisor as:

> a member of the first line of management responsible for work groups to a higher level of management. Traditionally supervisors have often been referred to as foremen, chargehands or superintendents and these are terms still used in a number of organisations today. However, with changes in working practices many organisations regard their supervisors as team leaders (1) and first line managers and use these terms to describe them. Whatever their title, supervisors direct and guide others in the performance of tasks. They do not normally perform the tasks themselves, although in certain organisations there may be some job activities undertaken by the supervisor as well as members of the work group. (ACAS, 2003, pp. 2–3)

Within social care, the role has developed from the charitable organisations of the nineteenth century, which employed mainly volunteer workers (commonly known as visitors) whose work was assigned, coordinated and overseen by supervisors who were often paid agents of the charity. Increasingly, this role also involved decision-making upon the allocation of funds to particular cases, case reviews to ensure that work was carried out in an acceptable way, teaching, and the development and codification of standards (Smith, 1996).

So within an organisational context, the supervision role is defined as essentially managerial (having administrative, educational and supportive functions—Smith, 1996, pp. 2–3). Within counselling and psychotherapy, however, the supervision role has developed more from the role of educational supervisor, as early psychoanalysts undertook a form of apprenticeship in learning their craft under the guidance of a more experienced practitioner.

This may explain the apparent conflict in the role described by the British Association for Counselling and Psychotherapy in its *Ethical Framework for Good Practice in Counselling and Psychotherapy* (BACP, 2002) which states in paragraph 26 that 'There is a general obligation for all counsellors, psychotherapists, supervisors and trainers to receive supervision/consultative support *independently of any managerial relationships*' (emphasis added).

This creates a problem in practice for many counsellors and psychotherapists employed in health and care organisations where professional supervision has long been seen as a legitimate and central part of the line manager's responsibility. They hold delegated responsibility for the allocation of cases and resources, appraisal and development of team members, and for the delivery to clients of a service that meets the organisation's standards. They are required to ensure that the organisation is meeting its statutory duty of care through appropriate performance management and development.

The Argument for Separating Managerial and Professional Supervision

Whilst the BACP appears to be unequivocal about the need to separate managerial and professional supervision, there is little indication in their framework as to why this is deemed important. Nothing in its aims, values or principles indicates a need to separate out organisational and professional support interests. Indeed in its revised framework, the BACP acknowledges the implications of its increasing membership from practitioners operating within an organisational context. It includes managers in the definition of practitioners, and identifies one of the major changes in counselling and psychotherapy as the 'growth of services by practitioners working as teams' (which implies that these practitioners are therefore also likely to be operating as employees of organisations). It also incorporates among its fundamental values a commitment to 'Striving for the fair and adequate provision of counselling and psychotherapy services', which seems to recognise that many practitioners in this field not only work within organisations, but should be seeking to influence their organisation's decisions on the allocation of resources.

Page and Wosket (1994), commenting on an earlier edition of the code, offer as justification for the BACP's separation of professional and managerial supervision, the possibility that the managerial supervisor's responsibility for the resource needs of the organisation might adversely influence their ability to attend to an individual client's needs in supervision. Whilst this is not an unreasonable concern, it can be equally argued that someone with some direct influence on the deployment of resources within an organisation might be the best supervisor to consider an individual client's case. They would certainly appear to be in a better position to influence the commitment to fair and adequate provision of services given as a core value in the BACP's latest framework.

Some research evidence to support either proposition would appear to be useful before an arbitrary ruling is applied. This might seek to identify the degree to which managerial supervisors are influenced in their supervision of individual cases by the need to manage an organisation's scarce resources, and, just as importantly, their ability to influence positively the deployment of such resources to support a client.

Mearns (1997, p. 83) argues that the BACP is taking 'a distinctly person-centred orientation to supervision in advocating that the primary responsibility of the supervisor is to the counsellor rather than the employer'. He recognises that this is at odds with the supervision policy and practice of many health and care organisations where the professional supervisor is usually also the line manager 'with primary responsibility to the agency rather than to the worker' (p. 84).

Here we have a significant assumption about the nature of the employment relationship in general, and about the inevitable role of the managerial supervisor, whether referred to as line manager, team leader, or supervisor.

First, in UK common and contract law, all employees, regardless of role, contract voluntarily to provide certain services in return for an agreed remuneration and within specified terms and conditions, and have an implied responsibility to act generally in the interests of the employing organisation. The assumption that employees in managerial roles have more responsibility for this than employees in other roles is therefore questionable. Whilst the manager may have a different function from the therapist or clinician (though in many NHS settings, many managers are also practising clinicians), general responsibility to the organisation is shared equally amongst all employees.

Second, Mearns make an assumption about the nature of line management. Building on the understanding that all employees share a responsibility to their employer, the proposition that a manager's responsibility to the organisation undermines their ability to be appropriately available to their team members, would also logically imply that counsellors employed by an organisation cannot therefore be appropriately available to their clients (as they would be expected, as employees, to prioritise the organisation's needs). It also assumes that it is possible to be an effective line manager without giving due priority to the support and development needs of team members. This is counter to both current management and organisational thinking. Organisations are increasingly understood as complex systems, whose parts are interdependent to a high degree. The organisation can only provide a service through its employees, and therefore the support and development needs of those employees is key. Equally the organisation needs to optimise its use of resources and this may be at the expense of individual employees and clients. The manager's role is not to prioritise *either* the organisation's priorities *or* the practitioner's, but to find a way to meet *both* the organisation's requirements *and* the team members'.

Third, Mearns implies that it is possible to develop a model of person-centred professional supervision but not a model of person-centred managerial supervision. I will address this later in the chapter.

First, however, I should perhaps indicate where I believe there may be an argument for separating professional and managerial supervision:

a. Where the line manager lacks the necessary professional skills and knowledge to provide developmental support to the practitioner (e.g. where the practitioner is learning a new approach in which the line manager is not proficient).

b. During a period of major organisational restructuring where the line manager may be unable to ensure consistency of supervision during a period of instability.

c. Where there are governance issues within the organisation and where the practitioner needs an independent review of their practice.

d. Where there is a breakdown in the relationship between the line manager and the practitioner.

In all but the first of the above, I would see these as temporary solutions, the underlying issue needing resolution.

THE CASE FOR LINE-MANAGEMENT-PROVIDED PROFESSIONAL SUPERVISION

I have already argued that the management supervisor has a responsibility to ensure that the organisation's duty of care to its clients is carried out, and that they therefore have a specific responsibility to ensure that employees are enabled to fulfil this responsibility. This gives them a right and a responsibility to observe or review the practice of their team members.

To create a second, mandatory supervisory relationship creates a further demand on the organisation's already stretched resources, which needs to be justified in terms of specific added value to the client's care. The additional funding required for such a practice would reduce the funding directly available for client care. Only where this can be justified through the provision of differential services to the clients should this be considered (for example, where a practitioner is learning a new skill set or approach which may bring support to a different range of clients, or more effective support to existing clients).

Hawkins and Shohet (1989) acknowledge the potential impact of organisational demands on the supervisory relationship, but without assuming that this can or should be somehow avoided. They argue that the supervisor cannot afford to act as if the client-therapist-supervisor relationship exists on an island. There are professional codes and ethics, organisational requirements and constrictions, as well as relationships with other agencies, all of which need to be taken into consideration.

Indeed for Hughes and Pengelly (1997, p. 6):

> Staff supervision is a means of developing and controlling the quality of
> service, taking accounts of the needs and rights of users and the quality

of staff performance. The needs and rights of staff must also be attended to . . . the functioning of supervision is therefore inextricably linked to the way the organisation manages the tension between needs, resources and rights.

The tension is real and complex. The concept of universal provision of health and care services without a public debate about what should be included in this and at what cost leaves many practitioners within the NHS and Social Care agencies struggling in the face of an uncontrollable demand on a tightly limited resource. With responsibilities both for the therapeutic needs of the clients they are working with; concerns for those with severe and enduring mental health problems sitting on lengthening waiting lists, many of whom are acutely ill and may therefore be at risk of harming themselves or others; and a responsibility to protect the public; they frequently struggle to provide the service that they believe to be required and that they are skilled to offer, and many feel the increasing pressure to overextend themselves, which is in contradiction to the BACP requirement that they 'monitor and maintain their fitness to practise' and are 'taking care of their own health and well-being' (BACP, 2002, paragraphs 32 and 56).

Similarly many face conflicting demands between their therapeutic relationship with the client and their responsibility for public protection, particularly with some of their most vulnerable and disturbed clients (for example where they are working in Assertive Outreach teams or Secure units).

Increased regulation by both professions and government adds an additional burden of documentation to practitioners, which further reduces their available time for client contact. Many try to resolve this by working longer hours (in breach of the code of practice on self-care), or by de-prioritising documentation (in breach of BACP *Framework*, paragraph 5).

The tension created can then exacerbate the conflicting perspectives and values of different professions within multi-disciplinary teams (for example between psychiatrists and psychologists, psychiatrists and nurses, psychologists and counsellors, nurses and social workers). Such conflicts are to some extent inevitable as competing interest groups with diverse value bases seek to influence the distribution of scarce resources.

For staff providing services to severely ill clients in this environment, supervision is clearly an essential support service, enabling them to review and reflect on both their practice with individual clients, and their response to and strategies for dealing with their organisational context. The line manager should be familiar with the demands being made upon the practitioner and able to access resources to support them. Would this be true of an independent supervisor?

Whilst recognising that an independent supervisor may be able to bring a fresh perspective, it is also possible that they will further exacerbate the tension by highlighting further the difference between an idealised model of therapy and that which the practitioner finds themselves able to provide *in this context*. Similarly, without an understanding of the culture and political makeup of the organisation within which the practitioner is working, there may be a tendency to encourage the therapist to challenge what is happening without due attention to the risks involved in this for that practitioner. (This is not to suggest that practitioners should be deterred from raising concerns about organisational practices, but that this should be done in a considered way, recognising the political nature of the organisation and exploring fully the risks involved.)

A PERSON-CENTRED APPROACH TO MANAGEMENT SUPERVISION

Although Rogers developed his approach within the context of counselling relationships, he was always interested in its wider application to other forms of relationship. His early work on encounter groups, used to train counsellors, was quickly evolved to train managers and he collaborated closely with Thomas Gordon who developed a Group-Centred Approach to Leadership and Administration (Gordon, 1951). Gordon summarises his approach as follows:

> the group-centred leader believes in the worth of the members of the group and respects them as individuals different from himself. They are not persons to be used, influenced or directed in order to accomplish the leader's aims. They are not people to be 'led' by someone who has 'superior' qualities or more important values. The group-centred leader sees the group as existing for the individuals who compose it. It is the vehicle for the expression of their personalities and the satisfaction of their needs. He believes that the group as a whole can provide for itself better than can any single member of the group. He believes in the group's fundamental right to self-direction and to self-actualization on its own terms. (ibid., p. 338)

Gordon (1977, p. 6) later went on to separate out the line manager's task (or production-centred) functions from their human relations (or person-centred) functions whilst recognising the important relationship between the two.

These ideas have been mirrored and further developed by a number of writers including Robert Greenleaf (1977) who articulated the concept of Servant Leadership in which the line manager's primary responsibility was to their team

121

members; and by Peter Block (1993) who proposed that the concepts of management and leadership be replaced with those of governance and stewardship, arguing for a service-oriented adult partnership relationship between employees and their employer: 'Stewardship asks us to be deeply accountable for the outcomes of an institution, without acting to define purpose for others, control others or take care of others' (Block, 1993, p. 18). Block argues that the traditional command and control concepts of patriarchal management, which are essentially parental and infantilising, be replaced by the concept of partnership:

> In an organisation where those around us are all adults, taking responsibility for other's performance, learning and future is a care-taking role that undermines the most effective distribution of ownership and responsibility... This is why partnership is so critical to Stewardship. It balances responsibility and is a clear alternative to parenting. The questions 'How would a partner handle this?' and 'What policy or structure would we create if this were a partnership?' are the two most useful questions I know in the search for the alternative to patriarchy. (p. 27)

Block goes on to identify four key requirements for the creation of real partnership:

• Exchange of purpose
  Whereby every stakeholder has a voice in what kind of institution we are creating. (Having facilitated the local staff consultation exercises in one NHS organisation for the creation of an NHS Plan, and participated in some of the local and regional community consultation events, I have seen this in action within the NHS. The resultant NHS Plan (DoH, 2001) and associated service modernisation agendas bear a remarkable resemblance to the vision and ideas identified by the staff and community groups with whom I worked.)
• The right to say no
  Block recognises that there may always be an imbalance of power between manager and managed, but suggests that this can be a 51:49 split, and that, even so, partners always retain the right to have their voices heard.
• Joint accountability
  The price of freedom and adulthood is that each and every employee takes an individual and collective responsibility for the outcomes of and quality of co-operation within a unit and/or organisation.
• Absolute honesty
  Block recognises that this is difficult and frightening in practice, but argues that 'not telling the truth to each other is an act of betrayal' (pp. 30–1) .

This sharing of power, responsibility and purpose in a respectful adult relationship is central to the person-centred approach. The sharing of 'purpose' creates the conditions for a mutual empathic understanding, whilst the 'absolute honesty' and 'right to say no' acknowledge the importance of congruence in an effective relationship.

In exploring the person-centred approach to management, however, I find it helpful to return to the core principles to help to map out the territory to be explored. If Rogers' six conditions (1957/1959) are necessary and sufficient for a therapeutic relationship, and if the learning relationship is to be consistent with these, how might the conditions apply to a supervisory relationship?

1. Two persons are in psychological contact

Accepting that the supervisee's client and the organisational context are also part of the process, the here-and-now relationship within supervision is still essentially between two people. 'In every sense of the term, the counsellor is not bringing the client to supervision, but she is bringing *herself*' (Mearns, 1997, p. 89). Similarly with a more empowering/partnership model of management supervision, then the supervisee can be considered to be sharing with the supervisor the need to consider any action within an organisational context. Minimally, therefore, the relationship is between two persons—supervisor and supervisee, but with each aware of the needs of a wider group of interests in their relationship.

2. The first, whom we shall term 'the client', is in a state of incongruence, being vulnerable or anxious

In the case of supervision, does the supervisee need to be in a state of incongruence, or is it assumed that this applies solely to their clients? Hawkins and Shohet (1989) see the supervisory relationship as one in which a practitioner is allowed to feel the emotional disturbance of their work with a client, survive it, reflect upon and learn from it. In Stoltenberg and Delworth's 1987 model, described by Hawkins and Shohet (1989, pp. 49–53) the supervisee's level of anxiety may well depend on their developmental stage as a practitioner, with anxiety reducing as competence and confidence increase. If we add on the challenges and conflicts that can be presented to a therapist working within an organisation, then the supervisory relationship allows the supervisee to explore any apparent conflicts in values, the implications of scarce resources and political tensions, and to reflect upon and learn from these in a way that enables them to deliver the best service they can to their clients within this context. The challenges provided by working within an organisation may also reduce as competence and confidence increase, though this requires the development of political, as well as therapeutic, skills within the therapist.

Nevertheless, if we work from the premise that this is essentially a learning rather than a therapeutic relationship, then it might be more helpful to rephrase the condition to propose that the supervisee should be in a state of curiosity, as this covers both the anxious new learner and the self-reflecting master practitioner, and is an essential ingredient of a learning relationship. This also counters any concerns about a supervisee whose practice may be giving rise to concern. If they are in a state of curiosity then they will be actively interested in exploring the different perspective in their practice available within supervision, and will therefore be open to learning.

3. The second person, whom we shall term the counsellor, is congruent or integrated in the relationship

This means that all the supervisor's experience and knowledge including their awareness of resource limitations, power structures within the organisation, and political skills, and any concerns that they may have for the client, and/or for the reputation of the profession, training body or employing organisation, are available to the supervisee within the context of this relationship. This is a learning partnership. Where there appears to be any conflict, the supervisor will check this with the supervisee, not only in order to share their own different perspective, but with a view to challenging their own thinking in the discussion. Responsibility towards the client and the organisation is shared.

4. The counsellor experiences unconditional positive regard for the client

This implies that the supervisor regards the supervisee as a whole person, with intrinsic worth, regardless of current professional competence or organisational relationship. Unconditional positive regard does not mean that the supervisor has to ignore any conflict between the supervisee's reported behaviour and the client's or organisation's needs. However, it does mean that they genuinely and respectfully invite the supervisee to explore this conflict together from a perspective of curiosity rather than judgement. This is equally applicable whether the supervisor is a professional supervisor concerned with professional competence, or a managerial supervisor concerned with organisational codes of behaviour. The challenge is to stay alongside the supervisee as adults in partnership, rather than moving into a critical and controlling parental role. (Elke Lambers gives an excellent positive illustration of this in practice in Mearns and Thorne, 2000, pp. 200–11.)

5. The counsellor experiences an empathic understanding of the client's internal frame of reference and endeavours to communicate this to the client

Worrall (2001) argues that the primary task of supervision is 'to facilitate a supervisee's capacity to offer empathic understanding' (p. 207), and that empathic listening to his supervisees is the only way that he can learn anything at all about the way that they work. I concur wholly with the second and partially with the first of these statements (i.e. that facilitating empathic understanding is **a** primary task, rather than the sole primary task). Whilst Worrall is highly sensitised to the potential blocks to empathic understanding (e.g. the impact of his own differential experience on a supervisee's experience of empathic understanding, or the temptation to move into a policing role when the supervisee's practice poses a threat to a client, or to his own professional reputation), I think some of these risks follow logically from his assumption about his primary task.

The acknowledgement of the supervisory relationship as in some ways essentially different from a therapeutic encounter can allow the supervisor to engage in the relationship as an equal partner rather than solely as an understanding listener, with their own legitimate interests and concerns. As a managerial supervisor, I am interested in what the supervisee is experiencing and how they are making sense of this, of the choices that they identify and make. If their sense-making process, or choices, are different from, and potentially in conflict with, those required by the organisation (or profession or training body), then I am interested to explore both perspectives with an open mind. For me, a willingness to be profoundly honest (congruent) with a supervisee is as important in the relationship as my offering of empathic understanding. I don't see a conflict between understanding another's thinking and disagreeing with it. (For example, I am a pacifist. My husband is not. I understand and respect his position, and he understands and respects mine. He will drive me to a peace vigil and expresses his deep pride in my witness. I feel empathically understood by him, even though we don't share a common view on this.)

It can also be useful to support the supervisee in seeking to empathically understand the context in which they work. Practitioners in an organisational context need to develop political skills if they are to facilitate client access to services.

6. The communication to the client of the counsellor's empathic understanding and unconditional positive regard is to a minimal degree achieved
If this condition is met, then the relationship is good enough to allow the supervisee to feel safe enough to continue to explore their professional issues and concerns. This is equally valid whether the supervisor is a professional or managerial one.

Of course there is inevitably a divide between the theory and practice, rhetoric and action, within complex organisational systems. Nevertheless, many managers are now working from a more person-centred orientation. At root both supervisor and supervisee share a common concern for the quality of service that the client is receiving and the effectiveness of both managerial and professional supervision is dependent primarily on the quality of the here-and-now person-to-person relationship between the supervisor and supervisee. This is true regardless of whether the professional supervisor also carries managerial relationship. The dual role is not necessarily problematic, but becomes so when the relationship is compromised.

THE THORNY QUESTION OF POWER

It is perhaps in consideration of power and responsibility that we identify the area where trust, and therefore a relationship, may break down.

The issue of power has long been central to the person-centred approach. Natiello (2001) differentiates between authoritarian power, a coercive force, and collaborative power, the power to act in cooperation with others and for the greater good. She argues that the latter power base underlies the person-centred approach and I would argue that this is the power base which is invoked within more recent management approaches.

However, it is interesting to consider how far this approach is actually offered in the supervisory relationship; and what assumptions the supervisor makes about its prevalence in the rest of the organisation. As already mentioned, a lack of understanding of the distribution of power through an organisation can lead the supervisor to giving misleading, and possibly dangerous, advice to the supervisee.

For Buchanan and Badham (1999), theories of power in organisations can be identified in three groups:

• Power as the property of *individuals*
  This may come from both personal (e.g. interpersonal skill and competence) or French and Raven's (1958) notion of 'expert power', and is exercised by one identifiable individual in an attempt to influence the behaviour of another. Both supervisor and therapist can be seen as operating through this form of power as clients are likely to see them as, at best, a source of specific expertise, and, at worst, of arcane knowledge.

• Power as the property of *relationship*
  Identified by the extent to which individuals believe that other individuals do or do not possess a particular power base. This includes French and Raven's coercive, reward, and legitimate power bases, all of which are only as valid as the degree to which others believe that the holder is able to access and administer valued rewards and unwanted sanctions, or is entitled to give instructions.

- Power as an *embedded* property

Here power is held 'within the structures, regulations and norms of the organisation, perpetuating existing routine and power inequalities' (Buchanan and Badham, 1999, p. 56). An example of this is the disciplinary policy of an organisation or profession. Where such a policy is highly formal and legalistic, one party or another in the dispute must present evidence to prove that they are right and that the other is wrong. The outcome is either a dissatisfied complainant or the application of sanctions against an employee or practitioner. Wherever the burden of proof lies (whether on the client or on the therapist, for example), the disadvantage also lies. If with the client, then their vulnerability in the relationship, and lack of audio-taped evidence, contemporaneous notes, or recorded discussions with a supervisor, make it difficult for them to make a strong case. If this is compensated for, then the therapist becomes vulnerable to the problems of continual self-surveillance where they never know who can use what against them or when a statement, repeated out of context, will rebound upon them.

Such an approach discourages open disclosure and dialogue, and is unlikely to provide an effective vehicle for learning.

The question of disciplinary action is an important one as it is the supervisor's response to a supervisee when the supervisee is behaving in a way that causes the supervisor concern that is the test of how evenly power is distributed within the relationship. It is relatively easy to commit to an empathic, non-judgemental relationship when a supervisee is demonstrating self-insight and competent ethical practice, but what happens when they are behaving in ways that the supervisor considers to be unethical, or damaging to a client? What is the supervisor's response when their concerns and expertise are not heard? This is a test for any supervisors, professional or managerial, who espouse a person-centred approach. Can they maintain sufficient trust in a supervisee's learning process, and in the potential of their facilitative relationship, that such conflicts will eventually be resolved to their mutual satisfaction? Or is this the stage at which they move back into a more traditional power distribution on the basis that they are somehow more responsible for the supervisee's behaviour than the practitioner themselves? Does it make a difference if the supervisee is in training? Does that in some way lessen their inherent trustworthiness to carry full responsibility for their behaviour? I think these are key questions for both the professional and managerial supervisor.

Mearns suggests that there might be exceptions to the confidential nature of the supervisory contract where either a training organisation needed to confirm the regularity and quality of the supervision provided to the trainee; and/or where the supervisor was concerned about the ethical working of a course member

(Mearns, 1997, pp. 84–5). The underlying assumptions here seem to be that (a) the trainee cannot be relied upon to report their supervision hours and utilisation accurately; and (b) that the supervisor does not trust that the relationship established with the supervisee would provide an effective enough vehicle for the adequate exploration of ethical issues. Whilst I agree with Mearns that, if this is likely to be a concern, it needs to be clearly stated in the contracting stage, what message does this give to trainees (who are learning as much about the approach from what they experience as from what they are taught) about the nature of power in person-centred relationships? At what point do we move from partner to parent? At what point do we cease to trust the client/supervisee and take over responsibility for their behaviour? At what point do we cease to be a learning partner alongside the trainee and become an expert who ultimately knows best? The degree to which we are prepared to remain in an equal, power-sharing relationship with the supervisee is the degree to which we remain in a person-centred relationship with them. This does not mean that a person-centred supervisor cannot take independent action, but that they must continually check the assumptions underlying such action and how consistent these are with the person-centred approach.

I think Mearns is reflecting a real dilemma within the person-centred approach as it is faced with increasing codification within the counselling and therapeutic fields. The BACP's own disciplinary process seems to follow a formal and legalistic process aimed at protecting the client from malpractice and the profession from disrepute, but this inevitably leads to unevenly distributed power which can be viewed as ultimately more detrimental to practitioner, client and profession. There is considerable evidence from the review of the NHS' complaints procedure that prompt and informal mediation is more likely to result in a mutually acceptable outcome than such formal processes (DoH, 2001). The Listening Document produced as a result of this review acknowledges that the system also needs to work fairly for staff, whose work in the NHS is invaluable, and without whom there would be no service.

Within organisational literature, the focus on learning organisations places high value on the creation of a 'no blame' culture if real learning from mistakes is to be possible. The development of the Failure Tolerant Leader is now discussed within mainstream management texts (Farson and Keyes, 2002) as the key to organisational success. They attribute to IBM's Thomas Watson Senior the philosophy that 'The fastest way to succeed is to double your failure rate' (p. 3) and quote managers at 3M as 'routinely reinforcing the company's mistake-tolerant atmosphere by freely admitting their own goofs' (p. 6). The 3M approach would appear to be consistent with the person-centred approach, as the managers:

try to break down the social and bureaucratic barriers that separate them from their followers. They engage at a personal level with the people they lead. They avoid giving either praise or criticism, preferring to take a non-judgemental, analytical posture as they interact with staff. They openly admit their own mistakes rather than covering up or shifting blame. And they try to root out the destructive competitiveness built into most organisations.

In the hard-nosed world of commerce, such approaches are not proposed because they meet some preferred ethical standard, but because they are seen to produce better results for the organisation. Farson and Keyes (2002) discover the novelty that listening to staff is more effective than talking to them, and that praise as well as criticism can be counterproductive. They quote research that demonstrates that 'children playing games lose interest once they are rewarded or complimented for their play' (p. 5) and quote a study of science students in which those who were not praised (but where the teacher took an active interest and asked questions about what they were doing) did better than their peers who were praised for their experiments:

> The process is more collaborative than supervisory. Failure-tolerant managers show interest, express support, and ask pertinent questions . . . Conversations are less about whether the project is succeeding or failing than about what can be learned from the experience. When a manager and an employee are engaged in that discussion, both of them enter the same kind of high-performance zone that athletes do when they're operating at their best. (p. 5)

So the establishment of congruent, empathic, non-judgemental relationships in which both parties are energetically present is seen as crucial for the effective learning from experience, regardless of whether that experience has produced the results expected.

If the world of commerce is beginning to catch up with Rogers' thinking on the importance of collaborative power relationships, then I think that, as person-centred supervisors, we have a particular responsibility to stay faithful to our practice.

Supervising the Supervisor—the role of supervision for managers

Finally, with managers now included in the group of practitioners covered by the BACP's *Ethical Framework*, the requirement arises for their practice to be supervised also. Given the model of person-centred supervision proposed here, and the acknowledgement that this fits with the trend in management thinking, this should flow naturally within the organisation's line management arrangements. Where a professional supervisor would be expected to be skilled and knowledgeable in the practice supervised, a managerial supervisor's supervisor would presumably need to be skilled and knowledgeable in management practice; and not just in the skills required in a supervisory relationship, but in the management of the tension between the relational and production aspects of the role. The development of such supervisors will be an interesting challenge for the counselling profession.

Criteria for effective person-centred supervision

For therapists and other care professionals working in organisational contexts, effective management and professional supervision is clearly a significant source of learning and support. This supervision must encompass both clinical practice and an understanding of the context in which the practice takes place. This knowledge enables the supervisor to congruently offer an empathic understanding of the supervisee's work and context, and to make available to them expertise through which the practitioner can improve their practice through the development of new therapeutic and political insights and strategies.

The ability to offer a congruent, empathic and acceptant relationship to the supervisee is an essential feature of person-centred supervision whether it be professional, line management or both. The congruent sharing of potentially conflicting organisational and professional demands, and commitment to shared decision-making within the supervisory relationship, enable power and responsibility to be distributed more equitably between the supervisor and supervisee. This is equally relevant to the professional and managerial supervisor. Wherever a supervisor reserves to themselves the right to make a decision about the supervisee's practice and/or to share information about this practice outside the supervision relationship, they are stepping outside the person-centred supervisory relationship. I can only envisage this becoming necessary where the relationship between supervisor and supervisee has broken down and trust lost. (Drawing from my own experience, in 25 years of line management, I have only needed to resort to formal disciplinary action on one occasion, in a case where the team member and I were unable to establish sufficient shared reality to enable us to resolve the performance difficulties experienced by both of us. Although drawing intensively from my own supervision throughout, and unable to identify an alternative course of action at this time, I see this, as I see all formal disciplinary action, as essentially a management failure. I still retain a question as to whether a deepened practice of the person-centred approach with this team member, and with a senior manager who was intervening within the relationship, might have helped me to maintain the relationship for longer.)

Although I am challenging the assumption that line management and professional supervision should be conducted separately, I am not proposing that line managers necessarily make better professional supervisors. I have received independent professional supervision for the last 13 years and benefited profoundly from it. However, I believe the question of competence to perform the role should be based on professional and political skill and knowledge criteria, rather than untested assumptions that serve to mask the more important issues of power distribution within the supervisory relationship.

REFERENCES

ACAS (2003) *Supervision*. The ACAS Online Publication Service. www.acas.org.uk/publications/B13.html

British Association for Counselling and Psychotherapy (2002) *Ethical Framework for Good Practice in Counselling and Psychotherapy*. (Revised edition) Rugby: BACP

Block, P. (1993) *Stewardship: Choosing Service over Self-interest*. San Francisco: Jossey Bass

Buchanan, D. and Badham, R. (1999) *Power, Politics and Organisational Change: Winning the Turf war*. London: Sage

Department of Health (2001) *NHS Complaints Procedure National Evaluation* and *Reforming the NHS Complaints Procedure: A Listening Document*. www.doh.gov.uk/nhscomplaintsreform

Department of Health (2001) *NHS Plan*. www.doh.gov.uk/nhsplan

Farson, R. and Keyes, R. (2002) The failure-tolerant leader. *Harvard Business Review, August,* Reprint R0208D

French, J. R. and Raven, B. (1958) The bases of social power. In D. Cartwright (Ed.) *Studies on Social Power* (pp. 150–67) Ann Arbor, MI: University of Michigan

Gordon, T. (1951) Group-centered leadership and administration. In C.R. Rogers, *Client-Centred Therapy* (p. 320–83). London: Constable

Gordon, T. (1977) *Leader Effectiveness Training*. L.E.T. New York: Wyden Books

Greenleaf, R. K. (1977) *Servant Leadership: A Journey in the Nature of Legitimate Power and Greatness*. New York: Paulist Press

Hawkins, P. and Shohet, R. (1989) *Supervision in the Helping Professions*. Milton Keynes: Open University Press

Hughes, L. and Pengelly, P. (1997) *Staff supervision in a turbulent environment: managing process and task in front line services*. London: Sage

Lambers, E. (2002) Supervision in person-centre therapy: facilitating congruence. In D. Mearns and B. Thorne, *Person-Centred Therapy Today: New Frontiers in Theory and Practice*. London: Sage

Mearns, D. (1997) *Person-Centred Counselling Training*. London: Sage

Natiello, P. (2001) *The Person-Centred Approach: A Passionate Presence*. Ross-on-Wye: PCCS Books

Page, S. and Wosket, V. (1994) *Supervising the Counsellor: A Cyclical Model*. London: Routledge

Rogers, C. R. (1957) The necessary and sufficient conditions of therapeutic personality change. *Journal of Consulting Psychology, 21,* 95–103

Rogers, C. R. (1959) A theory of therapy, personality and interpersonal relationships, as developed in the client-centred framework. In S. Koch (Ed.) *Psychology: A Study of Science. Vol. 3: Formulation of the Person and the Social Context* (pp. 184–256). New York: McGraw-Hill

Smith, M. K. (1996) *The Functions of Supervision: The Encyclopaedia of Informal Education.* Last update July 14, 2002, www.infed.org/biblio/ functions_of_supervision.htm

Worrall, M. (2001) Supervision and empathic understanding. In S. Haugh and T. Merry (Eds.) *Rogers' Therapeutic Conditions: Evolution, Theory and Practice, Volume 2: Empathy.* Ross-on-Wye: PCCS Books

CHAPTER EIGHT

FOCUSING-ORIENTED SUPERVISION

GREG MADISON

As an inexperienced training therapist, I was anxious about seeing my first clients, so I willingly acquiesced to the requirement of weekly group supervision. Supervision was a strange new activity that consisted of meeting with fellow students and a seasoned practitioner in order to explore what was *really* happening behind the closed door of therapy. I soon looked forward to these meetings as an opportunity to compare myself with my colleagues and to exchange real or imagined transgressions for the reassurance and advice of my more experienced supervisor. Unless my colleagues and I were entirely unrepresentative, such 'comparison' and 'confession' seems to constitute significant aspects of supervision, at least for training therapists.

However, my needs within supervision changed as I neared the completion of my training. This may be a logical and positive consequence of gaining practical experience as a therapist. The problem was that the supervision I was offered, or my use of it, did not evolve with these changing needs. Now as a training supervisor, I am conscious of looking for ways to enable supervision to evolve along with the needs of my supervisees so that our meetings remain personally and professionally engaging rather than merely compulsory. My question is: 'How can we develop forms of supervision that are responsive to the needs of supervisees at various stages of experience and thereby more likely to be of benefit to our clients?'

In some countries the expectation for regular supervision ceases when training is completed. Within other jurisdictions, however, regular supervision is accepted as essential to competent practice for counsellors and psychotherapists as long as they continue to see clients. In Britain, for example, ongoing supervision is now a requirement in the codes of ethics and practice guidelines of the British Association for Counselling and Psychotherapy (BACP), the United Kingdon Council for Psychotherapy (UKCP), and the British Psychological Society (BPS)—the principal accrediting/registering bodies for counsellors, psychotherapists, and counselling psychologists, respectively. This requirement serves to reify supervision as an essential component of the claim to professionalism for counsellors and psychotherapists. Even the BACP's *Ethical Framework for Good Practice in Counselling and Psychotherapy* (recently updated and less prescriptive than its previous codes) states that 'all counsellors, psychotherapists, trainers and supervisors are required to have regular and ongoing formal supervision/consultative support for their work in accordance with professional requirements' (BACP, 2001, p. 6).

With supervision being so embedded in training programs and continuing professional practice, how do supervisors and supervisees keep their discussions challenging, spontaneous and useful, and avoid supervision becoming a reluctant obligation or professional habit? What, in fact, comprises our supervisory time, and how central or ancillary is it to our actual work with clients? How can we make supervision sessions more directly relevant to our work with others and to our own personal development?

In this chapter I propose that, regardless of therapeutic orientation or years of experience, incorporating the experiential dimension of Focusing into supervision may enhance the awareness of the supervisee/therapist and carry forward the work of therapy. I am not suggesting that Focusing, as outlined by Eugene Gendlin (1981), should replace all other aspects of supervision, but that it offers a major avenue of exploration within it.

Incorporating Focusing into supervision sessions may address some of the questions raised above by reducing what I perceive to be a common obsession with the content of the client's narrative—or the supervisee's, for that matter. Supervision can at times concentrate so much on the client's story that we may well ask ourselves: 'Although with the best of motives, are we just gossiping about the private struggles of another human being?'; 'Are we only impressing ourselves with the depth of our concern and compassion for others?' The assumption may be that these discussions of content affect the supervisee's awareness in some way and *thereby* their work with their client. Doubtless this can sometimes be the case. However, I have taken part in too many long (sometimes theoretically based) conjectures about clients not to wonder if these are really of use in developing supervisee awareness. Depending to some extent on one's theoretical orientation, such supervision sessions are more or less likely to evaporate into the ethereal air of intellectual theorising or descend into the dark undifferentiated mysteries of synchronicity, parallel process, or intersubjectivity. The question is whether and how we are able to transfer these speculations back to our therapeutic relationships in a way that is beneficial to our clients, and not only intellectually or emotionally satisfying to ourselves. Without explicitly exploring how to take supervisory discussions back into the actual process with the client, how does this kind of supervision help with what happens in the next therapy session?

A Focusing stance may help address these tendencies to overemphasise content, to adopt a paternalistic attitude to clients, and to apply general theories to intricate human processes. Focusing may contribute towards a 'demystification' of supervision, and of therapy in general. It could offer a kind of supervision that is more 'grounded' in the *process* of what is being experienced between the two people in therapy as well as the people in the supervision session. This emphasis remains responsive to the supervisee's needs as they are presented session by session. Received knowledge and common therapeutic assumptions may be challenged by this return to how we are actually living our situations. In this chapter I outline some commonly held ideas about supervision and will follow this by a short description of Focusing before giving examples of how Focusing might function in supervision sessions.

SUPERVISION

Supervision aims to provide a space where counsellors and therapists can review and explore their way of being with clients. It is an opportunity to reflect upon (and re-experience) the processes of relating that occur in the therapeutic encounter in order to ask what this reveals about the therapist, what it may suggest about the client's responses to life, and what it implies about human existence generally. One assumption is that this exploration and reflection in supervision benefits the client in part because it can generate a return to openness for a therapist who may have jumped to conclusions regarding client issues, themes, or even 'pathology'.

In order to facilitate open exploration of the supervisee's work, the atmosphere of the supervisory session is crucial. Ideally, supervisees will experience their supervisor as supportive of the way they are trying to practise so as to facilitate honest self-disclosures. Otherwise, supervisees may resort to presenting 'successes' in order to gain the approval of their supervisor, while simultaneously concealing what they perceive to be their 'mistakes' and 'failures'. This both hinders the development of the therapist, and also creates a secretive world of unsupervised practice or even malpractice. The supervisory atmosphere is ideally one of respect and mutual exploration in which supervisee and supervisor feel safe enough to admit mistakes, try out new ideas, and disclose personal issues. With inexperienced supervisees, it may be especially important to accentuate the positive aspects of their development, even when they present sessions that may make the supervisor cringe. Yet, at the same time, supervisors (and, in a group setting, fellow supervisees) need to be able to challenge constructively (as distinct from criticising) client work, assumptions, and the theoretical stances of their colleagues.

The supervisee is responsible for presenting, in as coherent a manner as possible, their work with specific clients. They may also bring general practice issues, personal issues that are impacting upon their therapy work and which they are comfortable exploring in supervision, philosophical and theoretical issues, frame and boundary issues, and issues relating to administrative tasks such as letter writing, clinical notes, data protection, and legalities. In responding to any of these issues during a supervision session, the supervisor's role functions in various ways. For example, supervisors take on the role of colleague, teacher, therapist, and may take the role of accepting clinical responsibility for the supervisee's work. This last role explicitly necessitates discerning when a supervisee's actions might be inappropriate or even unethical. The supervisor may at times give their supervisee information, suggest or request various courses of action, intervene in a way that is variously supportive, clarifying, problem-solving, all of which may perhaps result in cathartic or reflective experiences and increased awareness in the supervisee or, ideally, in both supervisee and supervisor. The way all this transpires in a particular supervision session will of course depend upon the individuals involved but it will also be determined to a significant extent by the theoretical orientation adopted by the participants.

In spite of there being as many orientations towards supervision as towards psychotherapy itself, in this chapter I will stick to what I believe pass for the most common components of 'good enough supervision'. Of course, some of this will fit more closely with one therapeutic orientation or another, but there seems to be broad agreement even among practitioners of different therapeutic orientations about what constitutes supervision, though what is emphasised certainly varies (see Jacobs, 1996). I will mindfully ignore issues regarding the basic assumptions of supervision, the difference between supervising trainees versus experienced therapists, and group versus individual supervision, in order to concentrate on how a Focusing-oriented supervision might address the concerns I raised at the beginning of this chapter. Before looking at how Focusing might augment the tasks of supervision, I will offer a brief introduction to Focusing itself.

FOCUSING

Eugene Gendlin is an existential philosopher who became interested in how humans symbolise raw experience. As early as 1952, this interest brought him into contact with psychotherapists and psychological researchers and lately it has culminated in his *Philosophy of the Implicit* (Gendlin, 1997a, 1997b). Gendlin saw therapy as a unique place where the process of symbolising experience could be investigated. According to Gendlin:

> A person struggles with and finds words and other expressions for unclear—but lived—experience . . . What was felt but undefined by the client was thought to be unmeasurable and incomprehensible and it made people uncomfortable to talk about such a variable . . . When it correlated with success in therapy while other variables did not, people began to try to understand it more seriously. (Friedman, 2000, p. 47)

This ability to stay with an unclear (but clearly felt) bodily experience constitutes a natural form of self-reflection that is now called 'Focusing'. Focusing can lead to surprising insights, therapeutic change, creative thinking, and daily living in close connection with our bodily experience. Gendlin and others found that they could teach this simple and natural skill to people who had forgotten it, lost touch with it, stopped valuing it, or who were just no longer aware of it. Focusing is a way of paying attention to one's being-in-the-world, one's *interaction* as it is experienced through one's body. The bodily felt experience is the intricate interaction of self and world, elaborated by perception and language.

The psychotherapeutic usefulness of Gendlin's philosophy is that it is 'methodologically individualised'. However, according to Levin (1997, p. 95), Gendlin is concerned that this might be 'misunderstood as individual rather than social or historical. The historical process is individual when we think further. History moves through individuals because only individuals think and speak.' Therefore, according to Gendlin, our experience is not 'subjective' or 'intrapsychic' but interactional. What we feel is not inner content, but the sentience of what is happening in our living with others. He calls this feeling the 'felt sense' and uses the ' . . . ' to indicate it: a ' . . . ' may come. Then one finds that one's whole life-situation was in this at-first murky body-sense. We see: The body-sense is not subjective, not just internal, not private, it is the implicit situation' (Levin, 1997, p. 241).

Life is not formed out of unrelated bits of perception or isolated internal objects: 'we humans live from bodies that are self-conscious of situations. Notice the "odd" phrase "self-conscious of situations". "Conscious", "self", and "situations" are not three objects with separate logical definitions' (Gendlin, 1999, p. 233).

137

Situations are process, and this is therapeutically useful.

Thinking and speaking from awareness of this ' . . . ' is exact and not arbitrary. I cannot convince 'it' to be something other than what it is. We find that such a body sense is more intricate than ambiguity—it is not a mish-mash of perceptions and concepts. It is my facticity, my thrownness, my living situation, and I may not like it at all, but I am not free to just change it, to mould it into something nicer or more acceptable.

In therapy, this ' . . . ' is revealed as the physically-felt sense of a situation. It includes emotion, history, meaning, intentions, but remains more than easily defined emotions, more than we can know or could ever say about the situation. I can pay attention to this felt sense in a specific way, as can my client. This allows what usually remains implicit to form in awareness so that we can access more information about our current interactions with each other, and our usual interactions in the world of other people. Rather than usual attention to content, this becomes a process which allows the bodily ' . . . ' to take steps forward. We are so used to thinking in terms of content and inner subjectivities that it can be hard to realise that a body sense *is* an implying of specific interactions. It can seem like content, but it is never permanent content; it is a process which 'points' to a way to continue living forward and this is clearly felt when we bring our attention to a felt sense. Language, when it speaks from this ' . . . ', is one way to live the situation forward: 'such sensitive phenomenological attention to an implicit speech which is "not yet formed" is precisely what is precluded by standard conceptual thinking about the body' (Wallulis, 1997, pp. 277–8).

My client speaks about his current trouble with his mother and how it reminds him of the tragic death of his father when he was a child. I can see he is feeling something as he talks but he does not pay attention to this ' . . . '. Instead, he does what most of us usually do, he keeps saying the things he already knows about these relationships. His talking could bring him closer to what he is feeling, but it could also keep him far away from it. I invite him to pay explicit attention to how he feels as he talks:

Client: *I feel angry. It's that old anger again.*
Therapist: *Where do you feel that familiar old anger?*
Client: *It's here* [pointing to his chest].
                 (This client has reflected this way before, so he knows immediately what I mean. Some clients might respond: 'What do you mean where do I feel it?' It is usually simple to guide a person into the middle part of the body where we typically feel our life situations.)
Therapist: *Does it feel OK to spend some time with that feeling there, the way it is right now?*

Client:	(He is quiet for a minute, sensing if it feels OK for him to spend time with this.)
	Yeah, it feels like a concrete block in my chest.
Therapist:	*So you can feel it's like a concrete block there. And does that word 'anger' still fit the way the blocked place feels?*
Client:	*Umm, well, no actually . . .*
	(There is a silence while he checks what word, phrase, image etc. would better describe his actual present experience.)
	. . . It feels more like sad.
Therapist:	(I can see colour coming to his face as he says 'sad' and suddenly there is a palpable feeling of sadness in the room—I can feel a sadness rising also in my chest.)
	That place in your chest, it's really feeling sad about something right now.
Client:	*Yeah.* [he begins to cry]. *I dunno.*
	(He is silent, now with his eyes closed.)
	I feel so alone, so isolated. I still miss him. I find it so hard to love now. I say I love my girlfriend but I can't feel it. It's easier to be angry . . . [sensing again]. *It's about trust, I need to learn to trust again . . .*

The session proceeds and the client continues to have 'deeply felt' shifts in the meaning of his experience. We spend the last part of the session talking about what he has realised and how this challenges the way he sees himself and his way of living. We could have stayed with just the word 'anger', and his interpretation of his experience. Perhaps then we would not have touched the deeper experience in a way that moved it forward from 'anger' to 'blocked' to 'sad' to a whole life situation that was current, past and future in its implications. We could have both missed the rich phenomena of his current actual experiencing and the forward movement implied from it ('it' as a living process, not as sedimented content). Focusing allows us to be with the intricacy of our life situations so that we feel more than we already know about them, including the *specific* way these situations are implying a living forward. Although this way of describing experience may seem strange to those who have not experienced Focusing, the efficacy of Focusing in therapy is well known and well researched (Hendricks, 2001). Focusing offers to therapeutic practice a phenomenological stance that arises from the therapist's embodiment rather than other's theories, resulting in an attitude of being-with rather than doing-to (Madison, 2001). Therapy and supervision are more than just Focusing, but I would like to suggest that Focusing could be as efficacious in supervision as it is in therapy.

Using Focusing in supervision

I recently commented to a supervisee that I wanted to begin to use Focusing in our group supervision sessions. His response was: 'But you do that already, it's obvious'. Upon reflection, I realised that I was weaving a Focusing style and attitude naturally into my work as a supervisor. However, there are also more explicit ways of adding Focusing to the supervision that we usually do. In the following discussion I will demonstrate how Focusing can expand upon supervision from various angles. You may wish to consider further how you could incorporate it into different orientations as well as how it could be a distinct orientation itself.

CHOOSING WHAT TO BRING TO SUPERVISION

As supervisees it can be difficult to decide which client or what kind of issue we want to present in supervision. We often think our problems with each client are discrete, about only that particular relationship and in some respects that is probably right. But we may find, by inviting a 'felt sense' of specific clients, that there is also a similar feeling to our work with more than one client and that by presenting our work with one client, we are in fact addressing aspects of our work with other clients as well. Using Focusing, we can often feel whether this is the case: we don't have to wonder 'Maybe this also relates to the way it's going with Mr Smith'; we don't have to make an intellectual link or take someone else's word for it; we can actually *feel* that our interactions with other clients have moved forward by staying with a felt sense of one client.

Rather than the supervisee consciously choosing what to concentrate on in the supervision session, he or she can ask themselves: 'What feels most important today?' or 'What feels most important about this client?' and wait for a felt sense to form, usually in the middle part of their body: throat, chest, stomach, or abdomen. It may be quite surprising what just *feels* most important and it may not seem to make much logical sense. What comes in the body in response to this invitation needs to be protected from doubting or critical voices that may interfere: 'What, that? How can *that* be most important?' A bodily felt sense includes more than we can put into words and what seems like an insignificant matter may be a better way into processing larger issues.

WHEN SUPERVISION TOUCHES UPON AN ISSUE FOR THERAPY

The distinction between therapy and supervision can be simultaneously both clear and flexible. It is usually apparent when someone is not bringing enough of

140

themselves into the supervision forum or when they are using supervision solely to explore their own personal issues rather than their client work. From a Focusing point of view supervision should, by nature, be deeply self-reflective and experiential and thus it will generate issues for the supervisee and supervisor to take to their personal therapy or personal Focusing sessions. So, at times supervision might, for some minutes, feel and sound a lot like therapy. Using Focusing, a felt sense can be explored while keeping private what personal issue it connects to. This means that a supervisee can choose not to just stop when material comes up that she would rather not disclose in a supervision session but which is still quite relevant to her client work. She can speak about what feels right to explore in supervision and 'mark' what is right to take up later in her therapy. This applies equally for the supervisor. The supervision session remains primarily a place to reflect upon practice, not upon the larger life issues of participants, though at the level of experience these are intrinsically linked. Often a supervisee might, after some personal exploration, close the discussion by saying: 'That feels like a good thing for me to take to my therapy'. This demonstrates a flexibility to explore how personal issues impact upon relationships with clients while distinguishing this form of exploration from the wider personal context of a therapy session.

THE SUPERVISOR'S ISSUES

Just as the therapist/supervisee's issues can affect the therapy, so the supervisor's issues can also affect the supervision, in a productive or adverse manner. In order to best manage this effect, Lees (1999) suggests that supervisors and supervisees should be seen as 'co-workers' rather than the classical view of supervisor as mentor or overseer:

> there are several interconnected principles which arise out of the work which I have described. First, the need constantly to strive to establish balance in the supervisory system between supervisor, supervisee and client. Second, the need to protect both supervisees and clients from supervisor power and narrow-mindedness. Balance is maintained by giving space to supervisee concerns about the supervisor, to client issues, to the supervisory shadow and by maintaining an awareness of the dynamics of the context. (p. 140)

For example, the supervisor may become aware in the session that she has a feeling about what is happening right now between her supervisee and herself. Exploring this can create a space that is potentially deeply self-revealing. It encourages both people involved to experience their connection and simultaneously their uniqueness, and to develop a working relationship based upon empathy across difference, whether personal, theoretical or cultural. According to Rapp (2000):

> 'differences within cultures' are at least as important as 'differences between cultures' and it may, in fact, be more difficult to remain aware that a supervisee or supervisor who has much in common with us is nonetheless an 'other', a unique and different individual. We would be wise to assume as little as possible about another individual's very personal understanding of themselves and their world. (p. 99)

The 'Focusing attitude' facilitates this non-expert and democratic openness to the other, whether the other is client, supervisee, colleague, or anyone. In Focusing, one's own 'point of view' is first acknowledged and then 'bracketed' in order to have space to understand the way the other really experiences something. Approaching people with a radical acceptance of what exceeds either person's understanding fosters a real sense of mutuality. However, as I'll explore later, there can be responsibilities in a supervisory relationship which may necessarily supersede such a democratic stance.

WORKING FROM THE IMPLICIT PHENOMENA

Taking a phenomenological approach to psychotherapy is more an attitude or intention than it is an accomplishment. Basics of this approach include describing rather than interpreting experience, bracketing our expectations and assumptions in order to approach immediate lived experience, and having no preset hierarchy regarding what is significant and what is trivial (see Spinelli, 1989). We can never access experience, ours or another's, free from prejudice, but the phenomenological attitude nonetheless enables us to be much more open than we would be if we were explicitly bound to a preset theory. Focusing enables supervisors and supervisees from any theoretical orientation to work phenomenologically. This supports our intention to stay close to the client's experience rather than intellectualising, generalising, or distancing ourselves with theories.

In supervision, for example, we can ask a supervisee: 'Imagine what it really feels like to be with that client. Forget for a moment all the things you could say about that person and just let yourself feel again what it's like to be together with him.' This enables the supervisee to focus directly on the experience of being with a specific client rather than trying to figure them out or continuing to recount their story. The relationship that therapist and client co-create in the session is thereby directly available in the supervision session, in some form, from one participant's point of view. We won't assume that by doing this the supervisee has privileged access to the way their client feels, but I have often seen supervisees gain surprising insights into themselves, their client's issues, the context of their sessions, or even the supervision group, by inviting and then staying with a felt sense of a particular client session. Some of these insights might completely contradict their understanding up to that point.

If the supervisee is having difficulty opening to her client's experience, this can also be explored using Focusing: 'Can you ask yourself, down in the middle of your body: What's in-between me and my client?' In this way, some of the supervisee's own assumptions, fears, and prejudices can be made explicit by paying attention to the way they actually arise in that client interaction rather than by cognitive speculation and analysis of what she already knows about herself. If something new arises in this way, it can then be explored in terms of how it impacts upon the therapeutic relationship and again later in the supervisee's own personal therapy.

If a supervisee, supervisor, or entire supervision group, is having difficulty in empathising with a client's position or behaviour, it can be helpful to invite all participants to imagine being that client. Based upon what they know of the client's history, how that client struggles with his life situation, or his way of being in sessions, participants can be invited to 'Really imagine being in that person's situation, imagine you were living his life. What feeling comes in your body as you do that?' Our experience may be very different than his, but we will have *an* experience. The felt sense that forms reveals something about the supervisees, something about human life in general and may therefore perhaps contribute to an increased understanding of the client. From a felt sense we have more information to work with, perhaps something new will emerge, perhaps he will begin to make some sense to us or new questions may emerge for the next session. What arises in this way exceeds our preset concepts, assumptions, and theories. It is not the whole story, but it is more than we had before, and in the phenomenological tradition we would lightly hold anything that came and not use it to make conclusions or reduce our openness to the client.

PLAY IN SUPERVISION

I have described a few ways of using Focusing as a phenomenological method, but there are many ways that Focusing awareness might be incorporated into supervision. Supervision sessions can be lively and creative. They do not need to be heavy, sitting still in chairs, talking seriously with long faces. Playing with images, thoughts, trying out the client's posture, working with dream images, songs, or drawing, can bring out new aspects of experience. Any of these activities can be done from a felt sense so that any movement arises spontaneously from more than what one is already aware of. For example, if a client regularly taps her foot while affirming how relaxed she is, try doing that, saying to yourself: 'I feel completely relaxed' while tapping away. Don't think about it, don't analyse the apparent contradiction here. Just allow your attention to go down into the middle of your body and ask in there: 'What does all this just *feel* like? What does it feel like to be a person doing this while saying that?' and wait. Let a feeling come. Then let a word or image come that fits that whole feeling. Of course, again we won't assume that the supervisee's experience and their client's will be identical. We don't want to reach any conclusions. If something seems to become clearer during this, *then* see if it makes any sense to apply that meaning to what you know of your client's life. While you do this, your supervisor can also Focus on what it feels like to be across the room from a person who taps her foot while insisting she is relaxed. This may give the supervisor some insight into what these sessions are like for the supervisee as therapist.

'PARALLEL PROCESS' AND OTHER OCCULT INFLUENCES

At times it seems as if the 'client's issues' are repeated in the supervisory relationship through the behaviour of the supervisee. This has been understood in various ways and is often referred to as 'parallel process'. For example, Lees (1999) writes about 'how the dyadic interaction between supervisor and supervisee may be influenced by the unconscious "pathology" of the client, using such techniques as parallel processing . . . to gain access to these unconscious influences' (p. 131).

Hawkins and Shohet's (1989) 'double helix model' of supervision includes concentrating on how the therapy process is reflected in the supervisory process. This includes exploring the therapist's countertransference and the supervisor's countertransference in order to examine the 'parallel process' that may occur. In parallel process, Searles (1955) says that the therapist 'is trying unconsciously by his demeanour during the presentation, to show us a major problem area in the therapy with his patient. The problem area is one which he cannot perceive objectively and describe to us effectively in words; rather, he is unconsciously identifying with it and is in effect trying to describe it by the way of his behaviour during the presentation' (cited in Hawkins and Shohet, 1989, p. 68).

Similarly, Page and Wosket (1994) offer this description:

parallel phenomena are, similarly, forms of unconscious material imposing themselves on the basic affective relationship but, as the term suggests, in this case there is a degree of parallel between what is occurring in the supervision relationship and what is taking place in the counselling relationship . . . An example of this would be a counsellor who, when working with a particularly passive client, starts to act in an atypically passive manner towards his supervisor . . . Most supervisors welcome such parallel phenomena as the resulting dynamics provide a more direct way of experiencing the counselling process than second-hand reporting by the counsellor. (pp. 103–4)

Parallel process supposedly occurs as a form of discharge towards the supervisor ('There, see how *you* like it!') and an attempt to resolve feelings by re-enacting them (Hawkins and Shohet, 1989). Focusing offers a parsimonious description of 'parallel process' and also allows us to invite this experience to occur more often. The phenomena of parallel process are not mysterious or especially surprising when we recall that our bodies can create a holistic 'felt sense' of our life situations. Just as the client might recreate the experience of actually being with his lover simply by talking about him or her in a session, so the supervisee can recreate the situation of a specific session simply by recounting it in supervision. Likewise, the supervisor will begin to live that session while listening to his supervisee's account. It is not necessary to assume that someone is *doing something* to someone else when so-called parallel process is experienced. Nor is it necessary to assume that this phenomenon displays a 'problem area'. It may simply be that in supervision our bodies each form a felt sense of *being in* that situation, so we sometimes more than recount it: we live it in a shared way (though crossed with the supervision situation). If this sense of the session being relived in the supervision is missing, it can be invited by asking ourselves the question: 'And how does it feel to be with that client in the room? How does it feel for us to be exploring that here, now? What happens between us as we talk about your client?' As always, *after* the experience is explored, it is possible to return to the context of our own theories if that is actually useful.

CLEARING THE SPACE TO SUPERVISE

The first step in Gendlin's original way of teaching Focusing is called 'clearing a space' (Gendlin, 1981). When applied to supervision, this involves checking which issues the supervisor/supervisees are carrying bodily from their own lives as the supervision session commences. Each person takes a moment to ask down into themselves: 'What am I carrying around with me right now? What's in the way for me, or what's in-between me and feeling as good as I could right now?' The task is not to list every issue, concern, problem, that can be thought of, but just to notice what is actually in the way now. Each issue or feeling that arises is gently acknowledged, not analysed, denied, or figured out. Each thing that is being carried in the body is then respectfully set down outside the body, gradually creating a sense of more space inside. These issues can of course be returned to after supervision, but for the next couple of hours or so it means that there is a little more space to concentrate on supervision issues.

The more a supervisor can be aware of her own issues and acknowledge or 'bracket' them, the more she is able to be open to listening phenomenologically to her supervisees. This 'state' of openness to experience is referred to as 'listening from a cleared space' or as 'being in presence' by some Focusers (see Cornell, 1996). Being in presence is the experience of being open to all aspects of personal experience without taking sides with any particular feeling, desire, or intention. It is a state of relative equanimity and may be the underlying requirement for developing what Hawkins and Shohet (1989) describe as an important therapeutic skill:

> the most difficult new skill that supervision requires is what we call the 'helicopter ability'. This is the ability to switch perspectives; to be able to focus on the client that the supervisees are describing; to focus on the supervisees and their process; to be able to focus on your own process and the here and now relationship with the supervisees; to be able to see the client within their wider context and help the supervisees do likewise; and to see the work within the wider context of the organisation and inter-organisational issues. (p. 37)

Through 'clearing a space' and integrating a Focusing style and a Focusing attitude, I believe that this 'helicopter ability' may more naturally develop and enhance the effectiveness of supervision overall.

SELF-SUPERVISION

Focusing is an easily learned and effective form of self-reflection. When leaving the consulting room after a session, or later while writing up notes, a therapist might become aware of a feeling related to the session. If she knows Focusing, she has the option of pausing and letting her attention drop down to where her body makes this feeling, and quietly staying with it until something emerges from the feeling itself. This again involves bracketing what one already knows and all the interpretations that might prevent anything new from arising. This slightly meditative style of self-reflection can form the basis of self-supervision during which one's understanding of the client-therapist relationship as well as oneself continues to deepen between supervision sessions. Also, during a session a therapist can naturally Focus in order to reflect upon and guide their way of being with the client. The importance of this development is also highlighted by Hawkins and Shohet (1989) and by Jacobs (1996):

> Supervision provides the opportunity to learn how to be a better therapist; but it also teaches the therapist how to monitor her or his way of working without always bringing it to supervision (it is impossible to talk about every client and every session). Such monitoring takes place after the session, when writing up notes, or thinking about the therapeutic relationship; it takes place with experience in the session, so that the therapist begins to function as her or his own 'internal supervisor'. (pp. 137–8)

VARIOUS MODALITIES AND ORIENTATIONS

Friedman (2000) suggests that 'Focusing is the way that the Heideggerian and phenomenological approach to the body enters the world of psychotherapy' (p. 225). While this makes sense, Gendlin himself (1996) also points out that Focusing can be added to any psychotherapeutic approach. There are different ways of being with people therapeutically and it is beyond this paper to discuss the differences and similarities between therapy orientations. Nevertheless, I assume that the Focusing emphasis of being respectfully with the intricacy of this specific person sitting across from me is not inherently incompatible with any orientation or approach.

Whether the supervision session uses the language of being-in-the-world, transference/countertransference, congruence, empathy, resistance, splitting, or parallel process, if this language is referring to anything actual, then there is an experiential dimension to be explored. However, this requires setting aside one's theory long enough to connect with the phenomena it refers to, knowing that it is possible afterwards to return to the theory in order to speak of the experience to colleagues. Pett (1995), an existential therapist, asks how one can 'hold' onto any supervisory model while doing supervision without impairing the supervisor's ability to 'be with' the supervisee. He follows the generalities of the framework of Page and Wosket (1994). Although the specifics of Page and Wosket's model can seem quite prescriptive, Pett finds its general outline sparse enough not to impinge significantly on his intention to work phenomenologically.

From his experience as a supervisor, Pett (1995) finds that while a supervisee presents their work with a client, 'very often this description will lead to a response "standing out" of the description, much in the way Gendlin's (1981) "focusing" leads to a "felt sense"' (p. 122). If something 'stands out' then we can refer to it directly and explicitly explore it further, not only through language, but also through the body. For example, a supervisee working from an existential orientation may recount a client who expresses two values that seem to be contradictory. Rather than assuming a contradiction and exploring how to challenge this, the supervisee could 'play with' the felt sense of each expression. Take, for example, the two values: 'I want to be independent' and simultaneously 'I want to belong'. It may be that the possible contradiction is at the level of symbolisation while, at the more intricate level of experience, there are nuances far too subtle for words. In Focusing on his own felt sense of these values, the supervisee might feel 'I want to be independent' shift forward to become something more like 'I want to reach my full potential', while 'I want to belong' may become 'I want to connect fully to others'. The apparent contradiction has moved to possible compatibility, not through arguments that reify the original positions, but by exploring the phenomena of the lived experience that gives rise to each value. This supervisee is now able not only to appreciate his own values more, but also to work with his client in a deeply phenomenological exploration of both implicit and explicit values.

Alan Cartwright (1996), a psychoanalytic therapist, emphasises the therapist's role in staying with the client rather than with theory or isolated verbal expressions. He says: 'I have increasingly come to believe that it is often the implications and verbal contexts of words to which the patient and therapist are unconsciously responding' (p. 51).

Prue Conradi (1996), a person-centred therapist, asks her supervisees how the session felt overall:

> I give primary value to this feeling dimension, which I believe keeps us more closely in line with the supervisee's immediate experience, and secondary value to thoughts about the session, which will almost invariably remove us somewhat from the immediacy of the experience . . . I do not believe new learning will arise without first looking closely at the experience itself, both for the client and for the supervisee. (p. 55)

From a cognitive behavioural approach, supervision will likely echo the structured approach of therapy sessions, with an agreed agenda and so on. Focusing could assist this collaborative approach by providing more information to work with, offering more resonance to situations that the therapist may have difficulty with, and creating a warm empathy that is just as important in cognitive behavioural therapy as in other forms of therapy.

Lees (1999) points out the limitations of attempting to supervise across modalities while remaining within the limits of his own theory. Here is the result of using his own psychoanalytic language with a person-centred supervisee:

> it was perhaps not surprising that our relationship eventually became stuck. Indeed, by session seven we really did not seem to be communicating at all and the sessions were tense and awkward, *leaving me with a feeling of tightness in my stomach. Both during and after the sessions I felt angry, and frustrated and anxious.* (p. 134, my emphasis)

Since it can be incorporated into supervision sessions without bringing in new theory or content, Focusing may form a basis for supervisors who want to be able to work across modalities and orientations. Lees' example above also highlights a situation where it may be useful for the supervisor to Focus, either on his own after the session, or later in his own supervisor's supervision.

CONCLUDING REMARKS

Focusing is our natural ability to 'be with' the unclear process that always exceeds what we can articulate in symbolised content (words, concepts, images, or memories). As humans, we can refer directly to this ongoing bodily experience, and in supervision there are specific activities that can be explicitly enhanced by Focusing. The resultant form of supervision would be *process*-centred rather than content-centred, regardless of whether that content originated from the supervisor, supervisee, client's story, or theoretical assumptions. Concentrating on the experiential process, as I have suggested, could give us forms of supervision that are responsive to the changing needs of supervisees, keeping supervision challenging, exciting, and relevant to our client work and our own personal lives.

There are other supervision tasks which require a different quality of discernment or even an imposition upon the experiential. These tasks may originate in part from the *context* of supervision—the codes of ethics and practice of various professional bodies, training institutions, placement settings, and organisations. Discussing contracts, offering advice on professional development or practice, conducting annual appraisals and dealing with managerial concerns may all be appropriate or imposed aspects of supervision. While approaching these tasks in a Focusing manner may be helpful, they also require imposing upon our work the external authority, knowledge, and judgement of the larger world of therapy, institutions, law, and accepted practice.

So, there may at times be conflicts and choices between the experiential and the expected. However, being aware of the times when our felt sense moves in one direction while our professional duties move in another, can provide important information. It may be that Focusing not only enhances the efficacy of supervision, but that it assists in keeping us reflective regarding the professional accoutrements of supervision and of psychotherapy as a whole. It may also be that following the intricacy of our lived experience may lead to unique developments in the way we formulate supervision and the context of our practice as psychotherapists.

REFERENCES

British Association for Counselling and Psychotherapy (2001) *Ethical Framework for Good Practice in Counselling and Psychotherapy*. (Revised edition published April 2002) Available on BACP website: http://www.bacp. co.uk/

Cartwright, A. (1996) Psychoanalytic Self-Psychology. In M. Jacobs (Ed.) *In Search of Supervision* (pp. 36–52). Buckingham: Open University Press

Conradi, P. (1996) Person-centred therapy. In M. Jacobs (Ed.) *In Search of Supervision* (pp. 53–74). Buckingham: Open University Press

Cornell, A. W. (1996) *The Power of Focusing*. Oakland, CA: New Harbinger Press

Friedman, N. (2000) *Focusing: Selected Essays*, 1974–1999. USA: Xlibris Corporation

Gendlin, E. T. (1981) *Focusing*. New York: Bantam Books

Gendlin, E. T. (1986) *Let Your Body Interpret Your Dreams*. Wilmette IL: Chiron Publications

Gendlin, E. T. (1996) *Focusing-Oriented Psychotherapy. A Manual of the Experiential Method*. New York: Guilford

Gendlin, E. T. (1997a) *A Process Model*. Available from the Focusing Institute website. http://www.focusing.org/process.html

Gendlin, E. T. (1997b) The responsive order: a new empiricism. *Man and World, 30* (3) 383–411

Gendlin, E. T. (1999) A new model. *Journal of Consciousness Studies, 6*, 232–7

Hawkins, P. and Shohet, R. (1989) *Supervision in the Helping Professions. An Individual, Group and Organisational Approach*. Milton Keynes: Open University Press

Hendricks, M. N. (2001) Research basis of Focusing-oriented/experiential psychology. In D. Cain and J. Seeman (Eds.) *Research Bases of Humanistic Psychotherapies*. Washington, DC: American Psychological Association

Jacobs, M. (1996) (Ed.) *In Search of Supervision*. Buckingham: Open University Press

Lees, J. (1999) An approach to supervision in health care settings. *The European Journal of Psychotherapy, Counselling and Health, 2*(2), 131–41

Levin, D. M. (1997) *Language Beyond Postmodernism. Saying and Thinking in Gendlin's Philosophy*. Evanston IL: Northwestern University Press

Madison, G. (2001) Focusing, intersubjectivity, and "therapeutic intersubjectivity". *Review of Existential Psychology and Psychiatry,*XXVI (1), 3–17

Page, S. and Wosket, V. (1994) *Supervising the Counsellor. A Cyclical Model.* London: Routledge

Pett, J. (1995) A Personal Approach to Existential Supervision. *Journal of the Society of Existential Analysis*, 6(2) 7–26

Rapp, H. (2000) Working with difference: Culturally competent supervision. In B. Lawton and C. Feltham (Eds.) *Taking Supervision Forward. Enquiries and Trends in Counselling and Psychotherapy.* London: Sage

Searles, H. F. (1955) The informational value of the supervisor's emotional experience. *Collected Papers on Schizophrenia and Related Subjects.* London: Hogarth Press

Spinelli, E. (1989) *The Interpreted World. An Introduction to Phenomenological Psychology.* London: Sage

Wallulis, J. (1997) Carrying forward: Gadamer and Gendlin on history, language, and the body. In D. M. Levin (Ed.) *Language Beyond Postmodernism* (pp. 270–82). Evanston IL: Northwestern University Press

CHAPTER NINE

THE USE OF INTERPERSONAL PROCESS RECALL (IPR) IN PERSON-CENTRED SUPERVISION[1]

PENNY ALLEN

The individual knows best about the meaning of their own experience. Each individual is a unique authority about her/himself. (Kagan)

Every individual exists in a continually changing world of experience of which he is the center . . . this private world . . . can only be known, in any genuine and complete sense, to the individual himself. (Rogers, 1951, p. 483)

Interpersonal Process Recall (which from now on I shall refer to as IPR) is a process developed by Norman Kagan and his colleagues at Michigan State University in the early sixties. As a junior academic in a psychology department, Kagan videotaped eminent visiting speakers giving lectures in the department. Afterwards the speakers often wanted to see the tapes and, stimulated by watching the recording, they would spontaneously and uncharacteristically comment on a range of covert experiences they had been having at the time. Kagan was interested in this phenomenon and would ask a few respectful questions, which would

1. I would like to acknowledge my training in IPR with Norman Kagan and my continued practice with Peter Clarke who died in 1997 having just completed a rare contribution to the published literatureon IPR (Clarke, 1997). They were both generous in sharing material and workshop notes. I am also grateful to my two IPR colleagues, Jane Allen-Brown and Jon Scaife, for their support and continued involvement in the method and appreciation for the many hours of discussion and rumination we have shared together.

produce even more detailed recall, reflection and exploration. Over the years Kagan and his colleagues continued their research into methods for improving the quality of human interactions, and from this, developed a set of helpful questions called 'inquirer prompts', a protocol for an Inquirer Role and a structure to facilitate this form of self-study, which they called Interpersonal Process Recall.

Kagan believed that the potency and powerfulness of recall had to be experienced in order to be understood or taught and to enable one to be an inquirer for another's recall. For this reason he promoted the method through live workshops rather than through textbooks and continued to teach the IPR method through experiential workshops around the world until his death in 1994.

Coming from a person-centred background, Kagan assumed that people are responsible for themselves and will naturally move towards self-fulfilment unless blocked by fears. The underpinning philosophy of IPR as a self-learning tool is based on his beliefs that:

- People are intrinsically motivated to learn.
- People will only learn what they are ready to learn.
- People remember best what they discover for themselves.
- If you push, frighten or attack people, they will only learn how to keep you off their backs.

IPR is a self-reflective method of learning, a process of self-discovery. It is a way of enabling a person to look at the way they react and interact, and a way of studying aspects of interpersonal communication and our own process in these interactions. It is a safe, non-threatening way of creating a space in which to reflect, in the belief that each individual is a unique authority about herself and knows best about the meaning of her own experience. It is about expanding our repertoire of things that already work for us rather than about replacing what we already do with a new set of skills. I believe that it sits perfectly within the person-centred approach and is as useful for the experienced clinician, supervisor and trainer as it is for the novice or student.

In some ways, IPR more closely reflects the counselling model of the person-centred approach than some other supervision styles and models of supervision. The supervisor or, in the case of an IPR session, the inquirer is saying to the supervisee: 'I cannot tell you what you need to know and understand for your own growth and development, only you know that. But I can be alongside you and facilitate that process of discovery in you. I can help you to make sense of whatever you discover and support you in doing whatever you want to do with the knowledge.'

IPR is based on the idea that at any moment in time we are receiving and storing a multitude of feelings, thoughts, sensations, images and bodily reactions, of which we are not normally aware and which we do not have time to process in the moment, but which subtly affect the way we behave, react and interact.

Interestingly, the existence of this implicit memory and tacit knowledge or 'body-mind held memory', which many of us have known about subjectively, is now the subject of recent and persuasive research within neuroscience, particularly in the area of trauma (see Knox, 2001; Wilkinson, 2003; Pally, 2000).

If we can find a safe way to bring this information into conscious awareness, name it and examine it in a spirit of non-judgemental inquiry, then it can provide us with useful information about our own interactions, our mode of behaving in certain situations, the way we perceive others and the way they may perceive us.

This is clearly useful information for those of us who are trying to raise our level of awareness, for example as teachers, managers, clinicians, and especially as counsellors, psychotherapists and clinical supervisors or trainers of any of the above.

BRIEF DESCRIPTION OF WHAT THE PROCESS OF IPR LOOKS LIKE

Two people (person A and person B) make a video or audio recording of an interaction, a conversation. One of these people (person A), 'the recaller', then takes the recording and plays it back in the presence of a third person who acts as 'inquirer' for person A's recall of that interaction. The recaller stops the tape whenever anything occurs to her and the inquirer then aids her recall by prompting with helpful questions, thus facilitating the recaller to access memories of what was going on for her back then in the moment of the original interaction. This is a very brief description of an individual IPR recall and I will describe the detailed method of IPR later in the chapter.

Although people may profess a knowledge of the method, it seems that it is often the case that they have not fully experienced IPR in the 'classic' form which I describe. (This may be seen as being similar to the use of the term 'person-centred' as a vaguely understood ambition rather than the result of a rigorous training in the approach.) It is my belief that one does need to have this experience before fully understanding its powerfulness and the various possible applications.

The supervisory relationship
This model of IPR is not offered or intended to take the place of an ongoing supervisory relationship in which trust, mutual regard and genuine honesty are paramount, but it can be a useful tool to be used appropriately as one method of learning and enquiry. It is a method which can be incorporated into those things which we already know and do rather than replacing any existing knowledge or

skill. It can also be used as a stand-alone method for self-reflection, and its possible applications will become clearer later in the chapter.

It seems to me disingenuous to assume that the power in the supervisory relationship is, or can ever be, equal (or experienced as such), however much we might like that to be the case and however much our philosophy might subscribe to that as an ideal state. This can increasingly become an issue in these days of accredited training and validated courses where an accepted requirement of accreditation is a 'supervisor's report' and where trainees (quite properly) are required to find supervisors with an accepted training and qualification in supervision and the correct number of 'flying hours'.

It is almost inevitable that at times one sees one's supervisor as more knowledgeable, more experienced, more skilled, better qualified and more well-travelled in the world of counselling, therapy and professional practice. Indeed, a supervisee may well have chosen their supervisor for just those reasons. This is particularly true for a trainee who may be feeling deskilled and disempowered by the training process and for a beginning counsellor who may be feeling the anxiety and insecurity associated with being a novice in any new practice. There is an additional problem in that, in this country, regular supervision at a minimum of 1.5 hours a month is mandatory if working to British Association for Counselling and Psychotherapy (BACP) standards of practice. This means that a potential supervisee may not even go through the self-questioning stage along the lines of: 'Do I need supervision, and if so, why?'; 'What do I need to get from it?'; 'What kind of supervisor do I want?'; 'What do I not want?'

In a situation where the supervisor is not paid directly by the supervisee but is provided by the placement or employing agency, sometimes in exchange for free counselling hours in a voluntary agency, there is an added imbalance. If the client (in this case the supervisee) is making a direct payment to the supervisor for her services, there is a much clearer and more equal transaction. When contracting to work together, the supervisee may feel more able to state what they are hoping to get and what they need from their supervision. The supervisor can state what they can offer, how they will work and what the fee will be. If the contract is not met or is not working, ultimately either side can terminate. It may not so easily or clearly be the case where the supervision is provided as part of a package, and in these situations it is possible that issues of power and control can cloud the relationship and may affect honest openness and learning.

As a supervisor I believe it is honest to address these issues rather than pretend that they are not factors that we need to acknowledge, name, and work through.

There are, of course, occasions when the supervisor's experience enables her to take a dispassionate overview, to help a supervisee grapple with an ethical issue, to bring an understanding of the wider context of the work or to point the way to some further learning, theory or information which would be helpful to the supervisee in the understanding of their work. There are also times when an experienced supervisor is more able to provide holding and containment when it is needed, thus enabling the counsellor to do the same for her client. And this is entirely appropriate and desirable.

The downside, however, is that most of us carry with us memories of experiences in early life of being a small person in a big person's world: of bigger people around us knowing what is best, what is right—even when the big person's world appears to be unfair, illogical or clearly mad. We may carry memories of being tested, examined, called stupid, made to feel ashamed, told to accept another's authority without question, even when it has not been earned. These memories may or may not be conscious and recognised, and they may be in or out of awareness. Even for the most well-adjusted of us, such feelings, sensations, and memories can be easily activated in a relationship such as a supervisory relationship with someone we perceive as more experienced and wiser, someone from the big people's world, and especially at times when we might be feeling exposed or vulnerable.

This imbalance can of course be minimised in a good, trusting and genuine relationship where the supervisor is able to offer the core conditions and does not have a need to be seen as right, clever, wise and all-knowing; and where the supervisee is open to new learning, to self-discovery and is working in their own personal development or therapy toward a greater self-acceptance. But even in the best relationship, it would be rare for there not to be moments of transference from previous experience and I believe this is most likely to arise when the supervisee is feeling most exposed and vulnerable and therefore less grounded. For some of us, the detailed discussion of our work with clients can be just such a time of vulnerability, especially while in training or as beginning counsellors. I use the word *transference* here quite literally to mean the transferring of an old emotion or set of concepts from a previous experience onto a new and different but similar situation or relationship which may simply have been a trigger rather than a cause. This usually happens 'out-of-awareness' and I don't know of a better term than transference for this phenomenon which most of us recognise. Indeed, Rogers (1951) himself acknowledged the presence of 'transference attitudes' in the therapeutic relationship. The effect of the phenomenon I refer to as transference, may be experienced by both parties as incongruence and if acknowledged can be unpicked, named and worked through. In some ways this phenomenon can be a particular trap for person-centred supervisors who are striving to create facilitative conditions, who have genuinely good relationships with their supervisees and where both parties would wish for transparency and equality. In this situation it can be easy to miss underlying defences and performance anxieties which might be well hidden and 'out of awareness' to them both, but which nevertheless exist and may inhibit openness and new learning.

As Kagan put it in a workshop in Sheffield in 1992, 'if you offer people support and safe opportunities to reflect on their interactions with others, they become less fearful and more skilled in dealing with others'. Bearing all this in mind, if one of the functions of supervision is to facilitate honest, self-reflective practice, there are some questions which we, as supervisors, might ask ourselves:

- How can I be sure that I am allowing into awareness all that I need in order to look at and understand the process?
- How can I best enable my supervisee to extend her own self-learning and self-awareness, and to experience her growth and development?
- How can I do this in a non-threatening, non-punitive environment in which she can feel stretched and challenged rather than criticised or attacked?
- How can I encourage her to own and celebrate her own learning and good practice?
- How can I enable her to become more aware of her own tacit knowledge and sound intuition?
- How can I help her to develop an informed, alert and sure-footed 'internal supervisor' that she can believe and trust?
- How can I enable her to look at perceived mistakes or omissions honestly and to examine the reasons for doing or not doing, saying or not saying, things in the counselling relationship in a spirit of learning and inquisitiveness without her being overly self-critical, judgemental, punitive or negative; to be able to recognise 'stuck places' as a stage in the process to be worked through rather than as failure?
- How can I do any or all of this without re-enforcing existing conditions of worth and becoming the external locus of evaluation?
- How can I help her to strengthen her internal locus of evaluation?

In many ways these parallel the questions Rogers (1958) asks himself about creating a helping relationship. I believe that one of the methods which can greatly assist in this reflective endeavour is the use of IPR in supervision.

Taping

IPR requires the use of taped client sessions and I realise that the issue of taping is a contentious one for some people. There are ethical, professional and personal issues to be considered: how to introduce the subject of taping to clients without them feeling pressured or exposed; confidentiality; how the tape will be used; who owns the tape; whether the presence of a tape-recorder will alter the interaction in some detrimental way; introducing an agenda which is the counsellor's rather than the client's; coping with the technology; managing the anxiety of hearing ourselves on tape; dealing with our self-conscious and self-critical self; shame, and so on.

Nevertheless, I would argue that dealing with all these issues as they arise can be a valuable experience in itself, and help us reach a point where we can recognise that our learning is more important (and more interesting) than the maintenance of our own comfort-zone. Often, just not doing it and therefore not confronting or working through the issues would be much more comfortable. But addressing the issue could be seen as part of the process of being more open to our own experience, so that we can put those self-limiting things on one side and be more fully present for our clients. For trainers and supervisors, taping of sessions can also address some of the issues around assessment, safety and accountability and our responsibility to the safety of future clients by training safe, competent and aware counsellors. More detailed arguments for and against taping or not taping are set out in other publications (see, for instance, Scaife, 2001).

However, I am aware that, for some people, using and playing tapes of sessions can, potentially, be a nerve-wracking experience and should not be done for the sake of it without all three people, that is, the client, counsellor and the supervisor all having a clear idea about why they are doing it and how it will be used. With IPR there is a transparency of purpose, a clarity of method and a built-in safety for the counsellor which are some of the reasons why, as a trainer and supervisor, I like to use IPR as the preferred method for the playback of tapes whenever possible.

THE METHOD OF INTERPERSONAL PROCESS RECALL

IPR is a self-reliant and safe method of learning in which a person is in control of their own learning process. It gives that person the opportunity to examine in detail and talk about an interaction that they have already survived, using the safety and distance of a recording. In content terms, they already know the outcome so the worst that can happen now is that they will learn something new about themselves and the process. IPR can be used in many settings but for the purpose of this chapter in supervision it looks like this:

1. A counsellor makes a recording of a session or interaction with a client. This could be either an audio or a video recording, although most of us are more familiar with audio and the equipment is less intrusive. Video can offer an additional dimension in the form of visual cues but can also be distracting and, unless the subject is used to seeing themselves on the screen, it can lead

to unhelpful comment and self-confrontation.

2. The tape is then taken to supervision to do an Interpersonal Process Recall, with the supervisor acting as 'inquirer' to the counsellor's recall.

3. The inquirer (supervisor) should invite the recaller (therapist) to play the tape and to press the pause button when anything at all occurs to them: any thought, feeling, sensation, hope, fear, expectation, picture, memory, hunch, that they had at the time of the original interaction but that they did not have the time or space to stop and look at back then.

4. When the recaller stops the tape, the inquirer will prompt their recall with helpful questions or prompts. When the recaller is ready to move on, she continues 'play' until something else is triggered by listening to the tape at which point she stops the tape again. At all times, control for starting and stopping the tape rests entirely with the recaller.

The inquirer role

There are some essential elements to acting as inquirer:

- The inquirer needs to find enjoyment in the other person's learning rather than enjoying his own expertise.
- The inquirer offers structure and support without controlling the level of exploration or influencing the other's recall.
- The inquirer acts as a witness to the recall, and does not lead in any way.
- The inquirer prompts with open-ended 'What?' questions, not 'Why?' questions.
- The inquirer needs to be assertive in helping the recaller to stay in the past tense, attending to what was going on for them 'back then', not now.
- The inquirer should not interpret, evaluate, or assume superior knowledge.
- If the recaller strays into 'What if?'s or hypothetical opinions, the inquirer should bring her back to the tape.

Before starting the recall, the inquirer may introduce the IPR session to the recaller using a protocol such as the script offered here as an example:

> We know that we think and feel faster and with more complexity than we can ever give attention to or be wholly conscious of at the time. This is an opportunity to think about the original experience more fully than there was time to do back then.
>
> Listening to (or watching) the recording can remind us of:
> - things we had no time to say;
> - things that did not seem appropriate to say;
> - feelings, pictures, sensations we had no words for;

- risks for us in the situation;
- guesses about the effects we were having on the other person;
- things that got in the way of us responding in the way we wanted to.

Please stop the tape whenever you remember anything, when anything comes to mind, no matter how small.

The stop/start/pause button is always given to the recaller. If, after some time, they are not stopping the tape the inquirer may invite them to stop whenever the smallest thing occurs or just stop it anyway and see what comes up for them. If a question from the inquirer is not helpful or does nothing for the recaller she can just say so and move on. If the inquirer is not sure whether to continue with more questions he can ask the recaller, 'Is there anything more for you at that point in the tape or would you like to move on?' At all times the inquirer should respect the recaller's process and sense of what they need to do.

The questions used by the inquirer fall into various groups and I include below a set of questions which have been found to be helpful as 'inquirer prompts' and which can be used as a 'crib sheet' (see Box 9.1).

Box 9.1. Inquirer prompts in Interpersonal Process Recall (based on the Inquirer Crib Sheet, Kagan, 1980).

Self-exploration
- What thoughts were in your mind at the time?
- How were you feeling then?
- Do you recall any physical sensations?•
- If that sensation had a voice, what would it say?
- Were there any pictures, memories, words going through your mind?
- Did the setting affect you in any way?

View of the other
- Did you have any feelings towards the other person?
- How did you think the other felt at the time?
- How did you think they saw you?
- Did the other's appearance or posture have any effect on you?

Own behaviour
- Was there anything you were not saying?
- Do you know what that was about?

161

- Was there anything you would have liked to have said or done at that point?
- Why didn't you? What stopped you? Did anything get in the way?
- Was there any risk involved for you?

Values and assumptions
- Was there anything you liked about what was happening?
- Was there anything you did not like?
- Was anything taken for granted?
- Was anything important for you there?

Hopes and intentions
- Did you have any strategies?
- Was there anything you wanted to happen?
- What did you think the other expected of you, wanted to happen?
- How did you want the other to feel about you?

Links with past experience
- Was that a familiar experience/feeling for you?
- Had it happened before?
- Did it remind you of anything else in your life?

Reflection
- Any idea how you came to say/do/think that?
- Did you have any hunch about what was going on?

Closure
- Is there anything else for you there?
- Do you want to take this further or move on?

Usually one finds that just a few minutes of a taped interaction will take up a whole IPR session. Kagan always maintained that if there was an issue, a hesitancy, something not being said, a defensiveness, anything going on in the relationship, then it would come to the surface no matter where you stopped the tape and took a slice to recall. Instinctively one feels this to be likely and subjectively I have experienced it to be the case. This would support the view that what is discovered is not imagined or fabricated, but something which is already there (in implicit memory), just waiting to be brought into awareness. Of course, all memory is subjective and will differ from day to day, being amended and influenced by events and our previous experiences and information gained and stored since the original moment. But it does seem that this non-judgemental and value-free way of using a tape of the original interaction to kick-start a memory, has the effect of triggering and activating a fairly accurate memory that is richer, more detailed and more plausible than most other ways of reporting a past event.

The recaller may start the tape at the beginning or they may have a sense that it would be productive to wind the tape on to a particular place to start. The inquirer can check this with the recaller before starting the IPR inquiry.

Supervisors commonly experience some difficulties in the inquirer role. The main one is that the inquirer should be as neutral as possible and most of us find it very difficult not to get into our more familiar empathic counsellor or supervisor framework. This can be avoided partly by trying not to listen to the content of the tape but concentrating instead on the recaller's process when she has stopped the tape. It can actually still work perfectly well if the inquirer cannot hear the tape at all and this is sometimes a useful exercise when practising the inquirer role. Another problem which is experienced by supervisors in this role is in not having an agenda other than facilitating the supervisee's recall. This is especially difficult in the context of an ongoing supervisory relationship where, as a supervisor, we may have our own ideas about what would be helpful for the supervisee to explore.

In the Sheffield IPR Study Group we have had extensive discussions about whether the inquirer questions can be truly context-free, or indeed whether they should be. It is my view that this aspect should be negotiated at the beginning of the session. There are various ways to approach this. The supervisor can ask the recaller if there are any particular areas she wants to concentrate on, any particular types of question she would like asked. The supervisor can ask if it is OK for her to notice any areas not being attended to and to ask questions of her choice— always with the proviso that the recaller holds the power and need not answer them or can just move on. The counsellor and supervisor may have already identified a particular area needing attention and may have decided to do the IPR for this reason and in that case the inquirer questions will almost certainly not be context-free, but the emphasis will already have been negotiated and this will be understood by both people. However, I do think that in order to maintain the safety element of the recall, the protocol outlined above should be adhered to as far as possible.

As a supervisor I would not usually take a whole supervision session for the IPR but would leave time after the recall to return to our more usual mode. I would then use the remaining time (out of inquirer mode and back in supervisor mode) to discuss with the supervisee whether there are things that have come up in the session that she would like to attend to or to make a note of for future attention. If IPR is used regularly in supervision, there may be recurring themes or patterns which the supervisee and/or the supervisor notice and that they could then explore in normal supervision time. IPR is a particularly useful method for helping us to spot particular and recurring patterns in our way of being and for looking at whether these are helpful or necessary or not: patterns, for example, of rescuing, protecting, or not naming things for fear of intrusion. It also helps identify unspoken conditions of worth and taboos, or fears about saying or doing certain things; and can offer a way of trying out or rehearsing things we might have said.

Using IPR on a taped session between a client and counsellor will concentrate on that relationship and does not take account of the counsellor/supervisor relationship or any parallel process that might be present (see Chapter 4) although it can help to clarify where an issue originates, if there is one, and to whom it belongs.

Mutual recall

IPR can also be done as a mutual recall with both participants of the original interaction being present and recalling the session together. Either of them may stop the tape, and the inquirer then prompts each of them in turn. This has the advantage that each person both hears what was going on for the other person and can check out if that was anything like what they thought was going on. Each can also hear about the effect that their own behaviour was having on the other person at the time. It sometimes feels safer for the recallers if they have each done an individual recall first before doing a mutual recall.

Although we will not often have the opportunity to do this exercise with clients in our own practice, it is certainly possible to do it in training practice sessions. There can be enormous learning for a trainee counsellor to hear what was going on for their 'client', to find out how deep or accurate was their empathic understanding, and to learn how accurately either of them was picking up the meta-communications or how off the mark they were in the assumptions they were making about each other; about whether their guesses or hunches were accurate; and about whether the things they feared were actually risks for the client or were their own stuff. (For an example of this see Kagan, 1980b, Film C1, *Client and Therapist*.) Kagan also used IPR and mutual recall to great effect in the training of GPs, taping their first interviews with patients and then doing a mutual recall with the patient and trainee GP. (See Kagan, 1980b, Film F5, *Physician and Patient*.)

Group recall

A similar process can be used to tape a group interaction and then do a recall with the whole group. There is an interesting video of some early work Kagan did with a Health Practice Team in which a team meeting was filmed and then a group IPR was done with Kagan as inquirer (Kagan, 1980b, Film F7, *Health Team*).

In this country, Jon Scaife has used group IPR sessions effectively with teachers and their pupils (e.g. Lally and Scaife, 1995). Group recall seems to have the effect of resetting the power relations toward greater equality. Kagan believed that IPR could play an important role in conflict resolution and used mutual recall with couples and group recall with families (Kagan, 1980b, Film F2, *Couple, Man and Woman*, and Film F8, *Family Interview*).

Training

One of the difficulties sometimes encountered by trainers and supervisors of student counsellors in the person-centred approach is that some students come into training expecting *to be taught* how to be counsellors. Such students can be puzzled and confused when they are told that, instead, what they first need to do is understand themselves and bring their own processes into awareness. It can be difficult for them to make that leap and it is often not until they start practising and taking 'stuff' to supervision that they fully make the connection.

IPR taught as a method of self-reflection early on in the training can be an excellent and experiential way of getting this across. It can be a useful means for trainees to appreciate that their own process is as relevant in the relationship as the client's. In my experience of IPR training groups there is usually some point in the day when at least one person has that 'Oh, *now* I see' experience.

Some of the IPR questions can also alert us to our own patterns of organising our emotions, our habitually felt, bodily responses and what Kagan referred to as our 'interpersonal allergies'. No one can accurately guess at these for another person, as they are often hidden, developed as strategies earlier in life, or learned and copied and then internalised. We can only discover them for ourselves by careful observation of our own process with a willingness to bring them into awareness. IPR is a useful and non-threatening method for doing that at each individual's own pace.

For experienced therapists too there are those times when one feels 'stuck', uncreative and inadequate. At these times it is easy for many of us to slip into whatever is our own personal 'gremlin' or accusatory voice: 'If only I was more experienced in that speciality'; 'There must be a technique that would help'; 'Perhaps I'm not the best therapist/supervisor for this client'; 'Perhaps the person-centred approach isn't enough'.

At these times, if I am lucky, I am reminded of the title and subject of Sheldon Kopp's (1977) book *Back to One*, the title of which refers to the meditation practice of monkey-counting in which each time you lose the meditation you go back to one and start counting again. In other words, what I need to do at this moment is to stop trying to find an answer, theory or explanation that will get us out of this place, stop trying to know, to be clever, and simply to go back to one and be still and listen; to centre myself, look inward and examine what is going on in me: 'What information am I holding in my body? What can I see, hear, feel, sense? What is my experience at that moment? What is coming up for me? What is being with this other person at this moment triggering for me? Trusting in my intrinsic knowledge and wisdom and my ability to stay there, can I be fully present for this person and, if not, why not?'

If I have been taping such a session, then taking it to supervision and doing an IPR session will help me get at this information. It can help me to access the information held in my memory and my body; intrinsic knowledge which otherwise is not always in my conscious awareness or knowledge and which my desperate searching for an answer at the time has stopped me from noticing, accessing and naming.

If I have experienced incongruence, an IPR can help me notice and name what was going on for me, allowing me to observe and accept that information non-judgementally. I can often then move on into a more congruent place. Even if I have not been taping the session, my experience of the IPR method can be a helpful guide in processing a session for myself. I have the experience of knowing how to access stuff going on in me. Often that is all that is needed.

OTHER APPLICATIONS

As well as using IPR in the protocol I have offered here, I have found one of the most helpful side-benefits from using the method is that I have internalised the philosophy and the IPR questions. They are now an integral and enduring part of my 'internal supervisor' and inform the process work that I do on my own after a session.

Although I have illustrated in this chapter how IPR can be used in supervision, with the supervisor acting as inquirer for the counsellor or supervisee, it can be equally useful to take a tape of a supervision session to one's supervision of supervision to do one's own recall. Thinking of the complexity of the relationships: client/counsellor, counsellor/supervisor and supervisor/supervision supervisor, it is no wonder that it is sometimes difficult to disentangle where parallel process and one's own issues start and finish (see Hawkins and Shohet, 1989).

I think IPR can bring some clarity when waters become muddied in this area. In a recall it becomes easier to see which bits are mine and which are more entwined with someone else's process and experience. IPR is also an excellent model to use in peer supervision, where each person has an allocated time for recall and each can act as inquirer for the other.

The method also crosses all models and so can be used effectively and act as a unifying model for a supervisee and supervisor who are coming from different orientations or from vastly different work experiences and settings.

One of the dangers of a long-term supervisory relationship with a supervisor of the same theoretical orientation is that the two people can easily slip into a mutual comfort-zone. It can become cosy, and there can be collusion in familiarity. In this case, doing a tape and an IPR session occasionally can interrupt the familiar pattern and introduce some sharper self-reflective practice, highlighting any underlying issues.

If there is a particular need to examine a piece of work or an interaction and for some reason one does not have access to one's regular supervision, then it is possible to do a one-off IPR session with almost anyone who is willing to act as inquirer. This work need not of course be restricted to counselling relationships.

I have already mentioned that mutual recall can be used in couples counselling and in any conflict resolution situation where two people would benefit from hearing what is actually going on for the other person when they interact. Group recall can be used effectively where any group of people have identified a desire to understand better the underlying processes within the group. Kagan used IPR with organisations in the USA such as the military, the fire-service and GPs.

IPR can be especially helpful in training in sensitive and specialised areas such as gender, race and disability issues where people might wish to identify and work with their own prejudices and sensibilities.

IPR as a research tool

There are many examples of IPR being used as a tool within a research project to bring some clarity, particularly where basic assumptions need to be identified and understood. See, for instance, Elliot and Shapiro, 1988; Ball, 1994; Lally and Scaife, 1995; Cowie, et al., undated.

IN CONCLUSION

The power of a recall experience seems to be twofold: that it allows us to access information we might not normally notice: bodily feelings, sensations, fleeting thoughts, and so on; and that freedom from anxiety allows us to do this in more detail and at a deeper level than is normally the case.

There has been much discussion about how the process of IPR builds such high levels of safety. The method seems to offer safety in several ways:

- Listening to a tape gives some distance.
- The recaller herself is in control of the process and is not being asked to do anything other than take responsibility for her own learning.
- Finding words for difficult feelings and experiences and naming them tends to reduce their power and fearsomeness.
- Both people have survived the original interaction and therefore there are no further adverse consequences from looking at it again. As a past interaction, the outcome is already known and the content cannot be changed. This is why it is particularly important for the inquirer to keep the recall in the past tense. If it strays into the present then a discussion or speculation can occur which changes the agenda and removes the safety.
- No one else can possibly know or even guess at another person's internal experience and so there can be no external locus of evaluation.
- IPR can also offer the recaller—in this context the supervisee—an opportunity to try out or rehearse saying difficult or frightening things which they might not risk otherwise.

Of course, IPR can only be useful and effective if undertaken willingly by the participants in an atmosphere of mutual respect and genuine inquiry with each person willing to own their own material and take responsibility for their own learning and growth.

IPR is respectful to both one's own learning and one's intrinsic knowledge. As Kagan put it at a workshop in Sheffield in 1992:

> what we learn through intrinsic motivation, we don't need external nagging to maintain. In order to learn well we need to address our own anxieties. Skills are easily learnt and as easily forgotten (*or denied*) if they put us into situations where we feel uncomfortable.

To this I would add: '. . . and if they put us into situations where we feel fear or shame'.

The experience of doing a recall can be very powerful and yet remain safe and non-threatening. The beauty of a good IPR experience is that it is a process of trusting in our own organism to give us the clues and information we need in order to understand a moment of interaction with another human being. It is not dependent on an externally imposed theory, an intellectual exercise, or an outside or superior opinion. We can have a sense of self-respect in opening ourselves up to notice whatever is there and to learn whatever we are ready to learn from that information. I think it sits particularly well within the person-centred framework and addresses many of the thorny issues around the taping and monitoring of practice in training and supervision.

REFERENCES

Ball, V. (1994) *Good Staff Sit Quietly: A Study of Health Care Team Meetings*. Masters Dissertation, Department of General Practice, The Medical School, University of Sheffield

Clarke, P. (1997) Interpersonal Process Recall in supervision. In G. Shipton (Ed.) *Supervision of Psychotherapy and Counselling: Making a Place to Think* (pp. 93–106). Buckingham: Open University Press

Cowie, H., Lewis, J., Berdondini, L. and Rivers, I. (undated). Debriefing cooperative group work: A strategy for enhancing peer relations in the classroom. Paper. Centre for Psychotherapeutic Studies, University of Sheffield

Elliott, R. and Shapiro, D. (1988) Brief structured recall: A more efficient method for studying significant therapy events. *British Journal of Medical Psychology*, *61*, 141–53

Hawkins, P. and Shohet, R. (1989) *Supervision in the Helping Professions*. Milton Keynes: Open University Press

Kagan, N. (1980a) Influencing human interaction: Eighteen years with IPR. In A. K. Hess (Ed.) *Psychotherapy Supervision: Theory, Research and Practice* (pp.262–83). New York: Wiley

Kagan, N. (1980b) *Interpersonal Process Recall: A Method for Influencing Human Interaction*. Houston, TX: Mason Media

Kagan, N. (1984) *Interpersonal Process Recall: A method of influencing human interaction. Instructor's manual*. Houston, TX: Mason Media

Knox, J. M. (2001) Memories, fantasies, archetypes: An exploration of some connections between cognitive sciences and analytical psychology. *Journal of Analytical Psychology*, *46*, 613–35

Kopp, S. (1977) *Back to One*. Palo Alto, CA: Science and Behaviour Books, Inc.

Lally, V. and Scaife, J. (1995) Towards a collaborative approach to teacher empowerment. *British Educational Research Journal*, *21*(3), 323–38

Pally, R. (2000) *The Mind-Brain Relationship*. London and New York: Karnac Books

Rogers, C. R. (1951) *Client-centered Therapy*. London: Constable

Rogers, C. R. (1958) The characteristics of a helping relationship. *Personnel and Guidance Journal*, *37*, 6–16

Scaife, J. (2001) *Supervision in the Mental Health Professions: A Practitioner's Guide*. London: Brunner-Routledge

Wilkinson, M. A. (2003) Undoing trauma: Contemporary neuroscience. *Journal of Analytical Psychology*, *48*, 235–53

CHAPTER TEN

SHAKING THE SPIRIT: SUBTLE ENERGY AWARENESS IN SUPERVISION

ROSE CAMERON

A particular incident from my own practice as a supervisor stands out for me as I begin to write this chapter. I was supervising a counsellor whose client had complained that she seemed distant. My supervisee, Razia, reviewed her behaviour and feelings towards her client, and remained puzzled by the feedback. She then tried imagining that she was with her client, rather than with me while we talked. Her body and her words suggested that she was still fully engaged with me, but I noticed a marked difference in the emotional atmosphere between us. She seemed distant to me too.

I had noticed what it was that she had done that resulted in this change, and, obviously, wanted to tell her about what I had noticed. At this point, I normally take a deep breath and wonder how on earth to put it. This is not because what I want to say is critical, which it isn't. I cannot find the words because they are hard to find in English. However, Razia speaks Urdu as well as English, and I happened to know two words of Urdu that could help me tell her what she had done that had left me feeling out of contact with her. We discussed how she might relate to her client differently, and what effect this might have, not only on the therapeutic relationship, but on Razia herself. I expressed concern that Razia may become vulnerable in a way she had not been before, and was able to draw her attention to something she might already do out of awareness, that if done with awareness would help her look after herself. The words I used were '*rhu*' and '*kamp*'. *Rhu* translates as spirit, and *kamp* means shiver. Together—

171

'*rhu kamp*'—the words mean shivers of the spirit.

Rhu ر و ح Kamp کانپ

This chapter explains why such a phrase would be immensely useful in the practice of person-centred supervision. I will begin with my supervisee's initial concern—the quality of the therapeutic relationship, and then go on to discuss ways in which the helper (whether supervisee or supervisor) may manage the effect their work has upon them, and maintain their own well-being.

THE WELL-BEING OF THE THERAPEUTIC RELATIONSHIP

When Razia imagined that she was with her client, rather than with me, the change in emotional atmosphere, in the quality of our psychological contact, was immediate. I might well have simply told her that I no longer felt as deeply in contact with her, or I could have remarked that she seemed to have withdrawn. However, neither of these responses would have been specific enough (and there is often a problem with concepts such as psychological withdrawal or contact in supervision, or training, in that they only make sense to those who are familiar with feeling, within themselves, the difference between being psychologically present and psychologically withdrawn. They make little sense to those who are habitually somewhat withdrawn.) Had I said I no longer felt as deeply in contact with her, I would have been describing the *result* of what I noticed her do, rather than the thing itself. It was as if I had felt her move away from me: there seemed to be more physical distance between us. The air in front of me felt different, as if there was a chasm in it that had not been there before. I more commonly demonstrate rather than verbalise this when working with a supervisee who doesn't speak Urdu. Sometimes I suggest that they try the following exercise:

> Imagine that someone towards whom you feel abundant and unreserved warmth is in another part of the room you are in, and gently focus on them for a few moments, describing to yourself any sensations that you experience.

> Now imagine that they have been replaced by someone you dislike, or feel cool towards, and notice any sensations you experience.

Now give yourself a shake [this part is important] and think of something pleasant.

Usually my supervisees experience sensations of opening, expanding, extending, flowing, softening or melting, etc. in the first part of this exercise, and of shrinking, closing down, stopping an outgoing flow, creating a barrier, or withdrawing, in the second. We do not, in English, have any particular word for sensations such as these, and so may be disinclined to think of them as a category of response.

It is, perhaps because we have no term for this level of response, tempting to think of it as a private thing that happens within ourselves, and that it will not be perceived by others. But other people do notice. I also do a version of the above exercise, and ask my supervisee to give me feedback on how they experience being with me whilst I do it. My version does not involve imagining people I like or dislike, but simply allowing my 'edges' to 'soften' and flow towards my supervisee, and then 'pulling myself back in'. (Later I will introduce a concept that makes some intellectual sense of 'edges' and 'soften', and meanwhile suggest that such words do make sense at an experiential level.) My supervisees notice the instant I silently draw myself back in. The feedback is mostly that they experience me as fully present and engaged with them when I am expanding towards them, and as distant, remote, or cool when I pull myself back in. (There are important exceptions to this general trend that I will discuss later on).

Participants in one workshop, convinced that they were reading subtle visual cues when doing this exercise, experimented with closing their eyes and then trying to determine whether their partners (who were careful to breathe as silently as possible) were extending or withdrawing. Nobody's perception was impaired by not being able to see, and those whose perception had formerly not been particularly accurate, found that they were more accurate with their eyes shut. These sensations of extending and withdrawing, or opening and shutting down, may happen within the privacy of our own skin, but the energetic movement that gives rise to them can be perceived by others, whether or not we also give out aural and visual signals. Our ability to move in this way, to extend or contract, seems to have an objective as well as a subjective reality. It is also an everyday experience, yet, certainly in the West, we do not think of ourselves as really being able to flow towards another person or literally draw ourselves away because we perceive ourselves to be contained by our bodies and boundaried by our skin. We seem to have no concept or word for an aspect of ourselves that can expand beyond the skin. Because we have no commonly understood word or concept, it can be difficult to symbolise in awareness the feeling of expanding beyond our skin, or drawing back, and more difficult still to communicate about it.

Finding the word

In the supervision session with which I introduced this chapter, I used the word *rhu*. Razia understood perfectly what I meant when I said that she seemed to have pulled her *rhu* in. Many non-Urdu-speaking supervisees understand me when I say that they seem to have pulled *themselves* in. However, it would be difficult to explain, in words, to someone who did not understand what I meant by this, as consensus reality in the West does not include the idea that the self can literally move out of the body and be pulled back in. (Although many people use phrases such as 'not in their body', few claim to mean them literally.) I sometimes suggest the exercise described earlier which induces the everyday experience of feeling oneself silently reach out to someone, or silently pull back, to bring a supervisee's awareness to the unnamed aspect of ourselves that we can expand beyond our body. We can then both understand and agree on exactly what it is we are working with, without necessarily naming it. When I feel that suggesting an exercise may be detrimental to the process of establishing an equal relationship with a supervisee, I make sure I pay attention to what they are doing with their hands, as many people talk confidently and fluently about this level of relationship using hand gestures.

I had, prior to the session with Razia, often wished that I had words that were commonly understood to symbolise these subtle processes. Truth to be told, '*rhu*', although perfectly accurate, was also a lucky approximation as it is, like 'spirit', not quite specific enough. *Sukshama-sharira* would have been a more accurate word, but Razia would have been less likely to be familiar with it because it is Sanskrit, and a technical term from the metaphysics of Yoga. 'Sukshama-sharira' translates as 'subtle body', a term also used in Western metaphysics. It is used in both Indian and Western metaphysics to describe a body of essential energy that exists in the realm between the material and immaterial and unites psyche and soma. 'Subtle body' is my preferred term as '*rhu*' or 'spirit' do not necessarily imply, to modern ears, the idea of a realm between the material and immaterial. Alchemists called this the realm of the *imaginatio*, a level of reality in which internal and external are not distinct from each other. Some change occurred within Razia when she pretended she was with her client rather than with me, and I felt it directly. I did not infer it from her posture, expression, gesture, or tone, although any of these may have helped me interpret it. It was an inner event that I, another person, experienced.

The alchemical concept of the subtle body is one note in a murmur of discourse whispered since the beginnings of Western culture. The notion that we have a 'luminous body' has been posited since the first period of Greek philosophy, and very probably before that. The concept was highly developed by alchemists, and has reappeared as the 'radiant body', 'sidereal body', 'energy body', 'aura' or 'energy field' in the work of various mystics and healers since. It has, for centuries, been the foundation of the healing and spiritual practices of many other diverse cultures, and is one of the unifying theories within the contemporary mind/body/spirit movement. Obviously concepts produced by very different cultures and in different historical periods vary, but the various concepts of an energy body also have a remarkable amount in common. Most relevant to this chapter is the shared understanding that the subtle body is composed of an omnipresent subtle energy that is the essence of all things, and of the individual. This subtle energy, variously called pneuma, prana, qi', mana, huna, etc. is understood to be the life-force of both the person and the cosmos, pulsating and vibrating as it flows in and out of each individual with the breath, becoming their life-force, their essence, their spirit, their energy. It is differentiated from other pulsations in the environment only by the fine vibrancy of the subtle body, which contains it, and gives it form, but no ultimate boundary. Our energetic boundaries exist where we choose to create them. We may energetically withdraw, as Razia did, by pulling our energy field in, or we may extend it outwards. Whatever we do at this energetic level, and the responses we get, constitutes the energetic relationship supervisees have with clients and supervisors with supervisees.

The energetic relationship

My understanding that the word *rhu*, like subtle body, expresses something of our felt sense of ourselves as well as describing an abstract concept, enabled me to find a word from Razia's frame of reference that named what I had sensed. The idea that at an energetic level we really do extend towards others, or pull away from them in a way that they too experience, also helped me stay aware that although I knew Razia had withdrawn her energy, I did not know why she had done so. Without a concept such as the subtle body or energy field, it is much more difficult to pause between noticing what has happened and interpreting it. Earlier, I described asking supervisees for feedback as I energetically expand out towards them by 'softening' the 'edges' of my subtle body or contract away from them by 'pulling myself in'. Most say they experience me as fully present and open, when I am expanding towards them, and as interested, welcoming, and warm. Most say they experience me as remote, distant, closed off and cold when I pull myself back in. The perception that I am fully present and open, or distant and closed off, may be, in energetic terms, absolutely accurate, but the assumption that this is because I am interested and feel warmly towards them, or that I am uninterested, are interpretations, and, certainly in the context of this exercise, incorrect. When I do this demonstration I am simply moving my energy field: my feelings have not changed (although I suspect that warm feelings would probably arise within me if I remained expanded, and that I would feel disengaged and uninterested if I remained contracted).

Obviously, this is a somewhat artificial situation. Normally we expand because we are having 'expansive' feelings such as delight, joy, happiness, compassion, love, tenderness, and contract because we feel boredom, disgust, horror, shock, anger or fear. When I ask workshop participants to imagine someone they feel very warmly towards, the overwhelming majority of people expand instantly. A tiny number do not change energetically, but no one has ever contracted. Our inherent inclination is to extend out to make contact with what is attractive. Likewise, we tend to recoil away from anything we find unattractive. Not surprisingly, most people interpret energetic expansion positively, and contraction negatively. We sense that someone is holding themselves back, and assume, perhaps, that they don't like us. Or we sense someone suddenly recoil energetically, and believe that they are shocked by what we have said. They may in fact feel intimidated rather than hostile, or fearful rather than shocked. Or they may be contracted for some other reason that has nothing to do with us.

Energetic boundaries

I mentioned earlier that there are exceptions to the general rule that most people respond positively to expansion, and interpret contraction negatively. Everyone has different energetic boundaries, and what may be a welcoming surge of warmth to one person may be invasive and threatening to someone else. Much also depends on the energetic state of each person prior to an energetic change. I learnt this doing a demonstration at an impromptu workshop given during a conference. I had expanded and was expecting the customary feedback that most people experienced me as warm when I expanded, with perhaps a few finding it invasive. I was surprised when a couple of people said that they had lost all sense of me, and did not feel in contact with me at all. I realised that I had been in a much less focused state than usual when I began, and that my energy field was more expanded and diffuse than it would normally be prior to doing this demonstration. When I expanded my diffuse energy field it dissolved into nothingness for some people. Others could still sense it, and felt in contact with me. The difference seemed to be dependent on where their own energetic boundary, or 'skin', was at the time. Those who did experience my presence were fairly expanded themselves, and those who felt out of contact were less so. Either way, each person valued the experience depending on the level of contact they were comfortable with. Most of those who could still feel my presence welcomed it, whilst a couple of people found it invasive. Perhaps some of those who welcomed my expansion would have felt overwhelmed or threatened had they felt my more focused presence at another time.

Energetic encounter

Those who found my presence invasive probably recoiled energetically, and those who welcomed it probably extended out to meet me. Whatever the reaction, we had an energetic interaction of some kind, and, under normal circumstances, this would set the tone of our relationship over the next while. Several things happen in the process of an energetic exchange. Each person feels the energetic presence, or absence, of the other, very probably interprets it, and also makes an energetic response (or has an energetic reaction) in keeping with their interpretation or their own energetic boundaries, or both. And then the other person interprets and responds to this, and so on.

Relationships that are mysteriously difficult and beset with misunderstanding often make sense when explored at an energetic level in supervision. When I observed to Razia that she had pulled in her *rhu*, she said 'ah!', and her client's feedback about being distant finally became meaningful to her. Of course, it might have been that Razia did not want closer contact with her client, and if this had been the case I would have worked with that. However, she had been trying her hardest to understand what was missing for her client, and to be as congruent and available in the relationship as she could. We discovered where the incongruence was when we explored what was happening at an energetic level. The client had been somewhat prickly in the early days of their relationship, and Razia somewhat cautious. She had chosen (albeit out of awareness) to hold herself in energetically so as not to invade her client's space, and also to protect herself from the client's energetic prickliness. Holding her energy in had become habitual—how she was with this client. With this awareness, she was able to hear her client's request that she let go and allow her spirit to take up more space. All she had to do was relax, stop trying, and just be. In contrast, another supervisee found that the warmer and more accepting she tried to be, the more distant a particular client seemed to become. When she explored the relationship from an energetic perspective, she realised that she may well have been violating the boundary of his subtle body by energetically gushing at him, and so decided to take a step back energetically to make some room for him.

Looking at the energetic relationship

Razia identified the energetic response she had to her client by imagining herself to be with him and then getting feedback from me on the change I observed in her. Although it was useful, working in this way does not allow for the possibility that I, the person giving feedback, might distort what I perceive, or that the energetic relationship between myself and the supervisee might interfere with what happens energetically when they imagine being with a client. If a supervisee has a sufficiently differentiated awareness of their energetic process, they can imagine being with a client (or supervisor, line manager, etc.) and then observe and identify for themselves what they do energetically—this is particularly useful in self-supervision.

Such self-awareness is often sufficient, as it was for Razia, to throw light on what is impeding the therapeutic relationship, but this is not always the case. Had her client not said that she felt their relationship was too distant, the significance of Razia's energetic withdrawal might not have been so obvious (such a holding back was probably perfectly appropriate at the beginning of their relationship). Sometimes it is useful for a supervisee to 'look' at the whole energetic relationship, and not just their own part in it.

Had Razia 'looked' at the energetic relationship she had with her client, I presume she would have seen the client reaching out to her energetically while she remained somewhat withdrawn. She would have symbolised this in her own way—perhaps she would have seen two misty ovals of light not quite interacting, or two animals, or seen strands of colour. Common sense, or our common understanding of how the world works, may tell us that such looking tells the seer only about their own point of view, their own experience, yet research carried out by Henry Reed (1996) with thousands of workshop participants suggests otherwise. Reed (1996) asks participants, who work in pairs, to 'surrender [their] flow of imagination, to let it be spontaneous and natural' (p.11) as they close their eyes, and make 'mental contact' with their partner. Afterwards, he asks them to share with their partner the sensations and images that arose. He asks the participants if their discussion with their partners revealed any indication that what they had experienced during the contact was more than 'just imagination':

> The overwhelming majority of their hands fly up *amidst a flood of laughter.*
> Their reaction shows that they well understand the irony, and the
> ambiguity of the phrase 'just imagination' . . . Discussion and feedback
> with a partner confirms what seemed subjectively true during the contact
> experience—that it was a shared, mutual experience. (p. 30)

It is also possible to 'look' at an energetic encounter or relationship from a distance, and in retrospect, and so it is possible to do so in supervision. I facilitate this kind of 'looking' by suggesting that my supervisee close their eyes and allow an image to form of what their energetic relationship with a particular client (or colleague, manager, etc.) looks like. It is important to allow the imagination to be receptive rather than active. Actively visualising is the process of symbolising our own perception, whereas perceiving a shared reality involves being receptive to the unexpected. I suggested to a supervisee who was experiencing difficulty in working with a client who seemed somewhat disengaged that she have a look at the energetic relationship. She was not surprised to see that the client seemed to be floating away from her, but was surprised to see that she was also floating away from the client. She started checking that she was firmly centred in her body in their sessions, and that her mind was not wandering. She noticed that she became infinitely more present and congruent in the relationship, that the client seemed to respond to this, and their work together became much more 'here and now'.

A colleague in a workshop reviewed her relationship with all her clients in this way, and was horrified to realise that she was protectively encircling them all, while believing that this kind of relationship would be appropriate and helpful to only a small number of the people she was seeing. In her imagination, she withdrew her encircling gesture from the majority, and stood alongside them instead. When she returned to work the following week she found that several had sensed something change in their relationship, and that it was important for her to acknowledge that she had made a change in her deepest attitude towards them. The *imaginatio,* as the alchemists (and also some Jungians) call the realm of the subtle body, has an intersubjective reality. Any changes made in the *imaginatio* are likely to be experienced by the client, and should therefore be undertaken with care. I usually avoid doing so unless there is some need for protection—a subject I discuss in more detail later (see pp. 182 and pp. 186–7). I generally encourage supervisees to use the images they get as information only. Changing the image in some way is very powerful indeed, and changes the relationship in ordinary reality. For this reason it is not something to be done casually, or without considering whether there may be a therapeutically richer way of working with the issue. Furthermore, it would not be ethical to change or manipulate the image that represents the client as this would be interfering with their state of being without their knowledge or permission. In my own self-supervision, I use 'imaginal sight' (the term Reed uses for looking at the energetic relationship) in order to increase my understanding of what is happening in the relationship, and then make any changes to my energetic state in the session where they can be negotiated and discussed with my client or supervisee.

Self-awareness

Our energetic state affects the degree to which we are present in the relationship and therefore the degree of psychological contact made (Cameron, 2002a; 2002b; 2003). It affects both our ability to be receptive, congruent and empathic and the degree to which the client is likely to perceive us as accepting and empathic (Cameron, 2002a). If, for instance, we are contracted, or 'pulled in', the client or supervisee is likely to perceive us as reserved, holding back, not fully congruent or integrated in the relationship. It is also likely that they may interpret (possibly correctly) our contraction as disapproval, dislike or boredom. We are energetically further away from them than if we extend, less likely to pick up waves of feeling emanating from their energy body, and so unlikely to experience empathy at an intuitive or 'sensing' level (Cameron, 2002a; 2002b). We have little chance of becoming really in tune with them. If, on the other hand, we are relaxed, energetically open and expansive, they will probably experience us as more fully present, warmer, more accepting and more fully integrated within ourselves and within the relationship. Our ability to empathise at a more subtle level will also be greatly increased if the fabric of our energy field is less condensed and solid, more sensitive to the client's presence. Our energetic state affects both our ability to offer Rogers' therapeutic conditions and the client's perception of them.

The counsellor's energetic state has an enormous impact on the therapeutic relationship. It is therefore important to develop energetic self-awareness: supervision is an excellent forum in which to do this. Often a supervisee's—or supervisor's—energetic state is as it is because of their own psychological-energetic process, rather than being a response to the person they are working with. They may be more drawn in than usual following a meeting with someone intimidating, because they are unwell, preoccupied, or a host of other reasons. Although it may have nothing to do with the client, or supervisee, their energetic state will affect the relationship, perhaps because the client misinterprets it, moderates their own energetic state in response, or just because it limits the potential for intimacy.

Contraction is the most obvious way in which we may hold ourselves out of relationship, but by no means the only way. As I suggested earlier, when describing how some workshop participants lost all sense of me when I expanded, over-expansion can also keep us out of relationship, as can being disembodied in other ways. Most of us have habitual ways of holding our subtle body and particular energetic holds that we stay in for periods of time (Cameron, 2002b). These may be problematic for us or not. Becoming aware of our energetic process will almost certainly help us resolve those that are problematic. A trainee that I supervise was finding that very few clients came to see her more than once or twice. I asked if she knew 'where she was' when she was with her clients. Many people are already aware of what they are doing energetically in relation to themselves and to the client. They know that they are 'reaching out', 'have a barrier up'; that they are 'grounded' or 'beside themselves' or 'all up in the air', etc. This supervisee was not sure, and so I suggested that she move her energy field around until she did something that she recognised. She found the subtle sensations of having her energy concentrated in the top half of her body very familiar, and recognised it as something she did with clients, but knew that she also did something else. She tried expanding and contracting and neither was 'it'.

After some more experimenting, she identified that she had been withdrawing so extremely with clients that she was hiding behind herself, i.e. her energy body was behind, rather than interpenetrating, her physical body. She experienced the contrast between this state and being fully back in her body in our supervision session and realised that she felt wobbly and terribly unsure of herself in the out of body state, but calm and much more confident when she moved back into her physical body (thus reintegrating the two), and allowed energy to extend out through her feet.

She had found a way to manage her energetic and psychological state whilst with clients. Management, however, is only management, and so we spent some time talking about what the underlying issues might be, i.e. why she had been holding her energy in that way in the first place. She related it to being a beginner and really quite scared of her clients. She realised that she habitually pulled her energy upwards when feeling out of her depth, becoming 'all up in her head' and sometimes hid behind herself when she felt intimidated. Both of these strategies had been moderately effective when she was trying to keep a distance from her bullying father, or to think her way out of any encounter with him quickly. They were energetically protective and focused her mind, but only, she realised, for a short time before she began to feel ungrounded and panicky. She identified herself as re-contacting this old feeling of panic when she stepped outside herself and pulled her energy up. She committed herself to working on issues with her father in personal therapy, and in sessions with clients she made sure that she was fully inside her body.

Another, more experienced supervisee did a similar piece of work with a way of holding his energy that was not problematic, but was robbing the therapeutic relationship of depth. He had had feedback from colleagues about being 'camp', and he brought the question of whether this was something he needed to change to supervision. (Apparently, he expected me either to think that it was not very appropriate to be camp now that he was a counsellor, or to take a line 'If camp is who you are, then be it'.) I find his manner charming, but had no opinion on whether it was appropriate or not. I suggested that we consider how his camp mode might impact on his therapeutic relationships by looking at what he was doing energetically. Inwardly he 'camped it up' and observed what happened energetically whilst he did so. He identified that his energy rushed to the top of his body, and radiated out. I was able to give him the feedback that although my response to this was to smile and energetically extend towards him, it also gave him a somewhat giddy air. He then tried moving his energy downwards until he felt 'centred' and instantly felt very different. The change was also evident to me, both in the subtle visual cues he gave, and also how it felt for me to be in his presence. Some time later I had the opportunity to watch two video recordings of him working. One was made prior to this supervision session, and was good enough. The second was made afterwards. It was outstanding. He did not behave in a camp manner in the first, but his energy was light, and he seemed light-weight. The way he worked in the second session was not much different in terms of how often he spoke or the kinds of things he said, but his whole manner, his energy, had changed completely. He seemed so *solid*, relaxed, fully present, open, non-defensive and accepting. He was gently expanded and exuded confidence, gentleness and reliability.

THE WELL-BEING OF THE SUPERVISEE

Many supervisees (and supervisors) take a few minutes to centre themselves and get into the right state of being before beginning a session. They are practising energetic self-awareness, although they might not call it that. The concept of the subtle body, and the image of it as a semi-material, or vaporous 'body' that can extend away from the physical body or contract right inside it, gives us the conceptual tools with which to practise energetic self-awareness with more precision.

Encouraging energetic self-awareness may be viewed as fulfilling the restorative as well as the formative function of supervision (Proctor, 1988). Just as it can help supervisees understand more about the therapeutic relationship and the impact they have on it, so it can also help supervisees understand more about the impact the therapeutic relationship has on them. Getting grounded, or otherwise adjusting their energy before seeing a client, is helpful to the relationship, and hopefully to the client. Checking how they are energetically *after* seeing a client is helpful to the therapist, and to the supervisor after seeing the therapist.

There is much written in popular 'mind/body/spirit' literature about psychic protection, and unfortunately much of it seems to be based on the somewhat alarmist belief that other people are likely to harm us in some way, either by draining our energy, sending us 'negative' energy, or launching some other kind of 'psychic attack'. Whilst I do believe that such things are possible, and a problem when they occur, I also believe that we affect each other, and are affected by each other, just because we are in relationship, and that this is not in itself problematic. It is, however, prudent to become aware of some of the ways in which we may be affected. There are two that I want to discuss here: having an energetic reaction or response, and resonance. These are not 'bad': we have to respond or react to be in relationship; we feel 'in tune' with others when we resonate with them. However, both domains of influence may become problematic if we lack energetic self-awareness. We may become stuck in an energetic response we have had during the session; resonance may cause a supervisee (or supervisor) to manifest physical symptoms, or experience a change in mood that they do not welcome.

Holding an energetic response

Thus far, I have concentrated on energetic expansion and contraction, but have also referred to energy moving out of the physical body, and to energy moving up and down the body. Normally our energy body is in a constant state of change as we respond to what is happening around us and within us. Energy may move up, down, in, or out. There are a great many ways to become stuck within these four directions. We may become stuck in a contraction, or a kind of advanced contraction that I call a 'clench' (Cameron, 2002b), in which we pull our energy field in, whilst also pulling it down from our head and up from our feet, so that we have disconnected in every direction possible. This is often referred to colloquially as 'retreating from the world', or 'curling up into a little ball inside'. We may hold ourselves in an overly expanded state and be 'all over the place'; we may be 'down', our energy body having collapsed; or 'high' because our energy has risen upwards. We may have detached from the physical body and be 'beside ourselves'; or have 'jumped out of our skin'; or be 'not quite here'.

Holding a particular energetic state is likely to affect not only the relationship with the client, but also the supervisee's own mood. In holding a contraction, for instance, they hold onto the feeling that originally caused them to contract. It is likely that, being energetically more distant from the client, they will begin to feel somewhat cut off from them. They may find themselves less engaged, less empathic, and, if they continue to hold the contraction, will continue to feel disengaged as they go about the rest of the day. They will value the experience of being contracted in some way, perhaps negatively because they feel cut off, or positively because they like the emotional distance it gives them. It is also possible that they will access feelings from other periods in their lives, which again, they will value positively or negatively. They are becoming energetically stuck, unable to move on and respond afresh to the here and now. In other words, they are in a mood.

'Moods' are curiously absent from psychotherapeutic literature, including the PCA. We are more likely to conceptualise ourselves, our clients, and our supervisees as having something 'going on' or 'coming to the surface' than as being in a bad mood. Yet there is a difference between being in a bad mood and experiencing the effects of old issues that have been denied to awareness or distorted in perception. Bad moods often involve old issues, but a bad mood is more than having old issues reappear or feeling angry and upset. The issues and people that we have grumbled about have an astonishing ability to seem utterly different when we are not in a bad mood. We may have psychotherapeutic terms for many of the processes involved, but no real analysis of why we can feel so miserable so suddenly, and why we can snap out of it without anything obvious having changed. The unobvious thing that changes is our energy. This might change because someone is friendly to us, and we expand out of the contraction in response to their friendly extension, or any other chance occurrences. It is also possible to move energy voluntarily, and so choose to change our psychological state and attitude.

Rhu kamp

Moving one's energy is very easy to do, but difficult to explain, which is why I was grateful to be able to use the phrase '*rhu kamp*' when working with Razia. It refers to the sensation of shivers, but without the coldness, that many people experience when listening to music. Many people experience shivers down their spine when they hear something chilling or a tingly, shivery feeling when they are excited. *Rhu kamp* signals that our energy is moving, and that it had become stagnant. The best way I know of becoming aware of being in an energetic lock is to see if my energy will move. If I experience *rhu kamp*, I know I have been holding my energy, and simultaneously feel it releasing. (This kind of energetic releasing does not tend to lead to catharsis, although catharsis is very likely to result in energetic release.) Those familiar with the sensation of *rhu kamp* usually find that they can induce it very easily by moving their energy. Energy follows our intention, and this makes moving the energy body rather like moving the physical body: decide to do it and muscles that we don't have to think about do the rest. Intend to have shivers running down your spine, and, if there is any stagnant energy to shake out in a shiver, you probably will.

Moving energy

Energy can move without producing *rhu kamp*. Feeling different is the other major indicator that stagnant energy has moved. If an energetic lock has been held for a longish period, we are likely to feel quite different when our energy starts moving again. 'Getting grounded' is a common experience of this. The concept of grounding comes from subtle energy disciplines, where it means establishing an energetic link with the earth. It has been adopted into the parlance of the human potential movement, and is commonly, but loosely, used in therapeutic settings. Some people have specific processes that they use to ground themselves and may even be aware of these processes, whilst for others, it is a more hit-and-miss affair. Different people mean different things by 'getting grounded'—some are re-establishing an energetic link with the earth, whilst others are bringing their subtle body back into alignment with the physical, or relaxing and expanding.

It is useful for supervisees (and supervisors) to be aware of their typical energetic processes in order to move their energy with more awareness and precision. It is much easier to get grounded, or move our energy body in some other way, if we are aware of the ways in which we typically lock it in or out. I might hear that a supervisee jumped out of their skin, and ask if they know where they went when they did so. Some people say that they went out of the top of their head, others to another part of the room, some say they stepped out of themselves sideways. Knowing that they have gone out through the top of their head, or have contracted, overexpanded, let their energy collapse, etc. facilitates supervisees in bringing themselves back down through the top of the head, expanding out again, re-establishing an energetic boundary, or extending their flow of energy into the ground. Some of my supervisees just know what they do, others get clues from the direction in which their *rhu kamp* flows, and others experiment with moving their energy around in order to become aware of what is familiar to them. Others intuitively find ways of getting their energy flowing again by breathing differently, listening to music, dancing or giving themselves a shake.

Resonance

I was talking to Razia about *rhu kamp* because she decided to extend and soften towards her supervisee, and I was aware that this was likely to deepen the impact the client had upon her at an energetic level. Energetic expansion sensitises us, both in the sense of making us more sensitive towards other people, and in the sense of making us more sensitive to being impacted by other people's feelings. We may 'pick stuff up' more easily, in the sense of being more intuitively empathic, and also in the sense of being left with the client's headache or low mood. An energetically contracted state has a hard boundary that softens as we expand— we move into the *imaginatio*, and the differentiation between ourselves and others becomes less distinct. We can be more 'at one' with another person. There is great potential for intimacy, and for the depth of relationship that Rogers describes as his 'inner spirit reaching out to touch the inner spirit of the other' (Rogers, 1980, p. 129). However, such intimacy is only possible if the counsellor is sufficiently solid within themselves, otherwise their substance becomes too dilute and not only may the client lose a sense of them really being there, but the counsellor may also lose a sense of themselves and become confluent rather than intimate.

Energetic confluence may well result in the counsellor manifesting physical symptoms experienced by the client. I understand this to work in much the same way as audible resonance—a violin, for instance, will resonate if another is played in the same room by 'picking up' the sound waves and vibrating in tune. Energetic resonance is important to the understanding of relationship in all kinds of helping and healing because it concerns the influence of one person's state of being upon another: the untouched violin will resonate in tune with the one played, even if it was previously out of tune. In other words, the more integrated energy body will positively affect the less integrated body. Our very presence, our simply being there can have a positive effect on clients (and supervisees). Clearly we owe it to our clients and supervisees to be in the best energetic state we can at the time. We also owe it to ourselves since we become vulnerable to resonating with the client's energy body if our own is less integrated, and vulnerable to experiencing their mood or physical symptoms within our own body and psyche. In order to be energetically integrated and congruent, it is important to be integrated in the relationship in the usual sense of being congruent and fully present. If we are thinking of something else, holding onto an unexpressed feeling, or portraying something we do not really feel, it is likely we will become energetically dis-integrated, our subtle body no longer integrated with the physical. Similarly, if we have been holding our energy in a contracted or clenched state, or have floated out of our physical body, we will be unavailable for psychological contact of much depth. The subtle body also becomes disintegrated from the physical if we become ungrounded because we are under the weather, tired, or have not eaten enough. The subtle body inhabits the real between the body and psyche, and is affected by both.

There are numerous ways of building up energetic strength, practised by millions of people, particularly in China and Japan where energetic self-development through Qi' Gong, Aikido and martial arts is commonplace. The most efficient way I know of developing a strong, flexible energy body is an exercise from Aikido recommended by Henderson (1999). It works on the same principle as physical body-building in that it involves stretching and contracting energetic muscles—I call it the 'body-building exercise'. The advanced version involves expanding to encompass all of space and time, and then shrinking into a dot that disappears. I suggest a less ambitious form of deciding on a boundary—perhaps the walls of the room, or anywhere within or beyond them—and then expanding up to this boundary before contracting away from it. This can involve big pushes and pulls, tiny press-ups against it, and everything between. Many people, myself included, dislike contracting and it is not something I would recommend, other than for the purposes of this exercise, where it develops energetic mass, just as weight-lifting develops muscle. Expanding and contracting in a fluid way develops energetic flexibility. The energy body becomes more solid, but still flexible enough to be temporarily impacted by another and then bounce back into its own shape. I sometimes call it the 'jelly-making exercise' instead of 'the body-building exercise' because of the image of the energy body having solid yet flexible transparency like jelly. It provides an alternative to energetic withdrawal, and is useful, particularly to supervisees undergoing a turbulent patch of process, and in need of some emotional protection whilst they work on the underlying emotional issues. However, it is a very powerful exercise, and not one I recommend unless there is a clear need for it.

Some people seem to be energetically resonant as a part of who they are, rather than part of a passing process, and, being one of those people, I want to add something about living with a sensitive energy body. I have always been able to experience other people's emotions within my own body, and have had a tendency to pick up physical symptoms from clients. I learned, whilst training as a healer, how to protect myself energetically, and also learned various ways of clearing 'shared symptoms' (Wooding); I also worked, at a psychological level, on strengthening my boundaries and becoming more solid in myself. This was beneficial in many ways, but did not stop me picking up other people's physical symptoms. I checked, in supervision and therapy, whether I was identifying with clients out of awareness, but did not seem to be. Next, I consulted a Tai Chi teacher and learnt some very useful exercises, which I still practise. I also began swimming every day that I saw clients or supervisees in order to clear anything I had picked up energetically, and began drinking water during sessions. Again, this was all beneficial, but did not stop me picking up and sharing physical symptoms. Then I discovered the 'body-building' exercise above, and whilst it would no doubt help me build up energetic substance, and therefore greater emotional distinction from others, I found that other people, particularly strangers, reacted so strongly to my more substantial presence that I quickly felt the need to 'tone it down'. The only thing that I have really found helpful has been to change my attitude, and accept my tendency to pick up what is happening within the body or psyche of some clients. Instead of regarding it as problematic, I try to take more heed of what is happening in my body early on, and stay alert to the possibility that I am experiencing sensations or feelings that belong to my client. Catching what I pick up early, and then working with it to my client's benefit, rather than holding onto it, seems to stop whatever it is developing into anything that is problematic. I have learned to accept my ability to empathise somatically as an ability, rather than seeing it as problematic, or trying to prevent it.

CONCLUSION

It seems to me likely that as person-centred practitioners, intending to be in the client's frame of reference and to know something of their inner world, we may be particularly prone to picking up more than we might have expected. It is therefore important in supervision to find some way of exploring this, and of using what is discovered to the benefit of the supervisee's relationship with the client and with themselves. Energetic self-awareness, whether it concerns our own energetic process, or that of the therapeutic relationship, is helpful in understanding more of what is happening within our own being and how this affects our work. Supervisors can help raise supervisees' awareness that they may affect the therapeutic relationship, and be affected by it, in ways previously outside their awareness.

REFERENCES

Cameron, R. (2002a) In the space between. In G. Wyatt and P. Sanders (Eds.) *Rogers' Therapeutic Conditions: Evolution Theory and Practice. Vol. 4: Contact and Perception* (pp. 259–74). Ross-on-Wye: PCCS Books

Cameron, R. (2002b) Subtle bodywork. In T. Staunton (Ed.), *Body Psychotherapy* (pp.148–71). London: Brunner-Routledge

Cameron, R. (2003) Psychological contact: Emotional and subtle contact. In J. Tolan (Ed.) *Skills for Person-Centred Counselling and Psychotherapy* (pp. 87–109). London: Sage

Henderson, J. (1999) *The Lover Within*. New York: Station Hill, Barrytown Ltd.

Proctor, B. (1988) Supervision: a co-operative exercise in accountability. In M. Marken and M. Payne (Eds.) *Enabling and Ensuring.* Leicester: Leicester National Youth Bureau / Council for Education and Training in Youth and Community Work

Reed, H. (1996) Close encounters in the liminal zone: Explorations in imaginal communication. *Journal of Analytic Psychology, 41*, 81–116, 203–26. Expanded version available: http://www.henryreed.com/publications/close2you.htm

Rogers, C. R. (1980) *A Way of Being*. Boston, MA: Houghton Mifflin

Wooding, V. (unpublished) Applying for a miracle

CHAPTER ELEVEN

SUPERVISION AS HEURISTIC RESEARCH INQUIRY

TONY MERRY

In the first article published in the relatively new journal, *Counselling and Psychotherapy Research*, McLeod (2001) offers persuasive arguments for why 'research' in the counselling and psychotherapy field needs a radical rethink if the gap between 'research' and 'practice' is not to widen. Arguing for the development of a research tradition appropriate to counselling, McLeod suggests that, 'what is distinctive about counselling and psychotherapy, as a form of helping in modern society, is that it is collaborative, personal, respectful, and takes the goals and desires of the client as its starting point' (p. 8). Following from this, McLeod argues that the 'practices and values of counselling and psychotherapy include: the idea of human agency, collaborative and dialogical forms of meaning-making, the importance of feeling and emotion, the role of language in constructing realities, the capacity for reflexive self-monitoring, the validity of sacred experience' (p. 8).

'Supervision' is also a form of helping that reflects the values and criteria articulated by McLeod above. This chapter is an attempt to align supervision more closely with research, particularly qualitative research, so that it becomes a form of inquiry that has as primary goals, reflexive self-monitoring, personal meaning-making, and increased self- and other-awareness.

In this chapter, which is not about 'research' *per se*, I examine the extent to which adopting a 'research attitude' towards person-centred supervision can enhance its effectiveness, and, at the same time, encourage a questioning and

189

hypothesis-building orientation among counsellors in practice. I see this as important for a number of reasons. Firstly, supervision is, to borrow McLeod's words, a 'collaborative and dialogical form of meaning-making' in which feeling and emotion, language, self-monitoring and the validity of sacred experience all play vital roles. Secondly, supervision is, at its best, a collaborative inquiry dedicated to revealing what is hidden or only partially understood about a counsellor's relationships with his or her clients, and about the counsellor as a person. Thirdly, supervision is a means of reflecting on the central hypothesis of the person-centred approach, i.e. that there are six conditions that are sufficient and that must necessarily be present if counselling is to be effective. Finally, the supervisory relationship, if it is to be consistent with person-centred principles, is one that mirrors the counselling relationship and is, therefore, itself a testing ground for that central hypothesis.

A 'RESEARCH ATTITUDE'

The research attitude that I am exploring here is closely linked to the heuristic approach of Moustakas (1990). In brief, Moustakas describes an exploratory, open-ended method in which attention is focused inwardly on the feelings and emotional responses of the person/researcher to the outward situation, rather than on the components of that situation. In a recent discussion and critique of Moustakas, Sela-Smith[1] (2002) describes the heuristic method as one that 'invites the conscious, investigating self to surrender to the feelings in an experience, which carries the researcher to unknown aspects of self and the internal organizational systems not normally known in waking consciousness' (p. 59). This approach affirms the importance of subjective experience as a source of legitimate knowledge, and is in the developing tradition of qualitative methods finding increasing acceptance among psychology researchers.

Moustakas (1990) describes six phases of heuristic research, which I summarise as follows:

Phase 1: Initial engagement
The researcher becomes aware of a topic, question or problem that engages his or her intense critical interest. The researcher begins to engage in an internal dialogue to clarify the personal meanings contained in the question or problem.

---

1. Sela-Smith's criticisms of the Moustakas method, or her proposals for overcoming what she sees as weaknesses of the method are not explored here. Please see her article (2002) for a full discussion.

Phase 2: Immersion

Once the question or problem has been clarified, the researcher 'lives' with it, immerses him- or herself in it, and becomes intimately involved with it. This is not necessarily a controlled or planned activity. Rather it becomes a spontaneous aspect of the person's life. One example given by Moustakas (1990) is an investigation into the meaning of delight. Once the decision to investigate delight is taken, then delight seems to be everywhere in the person's life, and the researcher becomes intimate with it through living with it and experiencing it.

Phase 3: Incubation

During this phase, the researcher abandons any conscious focusing on the topic and allows an inner engagement with the experiences gained in the immersion phase. New insights, relationships and nuances may emerge, and new meanings may gradually become apparent. There is a sense of 'surrendering to the process' here, rather than of a consciously planned activity.

Phase 4: Illumination

When the inner work of the incubation phase breaks through into conscious awareness, themes and clusters of themes begin to evolve. The person may experience him- or herself in new ways and with novel or deeper insight. The relationships between aspects of the person's self and the research question emerge, and change at a deep personal level can occur.

Phase 5: Explication

This phase is characterised by a conscious examination of the layers of meaning that have developed in previous phases. There is a continuation of the 'indwelling' process of the immersion phase, and there is close attention given to self-awareness, feelings and beliefs. New understandings and new meanings, rooted in the subjective experience of the researcher, emerge into awareness.

Phase 6: Creative synthesis

The researcher's complete immersion in the heuristic process leads, finally, to a spontaneous creative synthesis that 'embodies an inclusive expression of the essences of what has been investigated. It tells the "story" that reveals some new whole that has been identified and experienced' (Sela-Smith, 2002, p. 68). Put another way, the researcher, through living with and fully experiencing the problem or question as he or she experiences it on a deeply subjective level, is transformed by the process at that same subjective level. The 'data' that has been gathered and organised by the process is in the form of personal meaning, insight and personal change.

Sela-Smith (2002) has usefully and briefly detailed the six key components she sees as intrinsic to heuristic inquiry, and which I summarise below:

1. The researcher has experienced what is identified as being researched.
2. The researcher makes reference to some intense or passionate concern that causes the investigator to reach inward for tacit awareness and knowledge.
3. The research indicates surrender to the question has taken place (living, waking, sleeping, and dreaming the question).
4. Self-dialogue, not simply a one-way reporting of thoughts or feeling is evidenced: to report a feeling is not the same as dialoguing with the feeling.
5. The search is a self-search.
6. There is evidence that transformation has taken place by way of a 'story' that contains the transformation and may transform those who 'read' it.

I am not advocating a wholesale importing of the heuristic method as a means of organising and conducting counsellor supervision. I am, however, suggesting that there is much to be gained from appreciating recent developments in qualitative research methodology, of which the heuristic approach is one good example, and using such developments to enhance and extend what can be gained from the collaborative exploration of counselling experience. In other words, I regard heuristics, in the context of counsellor supervision as an informing perspective, or an attitude of mind, rather than as a method. There are a number of reasons why I believe that supervision benefits from this perspective or attitude of mind.

First, I have previously described person-centred supervision (Merry, 2002) as a form of collaborative enquiry in which:

> two people (the supervisor and the counsellor) collaborate or cooperate in an effort to understand what is going on within the counselling relationship and within the counsellor. This moves the emphasis away from 'doing things right or wrong' (which seems to be the case in some approaches to supervision) to 'how is the counsellor *being*, and how is that way of being contributing to the development of a counselling relationship based on the core conditions?'

Moustakas' method outlined above is not a collaborative enquiry, but in essence it describes more or less exactly what happens, or at least what can happen, during the internal dialogue a counsellor has as she reflects on her experiences with clients. The collaborative aspect occurs as the counsellor engages with her supervisor and attempts to explore and make meaning from the complexities of her client/counsellor interactions. I believe that a supervisor who has some awareness of the heuristic method, or any of its variations, is in a better position to understand empathically the counsellor's internal dialogue, and, indeed, her own internal dialogue as she struggles with the material the counsellor is presenting.

Second, I believe that many counsellors (and supervisors) are uncomfortable with the idea of 'research'. Many view research as the process of objectifying experiencing and distancing oneself from it. Caught up in notions of research as a means of quantifying experience into 'data', many counsellors remain unaware of the strengths of qualitative methods in leading to personal understanding, the construction of meaning, and subjective engagement with what emerges during the counselling hour. In fact, I may not be alone in detecting a growing fear of research, with some justification, as a means of controlling and limiting what counsellors are able to do with their clients. The empirical 'gold standard' of research, particularly as it currently relates to outcome studies and evidence-based practice is creating anxiety among some person-centred practitioners who do not see how what they do can be reduced to empirical data.

As qualitative methods gain more respectability, as I believe is happening, more counsellors need to become familiar with the methods and processes that can illuminate the counselling process, from the points of view of counsellors and their clients, if they are to stay abreast of modern developments. The forms of inquiry that heuristic research methods advocate can complement empirical, quantitative approaches. As Elliott (2002) put it recently:

> . . . we need a richer, much more complex language, a language of human experience, meaning and qualities. (In fact, what we need is a language.) In other words, what we need is qualitative research, which considers things expressed in language as data and then tries to analyze these language data using methods of understanding and interpretation of similarities and differences and other various kinds of linking or connecting principles, such as intention, cause and narrative flow. (p. 107)

Understanding that supervision can be regarded as a kind of personal research project, in which the research question is: 'How can I be more effective with my clients?', and appreciating that there is a mass of 'qualitative data' available that can be expressed, analysed, understood and interpreted personally, may be a creative step towards demystifying the process of research among counsellors who hitherto have been suspicious of it. Rogers himself saw person-centred counselling as a process of testing the approach's central hypothesis anew with each client/counsellor interaction. Supervision is an opportunity to examine that hypothesis and extend understanding of its implications.

Third, person-centred counselling advocates the 'use of self' as part of the counselling process, yet many person-centred counsellors have only a vague understanding of what that might mean for them and their clients. 'Use of self' implies a subjective 'indwelling' into the counselling process, and a personal engagement with it that finds less emphasis in other approaches. As is evident in the above brief description of Moustakas' approach, heuristics demands an almost total use of self, and a commitment to allowing all experience into awareness using all of the person's resources, including feeling, thought, fantasy, imagination and creativity. In this latter regard, I see a heuristic attitude to the supervision process as a means of testing and refining a counsellor's use of self within a relationship, including a client/counsellor relationship.

Fourth, I regard heuristic research as a means of identifying and strengthening a counsellor's own 'internal supervisor', by encouraging a form of deep introspection in which the impact of a counselling relationship on the counsellor as a person is a legitimate source of personal inquiry.

Personal implications

In preparation for writing this chapter, I spent some time reflecting on how I do supervision (or, more precisely, on how I am as a supervisor). To aid that reflection I followed the Moustakas method in spirit rather than in detail. In other words, following my engagement with 'supervision' as a subject of personal meaning for me, I tried to immerse myself in the experience of 'being a supervisor', and to give myself time to let that immersion 'take hold'. After some time I began to become aware of recurring themes, and I began to recognise some new meanings and insights. What follows is a summary of some aspects of the 'creative synthesis' that emerged.

1. I experience supervision (as a supervisor) as a means of continuing my engagement with people at existential or relational depth. The experience is similar in some ways to my experience as a counsellor, but in other ways it is different. I am committed to a person-centred way of being in my practice and, as far as possible, in my general life. I see supervision as an opportunity to exercise my intellect, my 'emotional self', my imagination, creativity and curiosity, and I identify this as a theme for me. I enjoy relationships in which those faculties or competencies can find some expression, and I regard this enjoyment as a partial explanation for why I chose counselling and the teaching of counsellors as a career.

2. Related to this, I experience myself as having a need to communicate with others on matters that go deeper than the everyday interactions with which

we are all familiar. This may partly explain why I am writing this chapter. A theme that emerged from this, and other similar insights, is that I appreciate the time boundary that the supervision and counselling hour puts around my emotional and intellectual involvement. I cannot sustain intense relationships with a lot of people for very long, and being a supervisor and a counsellor enables me to enter into and leave intense relationships with a sense of personal security that I can 'lighten-up' and enjoy superficiality in-between times.

3. I realise that, generally, I am less empathic as a supervisor than I am as a counsellor. More accurately, my personal focus and attitude as a supervisor is less concerned with empathic understanding than it is as a counsellor. This does not mean, of course, that I am not concerned empathically to understand my supervisee's experiencing or my supervisee as a person at all. I am not sure if this is a strength or a weakness, or neither. I am as certain as I can be that my supervisees experience me as empathic at times, but not at others. (I am sure my clients feel the same.) It is a theme for me that in supervision empathic understanding sometimes loses out to my inner urge to create my own version of order from what I may sometimes experience as chaotic. This theme extends to my life outside counselling and supervision.

4. Other themes and clusters of themes emerged as I went through the process, but I intend the above to be illustrative only, not comprehensive. It occurred to me, mid-way through, however, that while the process was 'working' to some extent, it was missing a dimension that only a relationship with a second person could provide. In other words, I experienced this reflective process as solitary and introspective, and lacking in external dialogue and exchange. Put simply, I needed to hear myself saying these things out loud, and to have them received and understood by someone else, as part of the process, not as an adjunct to it.

IMPLICATIONS FOR SUPERVISION

As I remarked above, I am not advocating the transformation of supervision into a kind of mini-research project with an associated research protocol. In my supervision practice, which involves experienced person-centred counsellors and trainees, I do not explicitly set out to engage in a formal research project, neither do I explain the principles of heuristic research to my supervisees. I have not, however, dismissed the possibility of doing so. In fact, this chapter represents a tentative exploration of the extent to which my own supervision approach might be enhanced by drawing further on my understanding and appreciation of heuristic methods and other qualitative research methods.

My tentative conclusion, based on my experience of the heuristic method as I went through it alone, is that it can be enhanced through dialogue, though this radically transforms the Moustakas method into something which, while sharing some features and principles, has some significant differences. Moustakas has, I believe, provided a valuable service in describing a process through which a person journeys whenever he or she is personally, emotionally engaged in making sense from an experience that holds significant but hidden or partially hidden meaning for them. In other words, I regard the heuristic method as a natural process, that can be facilitated by the presence of a receptive, empathic other.

In this approach, then, the supervisor's role becomes one of facilitating a natural process that, left to itself, may proceed to a creative conclusion, but that also may become distorted or truncated. For example, Sela-Smith remarks that: 'if the topic is personally painful, the researcher may unconsciously resist the actual personal problem and consider something less threatening' (p. 65). Translated into person-centred terms, the implication here is that confronted with a potentially threatening experience, the researcher (supervisee) may deny the experience or distort their perception of it so that the threat is neutralised. In person-centred theory, the threatening experience is less likely to be distorted or denied if the person is in a relationship in which they experience non-judgemental empathic understanding. The extent to which this kind of relationship can be provided by a supervisor will determine, at least in part, the extent to which the supervisee is able to allow the experience into awareness and thus afford it non-defensive consideration. As an individual acting alone, the possibilities afforded by a person-centred relationship do not exist, and if the initial engagement with the problem, question or issue is in some way contaminated by the aroused defensiveness of the person, the outcome is less likely to be fruitful.

The non-directive attitude of the person-centred supervisor is also a critical factor in determining the outcome of supervision. Taking a heuristic approach requires the agenda for supervision to be generally under the control of the supervisee. If the agenda is under external control, by the supervisor or by institutional or professional demands, for example, it is unlikely that the supervisee will be able to connect at a deep level with the issue under consideration. In heuristic terms, immersion of the supervisee's whole self will be compromised, and heuristic self-inquiry will not proceed.

Non-directiveness is also essential whenever the supervisee is engaged in the 'incubation phase'. Here the person is allowing material to organise itself without the person deliberately and consciously controlling or directing that process. Such inner processes need to be respected as part of the person's 'organismic wisdom'.

A supervisor needs to know when to 'back off', and not insist on the premature movement towards resolution or conclusion.

I regard this 'method' as appropriate in supervision whenever a supervisee is experiencing an enduring difficulty with a particular client or issue, rather than as a routine approach to all supervision issues. In Phase 1, for example, close empathic attunement to the supervisee as her awareness of a problem in counselling begins to surface enables the problem to 'take shape', and its complexities to be appreciated. This process may continue over a number of supervision sessions, with the supervisee leaving the problem aside for a while, and then returning to it as 'immersion' and 'incubation' proceed.

It is in the final three stages that I believe a supervisor can be of most help. The 'illumination phase' can be experienced as personally threatening as it touches on the supervisee's self-concept, her personal assumptions about herself in relation to the client, and her concept of herself as a counsellor. As personal awareness begins to differentiate into sharper focus, the acceptant, congruent and empathic presence of the supervisor can enable defences or distortions to be dissolved. I view the main work of person-centred supervision largely in terms of a focus on the counsellor's way of being, self-concept, attitudes, values and personal qualities in relation to client work. This may be characterised as a 'personal growth' view of supervision, rather than a 'clinical' view, though this is not to say that other clinical and ethical aspects of supervision should be ignored. The 'heuristic attitude' taken to Moustakas's fourth and fifth phases is essentially one of a process of facilitating the internal struggle of the supervisee to gain clarity and personal meaning from her experiences with clients. The 'indwelling' process focuses on the subjective, personal world of the supervisee, and is concerned with self-awareness, feeling and meaning. The 'use of self' is enhanced every time 'the self' experiences a greater range of feeling and meaning and defences against entering at greater relational or existential depth with clients become weakened.

The final phase, 'creative synthesis', is one of integration, where new levels of awareness are integrated into the self-concept. This equates very closely with Rogers' concept of the development of personal congruence. The capacity of the supervisee to tell the 'story' of a particular relationship with a client, or of a specific issue with greater self-awareness and openness to experience is an indication of personal growth and increased congruence. 'Telling the story' to a receptive and empathic other, in this case the supervisor, is as much a part of the development process as any of the 'phases' that led up to it. To have one's expanded, inner world responded to empathically, and with authenticity and positive regard is, in itself, a therapeutic and growth-promoting experience.

CONCLUSION

I believe that a person-centred supervisor is well equipped to take a heuristic research attitude to the supervisory process, without any imposition on the supervisee to adapt what needs to be explored to fit a predetermined method. It is important that supervision does not become centred on 'the method', whether that be heuristic or any other. Supervision needs to remain explicitly 'supervisee-centred' or it runs the risk of violating a pivotal principle of the person-centred approach. The supervisor, however, is free to choose to adopt the heuristic perspective explicitly and explain it to supervisees, or simply to allow it to inform his or her attitude towards supervision. The second option enables material to be presented in supervision in ways that are natural and comfortable for the supervisee and consistent with his or her individual preferences and idiosyncrasies, whilst providing the supervisor with an additional framework for understanding the process.

The first option, however, has some additional strengths which may appeal to both supervisor and supervisee. It remains 'supervisee-centred' provided the supervisee gives informed consent, and provided the approach can be abandoned at any time if it proves to be intrusive. It provides a map that can help both participants understand the process in which they are engaged using a shared language that explicitly identifies and describes significant features of the territory. It can enable both participants to attend to and respect a natural process that is open to being facilitated in a collaborative environment of empathy and authenticity.

By identifying and describing a natural sequence of phases of inquiry, the heuristic method can help to ensure that important parts of the process are not overlooked or hurried. Control of the process remains with the supervisee, with the supervisor attending as an empathic companion and participant observer rather than as a 'research director'.

The outcome of the process is not pre-planned and is unpredictable, but takes the form of deeper self-knowledge, personal insight and expanded self-awareness. Concrete, 'objective' learning may result from the process, but this is not an explicit (or implicit) intention. Enduring change in behaviour, attitude and personal values are outcomes of personally meaningful self-discoveries, and the heuristic approach is dedicated to research into 'self'.

Finally, familiarity with heuristics and other forms of qualitative research can be transferred from supervision to other situations. Counsellors may be encouraged to inquire into other aspects of counselling and psychotherapy, including outcome research, adopting a qualitative approach once they understand and appreciate its value. While this is not a goal of a heuristic research approach to supervision, it is a welcome additional advantage.

198

REFERENCES

Elliott, R. (2002) Render unto Caesar: Quantitative and qualitative knowing in research on humanistic therapies. *Person-Centered and Experiential Psychotherapies, 1*(1 and 2), 102–17

McLeod, J. (2001) Developing a research tradition consistent with the practice and values of counselling and psychotherapy: Why Counselling and Psychotherapy Research is necessary. *Counselling and Psychotherapy Research, 1*(1), 3–11

Merry, T. (2002) *Learning and Being in Person-Centred Counselling*, 2nd edn. Ross-on-Wye: PCCS Books

Moustakas, C. (1990) *Heuristic Research: Design, Methodology and Applications.* London: Sage

Sela-Smith, S. (2002) Heuristic research: A review and critique of Moustakas's method. *Journal of Humanistic Psychology, 42*(3), 53–88

PART THREE

PERSON-CENTRED SUPERVISION ACROSS THEORETICAL ORIENTATIONS AND PROFESSIONS

CHAPTER TWELVE

ON SUPERVISION ACROSS THEORETICAL ORIENTATIONS

PAUL HITCHINGS

The title of this chapter suggests at least two questions:

• Might I, supervising a person-centred therapist, use concepts from other schools to further her understanding, whilst at the same time honouring her person-centred philosophy, values and practice?

• Might I, as a person-centred practitioner, supervise therapists from other orientations, whilst at the same time honouring my own person-centred philosophy, values and practice?

This chapter addresses primarily the first of these questions and focuses especially on the supervision of therapists (counsellors and/or psychotherapists) in training.

Aside from their professional and theoretical importance, these questions have become increasingly significant, as most trainees gain the majority of their counselling experience in agencies where they and 'in house' supervisors are allocated to one another, based more on practical or administrative constraints than on theoretical allegiance. Neither supervisees nor supervisors in these settings (e.g. National Health Service and private voluntary counselling agencies) have the same choice as those working in the private or independent sector.

Reflecting on this situation three core and interrelated questions emerge for me:

- Are there factors that might facilitate an effective supervisory relationship across theoretical orientations?

- Are there positive advantages to be gained from such supervision?

- Are there times when 'pure model' supervision is needed?

I address these questions within the context of a practitioner (supervisee or supervisor) holding a person-centred model, although some of the arguments are also likely to be applicable to other cross-model combinations.

A DIVERSITY OF PERSON-CENTRED APPROACHES

Before reflecting on the supervision of person-centred practitioners it is essential to acknowledge and understand differences within the approach. Given the clarity and economy of the theoretical model, it is easy to assume that person-centred practitioners are homogenous in their understanding and application of theory. However, as in all approaches to psychotherapy, the original model develops over time, and splits and subgroups begin to emerge. Lietaer (1990), for instance, identifies four discernible 'factions' and Sanders (2004) brings together five 'tribes' within the person-centred 'nation'. Rennie (1998) suggests that the essential differences between person-centred practitioners are between 'the literalists' and 'the experientialists'. The literalists take the stance that person-centred work derives from the necessity and sufficiency of Rogers' (1957, 1959) six therapeutic conditions, and the non-directive attitude on the part of the therapist. Worsley (2002) suggests a reading of Mearns (1994) as a clear account of this position, and other writers who represent this position include Brodley (1990), Bozarth (1998) and Thorne (1992). The experientialists, whilst generally arguing that they remain true to the core theory and especially to Rogers' therapeutic conditions, pay more explicit attention to the client's overall process and their own interrelated process. Where they depart from the literalists is in the apparent directivity of some of their responses. Amongst the major writers in this group are Rice (1974), Gendlin (1981), Greenberg et al. (1993), Rennie (1998) and Worsley (2002).

Sanders articulated, and then attempted to build bridges between, the different traditions within the person-centred and experiential family at the Fifth International Conference on Client-Centred and Experiential Psychotherapy (held in Chicago in June 2000). He offered a mapping of person-centred approaches based on a set of uniting primary principles, and a set of secondary principles. Further, he proposed that practitioners who identify with person-centred and

204

experiential approaches would commit to the primary principles, and select from among the secondary principles those with which they agreed. Following his presentation and discussion, the conference later adopted Sanders' work as the Chicago 2000 Position Statement (Sanders, 2000).

The primary principles (Sanders, 2000, p. 67) are:

• The primacy of the actualising tendency—it is a therapeutic mistake to believe, or act upon the belief, that the therapeutic change process is *not* motivated by client's actualising tendency.

• Assertion of the necessity of therapeutic conditions (1957 and 1959) and therapeutic behaviour based on *active inclusion* of these—it is a therapeutic mistake to *exclude* any of the conditions. *Passive* inclusion, assuming that such conditions are always present in all relationships, is also insufficient. This primary principle, which declares the paramount importance of the relationship in person-centred therapy, requires active attention to the provision of these conditions.

• Primacy of the non-directive attitude *at least* at the level of content but not necessarily at the level of process. It is permissible for the therapist to be an 'expert' *process*-director—it is a therapeutic mistake to direct the content of a client's experience either explicitly or implicitly.

The secondary principles of person-centred therapies (Sanders, 2000, p. 67) are:

• Autonomy and the client's right to self-determination—it is a therapeutic mistake to violate the internal locus of control.

• Equality, or non-expertness of therapist—it is a therapeutic mistake to imply that the therapist is an expert in the direction of the content and substance of the client's life.

• The primacy of the non-directive attitude and intention—it is a therapeutic mistake to wrest control of change process from client's actualising tendency in any way whatsoever.

• Sufficiency of the therapeutic conditions proposed by Rogers (1957 and 1959)— it is a therapeutic mistake to *include* other conditions, methods or techniques.

• Holism—it is a therapeutic mistake to respond to only a part of the organism.

This 'position statement' attempts to bridge the different groupings discussed previously by 'allowing' the possibility of the therapist being 'directive' at the process level. Unfortunately (in my view), and despite such a bridge, the separation between the two broad groupings of the 'literalists' and the 'experientialists' remains.

Worsley (2002) makes a passionate argument for the inclusion of a focus on 'process' in person-centred counselling:

> The key to all person-centred therapy is the offering of a genuine and respectful relationship based upon a close, empathic tracking of the client. There is no substitute for this through either skills-based portrayal of a relationship or through the use of tool-like interventions by the therapist.
>
> However, there is a marked divergence materializing between those who believe that the therapeutic relationship is based upon what is often referred to as a client-centred or classical style of intervention and those who take a more experiential approach. (pp. 3–4)

In response to the idea that the 'purist' or 'literalist' school is non-directive and consequently more solidly person-centred, he goes on:

> Process work is indeed selective of that to which the therapist pays attention. It is a category error to think that classical work is not. In classical work there is preference to choose content over process, as a matter of habit or principle; yet this is still a choice, and is directive, for the classical therapist deflects the client from the process-orientated aspects of her own frame of reference. (pp. 28–9)

We can glimpse aspects of this debate also in the work of Tudor (2000) who, in an article on the 'lost' conditions, reminds person-centred practitioners of the importance of the relational aspects of the approach. He argues for the relational nature of person-centred work, and suggests that both parties in the relationship co-create the presence of the six therapeutic conditions. This departs from the more common idea, found in most of the current literature, that the therapist 'offers' the three 'core' conditions: 'the client needs to have some self-regard and some regard for the therapist's regard, some empathy for themselves and some empathy for the therapist's empathy in order to receive these conditions' (p. 37). There is then a feedback loop between the two people in relationship and it is the 'betweenness' that creates the therapeutic healing: 'person-centred therapy is indeed, as Rogers (1942) first conceived it, "relationship therapy"' (ibid., p. 36).

These issues, concerning as they do the nature of the relationship in person-centred therapy, the content of what the client or supervisee presents, the processing of the therapeutic or supervisory relationship, and directivity, all have implications for how we conceptualise where expertise is located. It is to this issue that I now turn.

WHO IS THE EXPERT: THERAPIST, CLIENT OR NEITHER?

This question clearly has implications for the practice of person-centred therapists and for compatible supervision. In this, I am influenced by Safran (1998) who conceptualises the different stances that psychotherapists might take in relation to 'reality', and asks whether one person's view of reality is more privileged, or held to be more significant, than another's. His conference presentation is quoted by Gilbert and Evans (2000, p. 17), and he suggests that the different therapies might be 'grouped' according to which party in the psychotherapeutic encounter is considered to have the most privileged view of reality. He argues that such a privileged view might be considered to be held by the therapist, as in classical psychoanalysis; by the client, as in person-centred therapy; or by neither, as in relational therapies based on intersubjectivity theory. In the latter case the two people negotiate between two different subjectivities.

Applying this conceptualisation to the person-centred tradition we can see that the literalists locate 'expertness' solely within the client and see it arising out of and enhanced by a careful and close tracking of the client within a relationship characterised by the six therapeutic conditions. This might be termed a 'uni-perspectival' model. For the experientialists, particularly Worsley (2002), the expertise of the client is not so much located within the client, but emerges rather out of the process between client and counsellor. Essentially this is closer to an intersubjective approach to therapy. In this way, I consider that the debate within the person-centred approach is really about positioning person-centred therapy within a 'uni-perspectival' world or an 'intersubjective' world. Tudor (2000), Frankland (2001) and Worsley (2002) all seem to be close to a conception of person-centred therapy as an intersubjective process. As Worsley (2002) puts it:

> the classical approach can be misguided; it speaks of tracking the client with a knowledge that only the client is an expert on themselves. Of course, I wholly agree that the therapist cannot be an expert on the client . . . To the extent that the client is also limited by the way of knowing, it is surely the case that the client also has no privileged access to her own awareness. I object to the notion that clients are experts on themselves. (p. 62)

207

This certainly is my position and it has rich implications for appropriate supervision models. Taking such a position allows more bridges and compatible cross-connections to be made more easily with other approaches to therapy. Such a conception of person-centred practice allows a move towards embracing an 'integrative-relational' approach whilst still honouring person-centred philosophy, theory and values. For a fuller exposition of the divide within the person-centred tradition between 'classical' or uni-perspectival thinking and more experiential, process or intersubjective thinking the reader is referred to Worsley (2002). In my view, person-centred therapists need to know their philosophical and intellectual positions, both for the sake of the clarity of their practice and in order to receive compatible supervision.

MODELS OF PERSON-CENTRED SUPERVISION

This section relates the previous discussion on conceptions of the person-centred approach to available material on person-centred supervisory practice.

Rogers was clearly interested in the value of reflective learning for the person-centred practitioner. He embraced newly available technology to begin audio-taping therapy sessions with clients (Rogers, 1942). This practice of audio or video recording and subsequent exploration using transcripts has since become an established part of counsellor training and practice across many theoretical orientations. Allen in this volume suggests one particularly compatible way of using recordings in supervision. Whilst Rogers introduced such reflective, and training, methods he did not offer much specifically about the practice of supervision. For a brief account of his thinking, see Hackney and Goodyear (1984). There remains a general paucity of models of person-centred supervision, especially in comparison with the volume of writing on person-centred practice.

Most models within person-centred literature emphasise that appropriate and effective supervision of a person-centred practitioner needs to encompass the presence of Rogers' (1957, 1959) six therapeutic conditions as in the therapeutic situation. This is clearly in line with the idea that these conditions are centrally important in all healthy human relationships. However, the models, not surprisingly, also parallel the divisions evident in the practice of person-centred therapy. They can be placed along a continuum with the 'classical' or 'uni-perspectival' division at one end, and the experiential, process, relational or intersubjective division at the other. For the sake of simplicity, I will refer to each of these positions as the 'classical' and the 'relational' positions. The detail within each of these positions is, of course, more complex than this shorthand suggests, as previous discussion in this chapter has shown.

Whilst the literature on person-centred supervision is comparatively small, and underdeveloped in contrast to the literature on person-centred therapy, most of what there is seems to argue for and emphasise, implicitly or explicitly, a 'classical' position. It follows that these models seem most appropriate to those practitioners who identify themselves as classical practitioners. Expertise is seen as solidly residing in the supervisee and emerges through the offer of the three core conditions to the supervisee by the supervisor. These 'classical' models are still of value to those that see themselves more embracing of the 'relational' school of the person-centred approach but for such practitioners they are likely to have a degree of limitation. They will offer considerable experience of the 'way of being' of the person-centred approach to inform learning, but will probably under-emphasise much of the 'relational' nature of person-centred practice.

Patterson (1997), one of the earliest writers on person-centred supervision, is perhaps the most 'classical' in his approach. He seems to be at an extreme end of the 'classical' versus 'relational' debate, arguing that not only must the six therapeutic conditions be attended to, but also that both supervisee and supervisor must be 'committed to the same theory' (p. 194).

Lambers (2000) also seems to argue for a 'classical' approach:

> in person-centred supervision, the supervision relationship can be conceptualised as parallel to the therapy relationship: offering a context where the therapist can become aware of the processes taking place in herself in the relationship with the client and enabling her to become more congruent in that relationship . . . the supervisor has no other concern, no other agenda than to facilitate the therapist's ability to be open to her experiences that she can become fully present and engaged in the relationship with the client. (p. 197)

She seems however, to make a slight shift along the continuum when she draws upon the work of Rennie (1998) to argue for what appears to be an element of a more 'relational' model:

> So important is congruence to the supervision endeavour that the supervisor may even choose to give it a special focus. She may reflect and communicate about her experiencing in the supervision relationship in a much more systematic fashion than would happen in therapy. This kind of 'metacommunication' (Rennie, 1998) quickly brings into the open issues in the relationship which could become problematic if they had remained 'unspoken'. (p. 206)

In a similar vein, Worrall (2001), in his paper on supervision and empathic understanding, appears both to embrace the 'classical' position and reach out to a more 'relational' model. He argues (p. 209) that the provision of the core conditions (although he is more explicitly addressing empathy) in the supervisory relationship facilitates:

> a process conception of supervision which begins to look something like this: congruence (on the part of the supervisor) begets empathic understanding (on the part of the supervisor) begets a higher level of congruence (on the part of the counsellor) begets a greater capacity for empathic understanding (on the part of the counsellor).

In partial contrast to the above models, Frankland (2001) offers a model of person-centred supervision that seems to offer an explicitly outward-looking bridge to other compatible approaches. Frankland's model makes some connection with some of the generic models of supervision: the process model of Hawkins and Shohet (1989); the functional model of Proctor and Inskipp (1989, 1991); and the 'teaching' role within supervision of Carroll (1996). He also integrates working at the level of the symbolic or metaphorical. His seven-step model has essentially two overarching 'strands': the first within the person-centred tradition (steps i–iv), and the second (steps v–vii), embracing concepts present but undeveloped within the person-centred approach that can act as a bridge to other compatible traditions:

> . . . the 'first strand' derives from, and uses the language of the Person-Centred perspective. The 'second strand' can be expressed—in language congruent with the Person-Centred and other phenomenological/experiential approaches . . . what is being described here is not exclusively tied to any one approach. The core conditions and some concept of Symbolic/Metaphorical content, often evident through the Relationship, are present in a wide range of practices (e.g. existential, transactional, feminist and many integrative models), although they may be described in different languages and given different emphases. (p. 29)

Frankland's (2001) model of person-centred supervision

Seven-Step Supervision

(i) The worker raises what is important for them. I make no attempt to shape the way they explore this except to make it clear that I am not expecting (and don't believe we need) a full history of the person or account of the case. I try to listen with care and respect to the work that is being done, to the engagement with the client and what it is all doing to the worker/costing them, and their perceptions of difficulties (or whatever led them to bring this work to supervision). I absorb both the way of telling and the content and interject relatively little (occasional acknowledgements, clarifications, a little supportive 'joining in').

At this time I keep in mind the core conditions, and as I listen I check each of them. At the end of the initial account I will most often invite some discussion of each of these, or comment on what I have heard there of them i.e. invite exploration of:

(ii) Empathy (including its communication and reception)

(iii) Respect/Acceptance/UPR (including its communication and reception)

(iv) Congruence. Simply focusing on the core conditions is often challenging, and is thus a model of how providing these conditions may be a stimulus to the thinking and feeling of someone seeking assistance to enable change to occur. Exploration of what this worker is able to provide for this client frequently leads to the worker developing a new understanding, or experiencing a shift of feeling about the work; once they know what they want to do next the sequence can move directly to closure. Or (if not), on to:

(v) Exploration of symbolic/metaphorical material, often by commentating on what I have picked up or observed at (i) or through hunches about the client and the work or through an explicit exploration of parallel process. This may move to closure or:

(vi) There will occasionally be the need to explore ethical or best practice issues, or to offer techniques or knowledge (or the opportunity to explore or practise these). Such inputs tends to focus attention on decisions for action and hence closure.

(vii) The final step, whether closure comes after (iv), (v), or (vi), is clarification of what has been gained.

Frankland's model of person-centred supervision seems to offer a structure for the supervision of both those person-centred practitioners who conceive of themselves as being in the 'classical' school as well as those who conceptualise

211

themselves as being more in the relational mould. The former grouping may well emphasise his 'first strand' while the latter grouping embraces both strands.

Returning to my theme of 'the location of expertise', this is clearly located within the supervisee in the first strand of Frankland's model, but more clearly emerges in the relationship between supervisor and supervisee in Frankland's second strand.

Other models of the supervisory process in the person-centred tradition include Merry (1999), who writes about supervision as 'collaborative inquiry'. He outlines the general principles underpinning 'collaborative inquiry', some of which are that:

- ... both people involved are self-directed and both can contribute equally to the process.

- (it) ... is democratic in that it does not assume one person (usually the supervisor) to be more influential in the process than the other (usually, the supervisee). Both are equally influential, and each has a valid perspective to bring.

- Both cognitive and intuitive forms of knowing are available and can be explored.

- Evaluations of the quality of the counselling relationship can be made jointly because the counsellor does not feel threatened as a person ...

- The supervisor can be perceived as a 'co-worker' able to offer expertise, knowledge and experience in the pursuit of deeper understanding ... (p. 141).

Within the context of a solidly developed relationship of 'collaborative inquiry' the supervisor can then feel free to ask questions and offer suggestions. These latter activities are seen as supportive of the ongoing working alliance and the core conditions are seen as being maintained by such supervisor activities as opposed to the more common view that they would be transgressed. Merry's model (1999) is clearly more toward the relational grouping than the literalist end of the spectrum.

Discussing person-centred supervision, Villas-Boas Bowen (1986) differentiates and contrasts two major approaches: form-oriented and philosophy-of-life-oriented. By the former she means supervision that is overly concerned with the preservation of 'pure forms' of person-centred practice:

> The supervisee is discouraged from styles of expression that do not fit
> the supervisor's model. Although the atmosphere of warmth, empathy

and congruence may be present, a basic philosophical principle of the person-centered approach seems to be missing: the trust in the supervisee's capacity for self-direction and self-determination . . . (p. 293)

By the latter she argues (ibid., p. 294) for a supervisory engagement that is much more relational in nature with an emphasis on the unique relationship between each supervisor and supervisee:

> Like form-oriented supervisors, supervisors with this frame of reference believe that, in order to tap the client's resources, a climate of acceptance, empathy, and congruence is needed. But they also believe that the form that those necessary conditions take depends on the personality of the therapist, the personality of the client, and the type of interaction that develops between the two.

Her article seems to argue that this conception of the therapeutic relationship also needs to inform the supervisory relationship.

GENERIC MODELS OF SUPERVISION

Generic models of supervision map out broad areas of potential focus for the supervisor and the supervisee. Such models often emphasise that the supervisor is always faced with choices in their responses to what is being presented. This is true both across and within theoretical orientations. At best such models support a purposeful and choiceful supervisory process, and indeed can support the ongoing presence and development of the six therapeutic conditions in the supervisory relationship. If and when these conditions are acknowledged they can provide a common understanding of both supervisory and therapeutic relationships. When models of supervision are shared between supervisor and supervisee, they can enhance fluidity (as distinct from fixity and rigidity), choice, mutuality, and the application of theory to practice. Generic models which I find useful are: Hawkins and Shohet's (1989) process model of supervision; Proctor and Inskipp's (1989) normative, formative, restorative functional model; Clarkson's (1992) brief supervision checklist; Holloway's (1995) systems approach; Carroll's (1996) seven-tasks model; and Page and Woskett's (2001) cyclical model. (See Chapter 3 for summaries and discussion of these.)

One particular model, that of Orlans and Edwards' (2001) collaborative model of supervision, is worthy of some elaboration, as it stresses neither techniques nor formulae but offers a 'heart' to the process, based on the quality of the supervisory relationship. It takes an intersubjective and phenomenological stance, and while it is offered as a generic model it is also highly compatible with a person-centred frame of reference.

Orlans and Edwards focus on two broad areas: 'the supervisory relationship' and 'the learning process', which are, in turn, held by 'collaboration' as a key integrating principle. This model stresses the mutuality in the supervisory process in all its aspects, including an overt recognition of the learning to be gained by both parties, as contrasted with models which focus only on the supervisee's learning:

> We are proposing a model of supervision which challenges supervisors to emerge from fixed roles and responsibilities in a way which makes us fully available for a relationship characterised by transparency and by the principles of collaboration . . . in broad terms we are talking about a phenomenological attitude, where both supervisor and supervisee are willing to bracket their prejudices, attend to the description of what is available to the senses in the present moment, name 'unsaids' as well as other factors which might have a bearing on the relationship and on the work of supervision, and attend to the ebb and flow of energy as the process unfolds. (p. 47)

Such a model clearly has value to the person-centred practitioner and her supervisor, a value which can add to the understanding and quality of the person-centred approach by enhancing the presence of the six therapeutic conditions rather than detracting from them.

A PHENOMENOLOGICAL STANCE AS A UNIFYING FACTOR WHEN SUPERVISING ACROSS THEORETICAL ORIENTATIONS

Aside from the use of specific person-centred and generic models of supervision as discussed there is one common factor that can aid supervision across orientations: a base in phenomenological enquiry. (See also Chapter 8). Person-centred therapy is rooted in phenomenology, as are many other relational therapies, including most obviously, existential, gestalt, transactional analysis, most transpersonal approaches and a number of integrative approaches. Supervisors and supervisees who share this philosophical stance as a way of enquiry and knowing are well placed to create a successful supervisory relationship even across different 'school' allegiances.

The phenomenological stance of person-centred therapy is not particularly recognised. Spinelli (1989) notes that 'although most textbook accounts of Rogers' client-centred therapy fail to reveal his obvious indebtedness to the phenomenological method, Rogers himself made explicit reference to phenomenology as the primary basis for his approach' (p. 148).

Drawing upon earlier workers in the field (Ihde, 1977; Grossman, 1984) who adapted Husserl's (1931) phenomenological method of inquiry for use within the psychological sciences, Spinelli (1989) outlines three steps: The rule of Epoché, the rule of Description and the rule of Horisontalization (the Equalisation Rule) to achieve a phenomenological stance. These are elaborated below.

1) The rule of Epoché

Here we attempt as far as we are able to bracket off all our expectations, presumptions and preconceptions so that we can be as open as possible to our immediate experience. Whilst we will almost certainly not manage this completely we will remove a considerable barrier to our 'openness' to the other.

2) The rule of Description

This requires that we never explain or interpret, only describe. Even accurate description is difficult. It is in explanation that we bring to bear our own characteristic distortions of others' material.

3) The rule of Horizontalisation (the Equalisation Rule)

Horizontalise. Give equal weight to each aspect of what is being described. We attempt to remain open to all aspects of the other: to what is being said, how it is being said, body language, breathing rate, and anything else.

Spinelli (1989) argues that the foundation for the provision of the therapeutic conditions of empathy, unconditional positive regard and congruence is the phenomenological method:

> I would argue that client-centred therapy is a restatement of the essentials
> of the phenomenological method. The client-centred therapist, like the
> practitioner of the phenomenological method, attempts to bracket prior
> assumptions, biases and sedimented assumptions (the rule of epoché);
> focuses upon and describes (rather than seeks to interpret or explain)
> immediate experience (the rule of description); and avoids making
> hierarchical distinctions or judgements with regard to the value of one
> experience over another (the rule of horizontalisation). (p. 153)

The phenomenological stance, which is also the stance for the provision of the therapist conditions in person-centred counselling, invites us to approach 'truth' with humility, encourages tolerance of 'not knowing', honours subjectivity and intersubjectivity, and allows for the emergence of 'truths' from the 'betweenness' of people and their 'beingness' with one another. See Spinelli (1989) for a fuller exposition of phenomenological psychology, and Worsley (2002) for a discussion of the place of phenomenology in person-centred practice. This reminder of the foundations of person-centred counselling in the phenomenological method leads into the next question and section of this chapter: 'What might person-centred practitioners/supervisors have to gain from other approaches that share the same philosophical base?'

CONCEPTS FROM OTHER APPROACHES RELEVANT TO THE PROVISION OF PERSON-CENTRED SUPERVISION

Some person-centred writers, including Vincent (1999), warn of the dangers of utilising concepts from other approaches. The concern seems to be that the very act of considering that another way of working may be of some value to the person-centred practitioner implies that Rogers' (1957, 1959) therapeutic conditions are either unnecessary or insufficient or both.

I take a strong opposing line on this. Whilst I do believe that concepts from other models need to be translated into a person-centred language and frame of reference, to ignore what other compatible therapeutic systems might have to offer is, in my view, irresponsible. Furthermore it divides 'us' from 'them'; impoverishes and isolates person-centred practice; and lowers the regard with which the person-centred approach is held in the wider professional world. I have also experienced the damage that misunderstandings of other approaches have on trainees and supervisees working in the person-centred approach. This 'exclusive-inclusive' debate is a false one. It does not recognise the difference between the use of techniques (doing) in other approaches, which may be directive in nature, and the ways of understanding (being) derived from concepts within other approaches, which might aid and enhance the existence of the six therapeutic conditions in relationship.

It is my conviction and experience that there are numerous concepts from other orientations that may help the person-centred practitioner enhance the quality of the therapeutic relationship they offer. I explore below two concepts: the Freudian concept of the unconscious (Freud, 1949), which is at the heart of psychodynamic approaches, and the drama triangle (Karpman, 1968) taken from transactional analysis. Each is expanded with discussions about how their use in

216

supervision might aid and support good person-centred practice. There are undoubtedly numerous others that are embedded, especially within phenomenological approaches to therapy such as gestalt, transactional analysis and existential psychotherapy, and the reader is encouraged to find additional concepts that they may wish to apply to person-centred practice.

The unconscious

This concept is usually attributed to Freud but was current in much of the philosophy and literature of his period. However, it was his writing that gave it the currency that it has as a central concept in psychoanalytic thinking and application. Freud (1949) defined it as:

> Mental processes or mental material which have no easy access to consciousness, but which must be inferred, discovered and translated into conscious form. (p. 20)

He differentiated the unconscious from that which is conscious and easily available to us and from the 'preconscious' which can easily be made available. The value of the construct is that it suggests that human behaviour is at least partially motivated by forces that are outside of our awareness and that by making the unconscious conscious a person might lead a fuller and more choiceful life.

Reflecting on this issue and referencing Rogers, Villas-Boas Bowen (1986, p. 300) writes:

> He stated that material that is significantly inconsistent with the self-concept, although experienced at the subliminal level, cannot be directly and freely admitted to awareness. When this incongruity between self-concept and experience emerges without the person's awareness, then the person is potentially vulnerable to threat, anxiety, and disorganization. In order to deal with the incongruence, the person becomes defensive by distorting in awareness, or by denying into awareness, that material that is inconsistent with the concept of self. (Rogers, 1959)

She continues to offer a definition of the unconscious that is compatible with person-centred theory:

> . . . unconscious is defined as experiences that are not integrated with self or available to awareness, yet are powerful in affecting one's feelings, perceptions and behavior. (p. 300)

217

Clearly then the concept of the unconscious is more than sufficiently compatible with person-centred theory in that it relates to material which has not been fully symbolised. We also then create something of a paradox: how can I be congruent in relationship if aspects of my inner world are unconscious and so by definition not available to me? The core answer to this question in the person-centred tradition is by being involved in relationships where the six therapeutic conditions prevail. There are, however, other means such as being open to our own intuition, symbols and metaphor creation (see Frankland's model earlier in this chapter).

Drama triangle

This is a concept derived from transactional analysis that seems to have entered the mainstream language, at least amongst the therapeutic community. The original concept was developed by Karpman (1968) and refers to three 'psychological roles' which people can take in relation to themselves or towards others: Persecutor, Rescuer and Victim (Figure 12.1). Usually two people will take up complementary roles or 'fight' for a particular role in relation to one another and then switch roles (represented by the arrows in Figure 12.1). These roles need, of course, to be differentiated from their real equivalent. A war victim is a real victim, and not a psychological Victim.

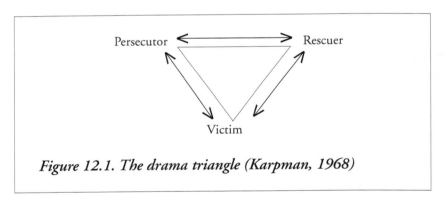

Figure 12.1. The drama triangle (Karpman, 1968)

Entry to any of these roles by the supervisor (or therapist) (which can also be understood as transference or countertransference transactions) will mean that at least one (and probably all three) of the conditions of empathy, congruence or unconditional positive regard has been limited. Usually such entry is only partially in awareness and not yet fully or accurately symbolised. For the latter reason, it must be remembered that such roles are not deliberate or intended but are usually reminiscent of old patterns learnt under powerful conditions of worth.

The supervisee, for instance, relates more and more detail about her client and his life circumstances without making any request of the supervisor. This is likely to be from a Victim position. The supervisor listens, apparently respectfully but eventually either gets irritated or withdrawn (from a Persecutor position) or begins to make connections for the supervisee (probably from a Rescuer position). The supervisee in this way comes to be dependent on the apparently superior 'wisdom' of her supervisor, and compromises her own learning. Alternatively there is some damage to the supervisory working alliance with the supervisee becoming fearful and potentially shamed.

The knowledge of such a simple but powerful piece of theory supports fuller symbolisation and a return to a more complete offering of Rogers' therapeutic conditions. Proctor (2000, p. 119) adds a useful reworking of this theory which she attributes to unpublished work by Hunt. This reworking offers a set of healthy equivalents forming what she calls the 'Beneficial Triangle', which involves, Vulnerability, instead of Victim; Responsiveness, instead of Rescuer; and Potency, instead of Persecutor. These healthy positions support the offering of the supervisor provided conditions of congruence, unconditional positive regard and empathy. In turn, these 'healthy' positions invite similar 'healthy' positions in the supervisee. There is then a 'healthy' feedback loop between the two people in relationship. Thus both parties in the relationship co-create the six therapeutic conditions. This is the essence of the relational aspects of the approach discussed earlier.

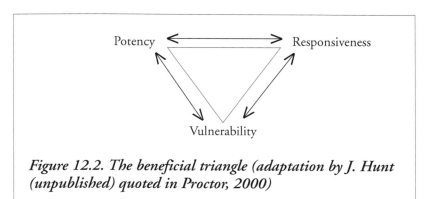

Figure 12.2. The beneficial triangle (adaptation by J. Hunt (unpublished) quoted in Proctor, 2000)

I now take each of these three 'healthy' positions in turn and discuss their impact on the three supervisor-derived conditions.

Potency
Congruence: my congruence as supervisor is enhanced if I hold my awareness of my own potency. My potency is my source of creativity, a trust in my own actualising tendency, and so I can empower myself to be aware of my internal processes. Also through such an awareness of my perceived potency by the other

(supervisee) I am able to modify my expressed congruence in the light of my empathy and unconditional positive regard of the 'other' (supervisee).

Unconditional Positive Regard: a holding of my potency is likely to mean that I express my unconditional positive regard and that I do so in a congruent manner. Also by holding my potency 'for myself' I am more able to offer myself as well as the supervisee this condition, thus managing to maintain my psychological contact and unconditional positive regard for the supervisee even through what may feel like difficult points in our relationship.

Empathy: again my holding of my potency means that I am less likely to become defensive and move more toward my own internal world. Instead I can remain more in my supervisee's world, and approach her experience phenomenologically.

Responsiveness

Congruence: if I can be genuinely responsive toward my supervisee, rather than rescuing her, then I am less likely either to hold back my appropriate congruent statement or to give a congruent response that is inappropriate. My 'responsiveness' will ensure that my congruence is well informed by my empathy and unconditional positive regard.

Unconditional Positive Regard: my 'responsiveness' again will help my awareness of when I have let this condition 'slip', or whether it has been perceived as intended or misperceived.

Empathy: my 'responsiveness' both toward myself and my supervisee again allows me to notice when I have missed him and to regain my accuracy.

Vulnerability

Congruence: an awareness of my own vulnerability allows me to be more internally congruent and for my outward expression to be regulated by an awareness of my supervisee's vulnerability also.

Unconditional Positive Regard: the recognition of the vulnerability we share in our common humanity supports the maintenance of unconditional positive regard towards self and the supervisee.

Empathy: a recognition of our common vulnerability again furthers my empathic stance towards myself and my supervisee.

The move away from the drama triangle positions to their healthy equivalents described above, shifts the co-creation of dialogue, from one that happens between two estranged self-concepts, towards one that happens between two organismic beings in co-created dialogue. Increasingly the supervisory relationship becomes that of two 'fully functioning' persons working together.

Taking the previously used scenario: the supervisee relates more and more detail about the client and his life circumstances without making any request of the supervisor. Either the supervisee seizes her potency and clarifies what she wants of her supervisor, or the supervisor utilises his potency and responsiveness to ask how and where the supervisee wishes to pursue this. In such a scenario the relationship is enhanced, supervision becomes more effective and the 'collaborative relationship' between the two people becomes strengthened.

SUMMARY

Returning to the questions posed at the start of this chapter:

• Might I, supervising a person-centred therapist, use concepts from other schools to further his understanding, whilst honouring his person-centred philosophy, values and practice?

• Are there factors that might facilitate an effective supervisory relationship across theoretical orientations?

• Are there positive advantages to be gained from such a supervision arrangement?

I believe that the answer to these questions is yes providing the following conditions are attended to:

• A genuine interest in both parties to develop a collaborative relationship

• A respect for the person-centred model and an embracing of phenomenological inquiry

• Clarity by both parties as to their placing on the 'classical' vs 'relational' position

• Willingness and ability to translate, rather than casually import, other concepts into person-centred theory

• Curiosity about concepts from other systems, and especially from those that are phenomenologically based, to enhance person-centred practice

• Open sharing between supervisor and supervisee of the model(s) of supervision being utilised

• Interest in healing the 'us' and 'them' divide between models of counselling and psychotherapy

Finally to return to the final question posed at the start: Are there times when 'pure model' supervision is needed?

Providing the above conditions are met I argue that such instances are likely to be rare. There is some argument for such 'pure model' supervision when the supervisee is wanting exam-focused supervision or when the supervisee has placed themselves at the 'classical' end of the 'classical' vs 'relational' dimension of person-centred practice. It might also be argued that even when a supervisee identifies at the relational end of the person-centred spectrum, classical person-centred supervision may provide a valuable discipline that will enhance those elements common to both the classical and relational person-centred practices.

References

Bozarth, J. (1998) *Person-Centred Therapy: A Revolutionary Paradigm*. Ross-on-Wye: PCCS Books
Brodley, B.T. (1990) Client-centred and experiential: Two different therapies. In G. Lietaer, J. Rombauts and R. Van Balen (Eds.) *Client-Centered and Experiential Psychotherapy in the Nineties*. Belgium: Leuven University Press
Carroll, M. (1996) *Counselling Supervision*. London: Cassell
Clarkson, P. (1992) *Transactional Analysis Psychotherapy: An Integrated Approach*. London: Routledge
Frankland, A. (2001) A person-centred model of supervision. *Counselling Psychology Review, 16*(4), 26–31
Freud, S. (1949) *An Outline of Psychoanalysis*. London: Hogarth Press
Gendlin, E. T. (1981) *Focussing*. New York: Bantam Books
Gilbert, M. and Evans, K. (2000) *Psychotherapy Supervision*. Buckingham: Open University Press
Greenberg, L. S., Rice, L. N. and Elliott, R. (1993) *Facilitating Emotional Change: The Moment-by-Moment Process*. New York: Guilford Press
Grossman, R. (1984) *Phenomenology and Existentialism: An Introduction*. London: Routledge and Kegan Paul
Hackney, H. and Goodyear, R. (1984) Carl Rogers's client-centered approach to

supervision. In R. Levant and J. Shlien (Eds.) *Client-centered Therapy and the Person-centered Approach.* New York: Greenwood Press

Hawkins, P. and Shohet, R. (1989) *Supervision in the Helping Professions.* Milton Keynes: Open University Press

Holloway, E. L. (1995) *Clinical Supervision: A Systems Approach.* California: Sage

Husserl, E. (1931) *Ideas: General Introduction to Pure Phenomenology, Vol. 1.* New York: Macmillan

Ihde, D. (1977) *Experimental Phenomenology: An Introduction.* Albany: State University of New York

Karpman, S. (1968) Fairy tales and script drama analysis. *TAB,* 7, 26, 39–43

Lambers, E. (2000) Supervision in person-centred therapy: facilitating congruence. In D. Mearns and B. Thorne, *Person-Centred Therapy Today: New Frontiers in Theory and Practice* (pp. 196–211) London: Sage

Lietaer, G. (1990) The client-centered approach after the Wisconsin project: A personal view on its evolution. In G. Lietaer, J. Rombauts and R. Van Balen (Eds.), *Client-centered and Experiential Psychotherapy in the Nineties.* Leuven: Leuven University Press

Mearns, D. (1994) *Developing Person-centred Counselling.* London: Sage

Merry, T. (1999) *Learning and Being in Person-Centred Counselling.* Ross-on-Wye: PCCS Books

Orlans, V. and Edwards, D. (2001) A collaborative model of supervision. In M. Carroll and M. Tholstrup (Eds.) *Integrative Approaches to Supervision.* London: JKP

Page, S. and Woskett, V. (2001) *Supervising the Counsellor. A Cyclical Model* (2nd edition). London: Routledge

Patterson, C. H. (1997) Client-centered supervision. In C. E. Watkins (Ed.) *Handbook of Psychotherapy Supervision.* New York: John Wiley and Sons

Proctor, B. (2000) *Group Supervision: A Guide to Creative Practice.* London: Sage

Proctor, B. and Inskipp, F. (1989) *Skills for Supervising and Being Supervised.* St Leonard's on Sea, East Sussex: Alexia Publications

Proctor, B. and Inskipp, F. (1991) This is not the truth. Unpublished workshop material, quoted in Frankland, A. (2001) A person-centred model of supervision. *Counselling Psychology Review,* 16(4), 26–31

Rennie, D. (1998) *Person-centred Counselling: An Experiential Approach.* London: Sage

Rice, L. N. (1974) The evocative function of the therapist. In D. Wexler and L. N. Rice (Eds.) *Innovations in Client-Centred Therapy.* New York: Wiley

Rogers, C. (1942) *Counselling and Psychotherapy: New Concepts in Practice.* Boston: Houghton Mifflin

Rogers, C. (1957) The Necessary and Sufficient Conditions of Therapeutic Personality Change. *Journal of Consulting Psychology,* 21, 95–103

Rogers, C. (1959) A theory of therapy, personality and interpersonal relationships, as developed in the client-centered framework. In S. Koch (Ed.) (1959) *Psychology, A Study of Science: Vol. 3. Formulations of the Person and the Social Context* (pp. 184–256). New York: McGraw-Hill

Safran, J. D. (1998) Workshop Presentation, SEPI Conference, Madrid, July.

Sanders, P. (2000) Mapping person-centred approaches to counselling and psychotherapy. *Person-Centred Practice,* 8(2), 62–74

Sanders, P. (Ed.) (2004) *Tribes of the Person-Centred Nation*. Ross-on-Wye: PCCS Books

Spinelli, E. (1989) *The Interpreted World: An Introduction to Phenomenological Psychology*. London: Sage

Thorne, B. (1992) *Carl Rogers*. London: Sage

Tudor, K. (2000) The case of the lost conditions. *Counselling, 11*(1), 33–7

Villas-Boas Bowen, M. (1986) Personality differences and person-centered supervision. *Person-Centered Review, 1*(3), 291–309

Vincent, S. (1999) What is a person-centred counsellor? *Counselling,10*(1) pp. 15–18

Worrall, M. (2001) Supervision and empathic understanding. In S. Haugh and T. Merry (Eds.) *Rogers Therapeutic Conditions: Evolution, Theory and Practice. Vol. 2, Empathy* (pp. 206–17). Ross-on-Wye: PCCS Books

Worsley, R. (2002) *Process Work in Person-centred Therapy*. Hampshire: Palgrave

CHAPTER THIRTEEN

ALMOST NOTHING TO DO: SUPERVISION AND THE PERSON-CENTRED APPROACH IN HOMEOPATHY

IAN TOWNSEND

Homeopathy is a 200-year-old alternative approach to health care. Success relies on its practitioners eliciting, and then understanding, the self-referenced nature of dis-ease present in the person seeking treatment, and using this understanding to select a single homeopathic treatment. Whilst homeopathy's body of theoretical knowledge and clinical evidence is well-established, its understanding of what happens in the consulting room, in the interactional process between practitioner and client, remains opaque. Homeopathic literature over the last 20 years hints occasionally and sporadically at links between this process and person-centred practice. Such links remain largely undeveloped.

In this chapter, I show how key components of the person-centred approach have parallels in homeopathic theory and with what happens in many a homeopath's practice room. I then comment on the way in which a relatively recent adoption and practice of supervision has served to expose this, and explore how a person-centred approach to supervision gently supports the emergence of a professional self, rooted in personal knowledge.

INTRODUCTION

I have been an educator for over 30 years, an independent homeopath in private practice for 17, and a teacher of homeopathy since 1988. When in 1997 I

225

discovered the formal practice of supervision it was with a sense of both relief and excitement. The relief? At last I had found a description, a set of words and a series of coherent models, that in some way described how I had been trying, intuitively, *to be* all my adult life. The excitement was at a barely sensed, but nevertheless gratefully acknowledged, level of experiencing. I had, in some indefinable way, 'come home'. Discovering supervision represented a shift in my awareness. I was not to know just how much of a paradigm shift it would prove to be, nor what insights were lying in wait.[1]

What is homeopathy?

The House of Lords Select Committee Report (2000) recently recognised homeopathy as one of the 'Big 5' complementary medicines. (The others are acupuncture, chiropractic, herbal medicine and osteopathy.) It is a system of medicine which originated in Germany as a result of one individual's lifetime response to the crude medical barbarisms of the day. Long before mainstream medicine had recognised the importance of hygiene, sanitation, exercise, adequate nutrition and thoughtful application of drug regimes, Dr Samuel Hahnemann was laying the foundation for much of what is now recognised as good (orthodox) medical practice.

His was a truly holistic approach. He considered the social, physical, mental, emotional and spiritual elements of the individual and joined them in a treatment programme which considered disease to be unitary, and which utilised a minimum dose of a single drug. He did this by recognising those elements as being based in, and reflections of, the energetic, individual, *vital force*.

So whilst an orthodox GP might diagnose an individual as having 'arthritis', 'migraine' and 'depression' co-present, and offer a different drug treatment for each illness, a homeopath would look for *the single pattern* in the individual, of which 'arthritis', 'migraine' and 'depression' were results. He would then treat that pattern rather than the outcome.

Before the advent of the 'germ theory of disease', before the so-called magic bullets of antibiotic therapy, Hahnemann had developed an energy medicine

---

1. One thing led to another, and five years of intensive study and practice later I am grateful to my colleagues (tutors and fellow students) within the international community of homeopaths: at the University of Derby Unit for Psychotherapy Practice and Research; and at both Temenos in Sheffield and Person-Centred Connections in Nottingham for their patience, support and challenge. I am also especially grateful to my good friend Sheila Ryan, who, more than any other person, has been responsible for bringing the practice of supervision to the attention of the homeopathic profession globally and to developing supervision in homeopathy; and, of course, to my supervisees past and present: they have been my teachers; the mistakes, as always, continue to be mine.

which was so successful that it spread rapidly throughout the world, almost becoming the medicine of choice in America (Coulter, 1984), where for the last 200 years it has coexisted as an alternative to the dominant medical model.

In my clinical experience, members of the general public have had widely differing perceptions of it. Some have mistaken it for something to do with herbs; others as involving the use of aromatherapy oils. There have even been occasions when patients in my consulting rooms have obviously been anticipating a massage treatment! The more knowledgeable have regarded it variously as an approach suitable only for the treatment of acute illnesses; more appropriate to chronic conditions; useful in some intractable maladies untouchable by modern medicine; or solely applicable to the physical condition. Others have insisted that at best it relies on some system of belief or faith healing; can be accounted for by placebo effect; or is, quite simply, a quackery that has no place in the twenty-first century.

Despite all the foregoing, homeopathy continues to grow in popularity, with patients presenting through the entire range of physical, emotional, mental, and spiritual conditions. Pool (1991, p. 113) puts it this way:

> In my practice many patients are seeking more than just a relief from physical, mental and emotional symptoms. They are looking for a purpose to their lives, a spiritual dimension which is not being met, and this seems to echo a spiritual crisis of our times. Speaking with my colleagues I learn that many of them are facing the same need within their practices.

Whatever the expectations, a patient's experiences of treatment will be remarkably similar. She attends for a consultation and tells her story. This certainly includes her own focus on her state of health, amplified through the practitioner's interest in its ecology: in other words, the links to her total experience and life history to date. She may be asked for many further details, is sometimes questioned on what seem to be strange and inconsequential areas, for example, food preferences, reactions to weather, her family history. She then eventually receives the homeopathic treatment: a small white pill containing, pharmacologically, nothing at all.

For the homeopathic practitioner, there is little or no patient expectation of referral to more expert sources, to specialists knowledgeable in one area or another. And unlike practitioners of the listening/talking arts, there is no expectation that *merely talking or exploring* will help relieve or resolve the situation.

There is an obvious, and expected, treatment outcome: that the patient's ingestion of that single white pill will result in an improvement in the state of health that has brought her to the practitioner.

Homeopathy has a clearly-defined methodology:

1. *The patient-practitioner interview*—which, partly free-flowing, partly structured, seeks to establish a set of patient- and practitioner-referenced data.
2. *A deliberative (often post-patient) process*—in which the practitioner considers the data received and analyses it to result in:
3. The selection and issue of a homeopathic drug;
4. *A follow-up evaluation system*—comprising subsequent interviews and observations of the patient post-medication, which enables the practitioner to assess the direction of movement of health.

For *this* therapy, the ultimate intervention is to offer the patient a single dose of dynamised medicine, which in its effect upon the physical, mental, emotional and spiritual levels of the organism mirrors back to her that which she is presenting. Hahnemann's *Organon* (originally published in 1842, and still homeopathy's seminal bedrock) lays down procedures for 'taking the case', i.e. carrying out initial and subsequent interviews, recommending that the practitioner adopt the bearing of an *unprejudiced observer* (or, for our purposes, one who offers *unconditional positive regard*); allowing the patient to tell her ever-deepening tale supported by practitioner attention, and, initially at least, unswayed by practitioner questioning. This has parallels with Bion's entreaty to 'stay empty with our unknowing, uncluttered by premature judgement, theory and interpretation' (cited in Hawkins and Shohet, 1989, p. 59).

Homeopathic success lies in the very quality of the information resulting from the therapeutic relationship, and it is surprising that so little attention has been paid to that relationship.

HOMEOPATHY AND THE PERSON-CENTRED APPROACH

At the heart of both homeopathy and the person-centred approach lies a belief in an actualising tendency (Townsend, 2002). Person-centred practitioners (PCPs) trust that if a client experiences certain relational conditions, then the individual's own tendency to actualise will take the opportunity for growth. Homeopaths model their own practice on an identical concept, the vital force, which can be stimulated by minimal doses of discrete energised (homeopathic) medicines.

Both have ideas about how limitations to actualisation occur. The notion of *conditions of worth* identified in the person-centred approach is similar to homeopathy's *central delusions* (Sankaran, 1991), *barriers to change* or *suppressions* (which also include ideas of inheritable, genetic, medical and drug-deadening limits). Both have a positive, pro-social, beneficent model of the human being with the concept of *optimal functioning* informing them, and a trust in the *internal resources* of the individual (possibly unidentified, unexplored or yet-to-emerge).

Whilst the person-centred model eschews diagnostic classification (Rogers, 1951; Lambers, 1994; Merry, 1999), the homeopathic model does focus on diagnosis, in a particular way. Homeopaths do not diagnose in the orthodox sense of naming an illness 'measles', 'bipolar disorder' or 'arthritis'. They use the individual's self-referenced description to recognise that person's holistic *energetic* state of being, at that moment in time, as represented in a 'remedy picture'. In this, the diagnosis *is* the possibility of cure. For if the homeopath perceives the patient as s/he *really is* in the moment, in the course of consultation (and the practitioner can only achieve this by offering a relational experience grounded in the core conditions), then by offering the mirror image within the homeopathic remedy, that person literally accepts themselves, and is restored.

Homeopathic remedies are made from plants, animals, minerals; from sound, colour, sunlight, radiation; from healthy and diseased human or animal tissue. There is, literally, nothing in the universe—or beyond it—that cannot be made into a homeopathic medicine. The process by which they are made, tested, and validated demands a book in itself (see Sherr, 1994). Suffice to say that on investigation a remedy reveals many aspects of the energetic, vital force/actualising potentials it holds within it, both those already known to the individual for whom it will be beneficial, and those still hidden from her.

Neither person-centred practice nor homeopathy seeks to guide or influence the individual's growth. In both cases, practitioners attempt to provide *unconditional positive regard* (PCA) or *an unprejudiced observer* (homeopathy) and are equally concerned to understand the interior meaning of the individual's experiencing: the homeopath carefully listening to the individual's story is as concerned to grasp the individual's *internal frame of reference* as is the person-centred therapist.

Whilst the person-centred therapist checks the accuracy of his or her empathic understanding through a process of continuous reflective listening, the homeopath does the same through energetic medicine. The end result can often be the same. As a homeopathic patient of many years standing, and someone now engaged in person-centred training, I am surprised that the process is so similar, even down to what I can identify as that pivotal, felt-sense 'click' or 'twist'—the moment I sometimes catch that represents a profound shift from what I was to what I am becoming.

Two examples from my own life:

I'd lived for more years than I could remember with a severe aversion to drafts. Open doors or windows *had* to be closed—*immediately*. Whilst this didn't rule my life, it certainly was something that friends and family noticed, and (kindly) pointed out. Even though I knew about it, I was unable to change it. One day, having just taken a homeopathic remedy (prescribed on the basis of a series of long interviews), I remember catching that internal 'click'—nothing conscious; simply a change from one state to another—and I automatically got up, opened every single door and window in the house and revelled in the breeze. Since then, I have lost the frantic desire to close windows and doors!

More recently, I experienced a change in a pivotal condition of worth that I had introjected 45 years ago: 'Don't be spontaneous, don't explore'. I had known about its situation (not its identified label) for many, many years but seemed powerless to understand or move on from it. Sitting in a residential person-centred group, experiencing safety and core conditions, I experienced that sliding pivotal moment—without conscious decision I suddenly identified 'what had been going on' and was able to give up that condition of worth and reintegrate a part of myself I had not only *not* experienced for those 45 years, but which had been completely and utterly lost to me, beyond my consciousness.

My point is that in neither of these cases did 'they' set out to cure me of condition A or B. In the one case an appropriate homeopathic medicine, in the other, the core conditions, were all that it took for my vital force or actualising tendency to help me grow, seemingly of its own volition, in a totally unexpected and beneficial way. It seems that in both cases, practitioner intent was remarkably similar:

> It is obvious to me, based on my work with many people, that therapeutic effects are produced when the therapist is free of specific intentions to produce effects on or in the client [and that] these effects seem to contribute in sometimes unexpected ways to accomplishing the general purpose and goal in the situation—the healing and growth of the client. (Brodley, 1998)

BACK TO BASICS—REVISIONING HOMEOPATHIC EDUCATION

Historically, the study of homeopathy, like that of many other practice-based disciplines, has been based on a curriculum model emphasising the acquisition

230

of a body of theory at the cost of its application, an education which emphasises quantity of knowledge over quality of experience. This is, in effect, an expert model, externally referenced and examined, with the locus of evaluation firmly external to the practitioner (Mackintosh, 1986).

Over recent years this model has been vigorously questioned within the profession's training and professional development dialogues, with a more interactional and interrelational one being proposed and increasingly gaining strength (Fordham et al., 1992; Brinkley, 1993; McMahon, 1993; Pollard, 1993; Ryan, 2003).

However, homeopathy has yet to develop an explicit and referenced model to inform the information-gathering stage of its process. In the absence of such a model the opportunity to develop, question, or refine this part of its art is denied. Other than the original, classic literature, there is only rudimentary awareness of this aspect amongst its modern teachers. Sherr (1986), for instance, developed *receiving the case*—a model in which the anticipative homeopath, within her therapeutic ambience, holds the client, and encourages through homeopath-inaction, the client's telling of her story. This (unpublished) model holds within it seeds of the person-centred approach in its respect for the client, her pace and her story. Some years earlier, Sanders (1984) was utilising a transactional analysis model to aid her understanding of case material, though it is unsure to what extent this therapeutic stance informed her actual process of case taking.

As for the general curriculum, there are ongoing developments which have yet to be organised and codified within the homeopathic literature (Ryan, 2003).

This leads, not unsurprisingly, to the situation where the challenge of the unsafe or potentially incompetent student remains one to haunt our educational process (Iliott and Murphy, 1999; Society of Homeopaths, 2002). We give our students the intellectual tools to manage the task of *being homeopaths* and wonder why some fail to engage with the daily practice of the discipline. We launch them on the unsuspecting general public ignorant of the rich tapestry that is the life of personal practice with its trials, tribulations and triumphs. Learning to be a homeopath, capable of sitting in a practice room, receiving the case history of a patient, and then prescribing, is different to '*learning* homeopathy'. The latter involves itself with facts and figures, remedy pictures and case management strategies; the former calls into being a set of skills which are all to do with being human—with knowing about, and caring for, oneself as well as others, and communicating that caring. It is a lifelong endeavour and takes more than a single training course to achieve.

It comes as a surprise to many students to find that there are different sorts of intelligences, different ways of learning (Gardner, 1999). They are usually all too familiar with *intellectual* intelligence, measured by how well they can write this essay, produce this assignment, remember these facts for an examination. However, practice-based disciplines require so much more than the remembering of facts and the ability to assemble intellectual arguments. How we are as practitioners cannot be divorced from who we are as people and this calls on us to become 'intelligent' in many other ways. So we find we need to become more knowing of ourselves. This *emotional* (intra-personal) intelligence consists of our becoming increasingly and appropriately self-aware: the desire to engage with our own process of development, the willingness to describe this to ourselves and others, and the ability to relate self to the other person.

A major part of being a homeopath lies in knowing about how we interact with people—knowing how to be with clients—and so we also value the growth of *social* (interpersonal) intelligence. How well do we tolerate others—their 'good' and 'bad' points? How well do we tolerate, understand, accept, these areas in ourselves—in work, group, and individual settings? The practice of homeopathy is a social endeavour—with the skilled practitioner coming to rely on her peers, her professional colleagues, for support, encouragement and challenge. Such interpersonal intelligence comes into play as a homeopath in our ability to relate to others and encourage them to tell us their story. Castro (1997) identifies such willingness to be aware of self in the practitioner-patient relationship as a mark of a profession's true maturity.

Homeopathy encourages the patient to speak, and the practitioner to wait patiently, and not to impose their own values on the patient. In doing this, it encourages active listening, practitioner receptivity, and a *trust in the process*. Given sufficient time the patient will deliver the most comprehensive and holistic account possible of her pathology. Homeopathy shares this emphasis on the patient's own experience of her presenting issues with the person-centred approach, and both differ from normal medical approaches which, as Mearns puts it (1994, p. 30), 'allow [the orthodox practitioner] . . . to set in motion a "treatment plan" which relates to the characteristics of the problem . . . a much less demanding process than having to treat each new client as an individual with a unique experience of the problem'.

Technician or Artist?: The place of the personal in the theory and practice of professional knowledge

One might expect that different aspects of the patient-practitioner relationship would have attracted wide attention within the literature of homeopathy, as they have within other practice-based disciplines; and that these would address the nature of the homeopathic interview process and investigate any parallels existing between this and other relational models. However, a literature review of the last 25 years reveals scant attention being paid to these vital areas. This, despite the fact that the very first Annual Conference of the Society of Homeopaths in 1983 invited a keynote address by Ian Gordon-Brown, linking soma to psyche in a presentation entitled *Symptom as Symbol* (Gordon-Brown, 1983). Later keynote addresses were to address supervision, relationship and power (Castro, 1988, 1990, 1992).

The need for self-awareness and familiarity with relational concepts had been admitted by both Richardson (1981) and Pool (1995). Richardson saw the clear link between the ability to 'perceive the case' and the practitioner's awareness of self:

> It is our commitment to see all the symptoms of the case as clearly and with as much understanding as possible. So I return to my starting place in saying that only through constant conscious work on ourselves, with the help of friends and teachers, and especially with the willingness to listen to the inner teacher of one's own unconscious and higher self, can we attempt to maintain the necessary clarity we all so dearly need. (Richardson, 1981, p. 63)

Pool's (1995) paper underlined this, adding an awareness of analytical concepts, without placing these within the wider context of an identified knowledge-base:

> How do we avoid projection and collusion, transference and counter-transference if we do not even know what to watch for? How do we maintain our own space and boundaries gently but firmly if we are unconsciously caught in the need to be needed? How do we hold our patients in their inner dark places and fears if we are afraid to look at our own? (Pool, 1995, p. 30)

A similar borrowing of therapeutic concepts continued with Mackintosh (1981, 1982) who eventually made the briefest of references to Rogers' core conditions in her 1986 paper. In the main, however, homeopathic writers do not identify from whence they draw their ideas. Pinto (1995), for example, admits that 'in the 15 years I have been practising I have spent a considerable amount of time looking at psychotherapy models in order to understand behaviour in patients and to apply this to homoeopathic case taking' (p. 15)—without clearly identifying these models!

In a published (and completely unreferenced) paper Roberts (1998) suggests that homoeopaths might benefit from an awareness of, and training in, therapeutic skills. He identifies eight 'counselling techniques' (listening skills, reflection, paraphrasing, empathy, probing, conditions of worth, challenging, goal-setting) which he states as relevant to the homeopathic process. Unfortunately his paper did not place these techniques conceptually within a counselling or homeopathic framework, nor did it offer a trans-theoretical perspective.

Coming closer to the present day, two interesting developments emerge: a resurrection of interest in the therapeutic relationship, and a willingness to place a homeopathic interview within a named process approach. Barzman (2000), writing from a depth psychology, Jungian-identified background, usefully points to the possibility of contamination resulting from relational aspects of the therapeutic relationship being ignored:

> What factors within the practitioner, within the patient/fellow sufferer, and between them, could lead to the voice of the symptoms being hushed? And what happens when that voice is hushed? In particular, what possible effects on the patient follow from this? (p. 14)

Furthermore, after 250 years where millions of patients consulted tens of thousands of homeopaths, Chatwin and Collins (2002) ask (for the first time): 'What is it that actually happens in the homeopathic interview?' Using the tool of conversation analysis they attempt to capture the distinctive feel of the homeopathic encounter, with the awareness that:

> At a basic level, patient/practitioner communication can have a direct impact on factors such as the degree to which a person feels satisfied with the therapeutic relationship, or on the level of commitment that they are willing to invest in their treatment. (p. 24)

Over the 25 years' literature reviewed, only three authors (Spring, 1990; Kaplan, 2001; Ryan, 2002) and myself (Townsend, 2002) have clearly linked the homeopathic interview process to the person-centred approach.

Beat Spring, a homeopath based in Berne, Switzerland, was the first person to remark on the similarity between Rogers' ideas and homeopathy:

> In a person-centred psychotherapy session, as taught by Carl Rogers in La Jolla, California, you very empathically listen to the report of the client. You abstain from any judgement or desire to give advice and literally try to understand and see the world through the eyes of the client. You may ask questions to get a better and deeper understanding of what he/she just said or give him signs of your understanding to encourage him. (Sounds like a

good prescription in how to take the homoeopathic case doesn't it?) . . . You are not leading. but just following the process very attentively. You are not in the position of knowing better than the patient what he needs. You just help him find that out himself. (Spring, 1990, p. 49)

Norland (1998) touches, unknowingly perhaps, on Rogerian concepts when he produced this metaphor for the homeopathic interview:

> I like to image a session as being like going for a walk with the other into their territory so that we are both experiencing this event together. This allows for empathy to coexist with objectivity, for they are showing me the sights, yet, if the going gets tough I am there alongside them. (p. 10)

This statement is not so different from that found in Mearns and Thorne (1994): 'right from the start of the relationship the counsellor endeavours to enter the client's frame of reference and walk alongside him in his world' (p. 43).

Kaplan's (2001) book is a landmark publication. For the first time in homeopathic literature we see a homeopathic practitioner identifying, applying and embodying the value of the person-centred approach within homeopathic practice. Ryan's most recent paper (2002) builds on more than 15 years experience and publication in homeopathic supervision, stressing the primacy of the person-person relationship within homeopathy. In doing this she clearly acknowledges the influences of both Martin Buber and Carl Rogers. I myself link the process view of homeopathy with the person-centred approach (Townsend, 2002) and am now developing this within the BSc (Hons) Homeopathy Degree at the University of Central Lancashire (UCL). This represents a radical departure from traditional training. Rather than placing subject knowledge at the centre of the student experience, it gives primacy to the idea of *student-centredness* (Rogers, 1969; Bondi, 2000). In doing so, the degree is congruent with the university's own Mission Statement 'to promote access to excellence and enable [students] to develop [their] potential' (UCLan, 2002).

Homeopathic supervision in context

Supervision in the homeopathic profession is an entirely British-led phenomenon, one which has taken 15 years to develop to its present level. Before that, it was unnamed: individuals developed practical skills by finding individual mentors or by gathering support from their peers.

The first definitive paper by Castro (1989) appeared more than a decade ago, followed by Fell (1989), Whitehead (1989), Pinto (1991), Sobol (1994), Morris (1996), Ryan (1996, 1997, 2002), Townsend (1999a, 1999b, 2001, 2003),

Havelock-Davies (2001), Larkman (2001) and Wood (2001). Now in the UK, a supervision process is established at student level, mandatory at practitioner registration level, and is an expectation post registration.

Since 1998 there has been regular publication by the Society of Homeopaths (SoH) (the largest and longest-established registering body in the UK) of a *List of Homeopaths Working As Supervisors* (SoH, 2002). Over a number of years the Society's Professional Conduct and Continuing Professional Development Departments have collaborated through a series of regional meetings, postal and e-mail feedback on versions of a *Code of Ethics for Supervisors* which was then launched as a working draft (SoH, 2001). The role of supervisor is increasingly being recognised, and becoming well-grounded in the psyche of the profession itself. The idea of supervision in British homeopathy in the twenty-first century is coming of age.

Despite that, with the exception of Ryan (2002), there has been no exploration in the homeopathic literature of models of supervision available to the profession, or of the roles which could be encompassed within it. The development of a thoughtful and public dialogue around questions such as whether or not homeopathy needs to develop its own unique model of supervision, or can freely borrow from existing ones, has yet to be addressed. This is especially important if, as Hawkins and Shohet (1989) claim: 'one's style as a supervisor is affected by the style of one's practitioner work' (p. 47).

Historically in homeopathy, supervision has been a case-bound approach. It has occupied itself with technical matters, addressing such questions as:

- Has the supervisee obtained sufficient information from the patient to enable the case to be analysed and the correct remedy found?
- Have all factors regarding prescription and case management been addressed?

For follow-up visits, supervisors address issues such as:

- Have the initial presenting symptoms (and later revealed symptoms) been thoroughly checked?
- Has the patient's response to the homeopathic prescription been correctly assessed?
- What now needs to be done?

Supervisory models and homeopathic process
A central question facing any profession willing to embrace supervision is this: to what extent does it develop its own subject-specific model of supervision, and/or to what extent does it draw from those models already available, but which may seem

external to it? (see Tudor, 2002). Assuming the profession is aware of the range of supervision models, understands their rationale, and can dialogue with them, it demands a willingness to consider the role of socialisation, the place of task-centredness, the location of evaluation and the nature of supervisee autonomy, the notion of developmental staging, the idea of a process basis, and a familiarity with the eclectic/integrative/pure model debate. In addition to this, such questions beg knowledge of models of adult learning and assume consistency of supervisor style.

The process of adopting supervision seems to be remarkably similar to the process of becoming a practitioner of any therapeutic orientation, and indeed has parallels in Stoltenberg and Delworth's (1987) developmental model of supervision:

1. The initial phase involves the practitioner asking questions such as 'Is this approach the right one for me?; 'How can I test its consistency to my central ideas/beliefs?'
2. Then, early stages are characterised by a focus on technique: 'Can I do it?'; 'How can I remember what to do?'; 'Is this how I do it?'; and a parallel emphasis on the technical: the learner needs to be able to make this intervention, or to plan that strategy, or to demonstrate their understanding of something else.
3. This is followed by a period in which the adopting person or organisation starts to wonder 'Is this all there is to it?' After a prolonged period of practice and thoughtful reflection, the practitioner realises that his or her proficiency is more related to state-of-being than adherence to any one particular set of skills. In other words, the locus of evaluation has moved, in Carroll's (2001) description, from a focus on the skills and tasks (in other words, functions) of supervision to the practice of an authentic, grounded way of being as a practitioner:

> The 'outside-in supervisor' . . . is an expert, a technician who is doing something to someone else. Their task and their work are not necessarily connected to them as a person. The inside-out professional is someone whose job comes from inside. The 'inside-out supervisor' knows that the beginning is always with self, not the other, that no matter how knowledgeable, skilled or competent you are, if you're 'not OK' inside then you won't 'be OK' outside. (p. 78)

The suggestion in previous sections of this chapter is that homeopathy has yet to develop within its discipline a coherent model of human interaction which can inform and guide its information-gathering stages. I suggest that the person-

237

centred approach comes closest to representing what homeopathic practitioners do when they are with their clients, and thus offers the most consistent model for supervision practice. This then begs the question 'Is there such a thing as person-centred supervision?'

WHAT ALREADY HAPPENS IN HOMEOPATHIC SUPERVISION ?

Over the last decade supervising pre-graduation homeopaths, I have noticed myself becoming more and more willing to trust the student. I have moved away from the largely *teaching* role of supervision with its focus on identifying areas where the student appears 'weak' and then engaging in remedial work on her, to just being: where I trust the student to be wise enough to bring her own issues to supervision, to know when she has the resources to move into this area, or that one, and to explore it with me. I found that keeping the belief in the authority of the person resting in that person rather than in an outside expert echoes what Patterson (1964) noticed almost 40 years previously: 'the student, if not interrupted, lectured to, criticized, with his mistakes being thrown in his face, will take the responsibility for analyzing and evaluating himself' (p. 52).

I have rarely been disappointed. It has been my experience that, in the face of this trust, students indeed know their 'weaknesses'—and are able to own and confront them authentically. This does not mean I abrogate my role of 'weakness spotter', for students are expected to present their casework in a formalised written academic format. Having such a format enables me to wonder, in their presence, whether they have addressed a particular area sufficiently. At first I was puzzled by the frequent response of relief, until students reported that such joint wondering triggered or made sense of a disquiet they had had about their work, but had not been able to put into context until this invitation to wonder arrived. Perhaps this represents an example of working at 'the edge of awareness'?

My biggest piece of learning, as a person-centred homeopath and supervisor, has been how powerful a sufficiency of therapeutic conditions can be. Time and time again I have been privileged to witness the flowering that this brings and to share the palpable sense of pleasurable surprise on the part of the supervisee as she owns the growth of confidence in her emerging self, and in the knowledge and skills she has learnt. The challenge, in this context, is to avoid the traps of working to an identified schedule or of being prescriptive: 'the therapist and the supervisor do not map out content areas that must be dealt with if changes are to take place' (Rice, 1980, quoted in Patterson, 1983, p. 24).

In homeopathic terms, the question we hold as our focus becomes this: 'How can we work together to ensure the supervisee becomes the best homeopath she can be?' The function of the supervisor is to create the atmosphere that will enable the student to find her or his own style of being a homeopath, by adhering to the person-centred ideal of offering the necessary and sufficient conditions, even in the face of the supervisee who appeals for help or who asks for instructions. Villas-Bowen (1986) acknowledges the temptations for the supervisor in the face of such appeals and requests:

> the supervisor may feel tempted to come to the rescue, offering prescriptions, suggestions, perhaps a theoretical explanation. By offering such a 'shortcut' through the supervisee's exploratory process, the supervisor is likely to maintain the supervisee in a position of powerlessness and giving in to her need to rely on the authority and power of the supervisor, instead of helping her to acknowledge her feelings of helplessness, stuckness and perhaps incompetence. (p. 207)

We mirror the working relationship in such a way that the supervisee comes to realise her own therapeutic potential (Lambers, 2000).

The challenge of evaluation

Developing a person-centred approach to supervision within an undergraduate programme raises the issue of evaluation. Examining the evolution of supervision theory over recent decades, the literature reveals a move from the insecurity of its earlier years with 'no consensus about the best ways to supervise in the midst of conflicting demands' (Lawton and Feltham, 2000, p. 7); from 'supervision is still little understood. There are few agreed definitions and certainly no agreed tasks, roles, or even goals of supervision' (Carroll, 1988, p. 387), to a determined focus on quality assurance: 'supervisors generally agree that the goal of supervision is to enhance the quality of the service to the client' (Gilbert and Sills, 1999, p. 162), a goal previously applauded by Page and Wosket (1994) who raise the maintenance, monitoring and evaluation of quality and competence to the status of ethical imperative.

Bradley and Ladany (2001) focus on evaluation as *the* central core of supervision, quoting studies which stress the importance of the supervisor providing corrective 'negative' feedback. And whilst some see *evaluation* as a vital part of the supervisory process, some texts ignore it (Martindale et al., 1997; Power, 1999; Barnes et al., 2000; Lahad, 2000; Lawton and Feltham, 2000; Shipton, 2000); whilst others pay it scant attention (Gilbert and Evans, 2000). Scaife (2001) addresses the supervisor's role as *evaluator* rather than the evaluation of the supervision itself (only one page referencing rating scales, all of which are drawn from a single citation). Van Ooijen (2000) proposes extremely simple tools for evaluation.

The problem for many supervisors and supervisees alike is that challenging or critical feedback is often perceived as negative and disempowering, whilst positive, supportive feedback is so unfamiliar as to be arbitrarily disregarded:

> Most people have emerged from such a shame-based educational process that any feedback which is in any way critical seems to 'devastate' the person, so that as trainers and supervisors we can become disempowered by this process. We may end up avoiding giving necessary feedback and confrontation of a trainee supervisor in order to spare their feelings while condoning ineffective work in this process. The experience of shame is undermining for the person in the learning context since it leads to people hiding their perceived weaknesses and faults so that they do not get the input that would most help them to develop effective assessment processes for their own work. Part of teaching evaluation becomes the healing of the wounds that people have incurred in previous learning situations where being assessed has led them to conclude that they are 'stupid', 'ineffectual' or even 'bad'. (Gilbert and Sills, 1999, p. 181)

However, evaluation becomes consistent with person-centred theory when it is requested by the supervisee, agreed as an essential part of his own development by the trainee, or is an agreed, accepted, and contracted part of the work setting (Bozarth, 1998). Whilst such a collaborative approach to evaluation is congruent with person-centred theory, does it risk ignoring those sticky issues lying in wait for all supervisors?:

> My own experience has been that a small but significant number of students are unable or unwilling to deal with the limit-setting and confrontation necessary to manage difficult cases, and that an overlapping group of students have difficulty maintaining appropriate boundaries . . . We have agonized over decisions for which more seemed to be needed than suggesting therapy. We have had to deal with students who were alcoholic, others who had personality disorders, and still others who were involved in legal problems that suggested possible psychological dysfunctions. It has helped, in such cases, to remind myself that I must not gloss over such difficulties. The profession holds us as trainers responsible for a student's current work with clients and also for damage that might reasonably occur to *future* clients if we graduate a dysfunctional or impaired student. (Davenport, 1992, p. 230)

For the development of the autonomous, responsible, self-aware and self-critical practitioner *within a time-limited period* a tension exists between the encouragement of that process and the need on the part of the supervisor to remain responsible also to the client and the graduating organisation. Over 45 years ago, Rogers (1957) observed:

> If the therapist conducting the training holds an orientation which is interventive and interpretive, or one in which guidance and coaching play a prominent part, then he will guide and coach the trainee and interpret to him his own dynamics in the therapeutic relationships. If the therapeutic orientation of the supervisor is facilitative, endeavoring to permit the individual to gain insight into himself and to develop his own modes of meeting life, then the supervisory contacts will be primarily a listening, facilitative understanding. (p. 86)

This attitude is consistent within the approach and has remained relatively unchanged over time:

> This places the onus on you to be as open and non-defensive as you can be in talking through the ways you think and feel about yourself in relationship with your clients . . . Your supervisor, if he or she is to be effective in person-centred terms, needs to work towards establishing a relationship with you that has the same qualities as the relationships you try to provide for your clients. Put briefly, the supervisory relationship should mirror the client/counsellor relationship in that it values the qualities of empathic understanding, congruence and unconditional positive regard and takes these as core conditions for effective supervision. (Merry, 1999, p. 137)

CONCLUSION

As far back as 1979, Bernard suggested three foci for the supervision process:

1. *Process*—How supervisee skills and strategies impact on therapeutic relationship;
2. *Conceptualisation*—The increasing refinement on the part of the supervisee to understand the patient against a theoretical model (and the supervisor to understand the supervisee similarly); and
3. *Personalisation*—The increasing ease with which the supervisee acknowledges the ways in which her attitudes, values and behaviours can affect the patient-practitioner or practitioner-supervisor relationship.

These, mediated via Proctor's (1993) 'formative, normative, restorative' model form is, for me, a useful adjunctive backcloth to working with student homeopaths in a person-centred way. I, and I believe the students I work with, are increasingly experiencing the transformative power of Rogers' simple way of being, and together are witness to Heyward's (1993) powerful observation:

> I believe strongly that we are genuinely healed, strengthened, and liberated only in-so-far as our relational energy is calling us both, or all, to life, to be who we are at our best together. Unless the healer is being transformed by the therapy process and the teacher being changed with her students, these relationships are not trustworthy resources for authentic spiritual growth or emotional well-being. (p. 11)

REFERENCES

Barnes, G., Down, G. and McCann, D. (2000) *Systemic Supervision: A Portable Guide to Supervision Practice.* London: Jessica Kingsley

Barzman, A. J. (2000) Containing the symptom's voice: on boundaries and practitioner self-awareness within the homoeopathic practitioner fellow sufferer relationship. *The Homeopath*, 76, 14–16

Bernard, J. M. (1979) Supervisor training: a discrimination model. *Counselor Education and Supervision, 19*, 60–8

Bondi, A. (2000) *Education Policy*, (2nd Ed.) Northampton: Society of Homeopaths

Bozarth, J. (1998). *Person-centered Therapy: A Revolutionary Paradigm.* Ross-on-Wye: PCCS Books.

Bradley, J. and Ladany, N. (2001) *Counselor Supervision: Principles, Process and Practice* (3rd Ed.) Philadelphia: Brunner-Routledge

Brinkley, J. (1993) Revisioning homeopathic education. *Newsletter of the Society of Homeopaths*, September, 13–29

Brodley, B. (1998) The non-directive attitude in client-centered therapy. *The Person-Centered Journal, 4* (1), 18–30

Carroll, M. (1998) Counselling supervision: the British context. *Counselling Psychology Quarterly, 1*, 387–96

Carroll, M. (2001) The spirituality of supervision. In M. Carroll and M. Tholstrup (Eds.) *Integrative Approaches to Supervision*, (pp. 74-89). London: Jessica Kingsley Publishers

Castro, M. (1989) Supervision: a homœopath's perspective. *The Homœopath*, 8 (9), 108–21

Castro, M. (1997) Homeopaths heal thyselves. *Homeopathy Today*, March, 10–14

Chatwin, J. and Collins, S. (2002) Studying interaction in the homeopathic consultation. *The Homeopath*, 84, 24–6

Coulter, H. L. (1984) Divided legacy: the conflict between homoeopathy and the American Medical Association. *Science and Ethics in American Medicine, 1800–1914, 3.* Berkeley, CA: North Atlantic Press

Davenport, D. S. (1992) Ethical and legal problems with client-centred supervision. *Counselor Education and Supervision, 31*, 227–31

Fell, A. (1989) Supervision and support group with Angela Fell. *Society of Homeopaths Newsletter*, September, 30–1

Fordham, R., Griffin, P., Scott, G. and Townsend, I. (1992) *Prospectus*. Otley: Darlington School of Homeopathic Medicine

Gardner, H. (1999) *Intelligence Reframed: Multiple Intelligences for the 21st Century*. New York : Basic Books

Gilbert, M. and Evans, K. (2000) *Supervision of Psychotherapy and Counselling*. Buckingham: Open University Press

Gilbert, M. and Sills, C. (1999) Training for supervision evaluation. In E. Holloway and M Carroll (Eds.) *Training Counselling Supervisors* (pp. 162–83). London: Sage

Havelock-Davies, J. (2001) Supervision: a journey of self-discovery. *Society of Homœopaths Newsletter*, September, 24–5

Hawkins, P. and Shohet, R. (1989) *Supervision in the Helping Professions*. Milton Keynes: Open University Press

Heyward, C. (1993) *When Boundaries Betray Us*. Cleveland: Pilgrim Press

House of Lords Select Committee, (2000) *Select Committee Report*. London: HMSO

Iliott, I. and Murphy, R. (1999) *Success and Failure in Professional Education: Assessing the Evidence*. London: Whurr

Inskipp, R. and Proctor, B. (1993) T*he Arts, Crafts and Tasks of Counselling Supervision: Part I - Making the Most of Supervision*. Cascade Publications

Kaplan, B. (2001) *The Homeopathic Conversation: the Art of Taking the Case*. London: Natural Medicine Press

Lahad, M. (2000) *Creative Supervision*. London: Jessica Kingsley

Lambers,E. (1994). The person-centred perspective on psychopathology: the neurotic client. In D. Mearns, *Developing person-centred counselling* (pp.105-109). London: Sage

Lambers,E. (2000) Supervision in person-centred therapy: facilitating congruence. In D. Mearns and B. Thorne, *Person-Centred Therapy Today: New Frontiers in Theory and Practice* (pp. 196-211). London:Sage

Larkman, K. (2001) *Supervision: Time to Widen Our Horizons*. Society of Homœopaths Newsletter, December, 45

Lawton, B. and Feltham, C. (2000) *Taking Supervision Forward: Enquiries and Trends in Counselling and Psychotherapy*. London: Sage

Mackintosh, E. (1981) Exploring homoeopathy and modern psychotherapy, Part I. *The Homoeopath, 2* (2) 55–60

Mackintosh, E. (1982) Exploring homoeopathy and modern psychotherapy, Part II. *The Homoeopath, 2* (3) 90–5

Mackintosh, E. (1986) The Language of Homoeopathy. *The Homoeopath, 5*(4) 147–9

Martindale, B., Morner, M., Rodriguez, M., and Vit, J-P. (1997) *Supervision and its Vicissitudes*. London: Karnac Books

McMahon, T. (1993) Responding to the Challenge. *Newsletter of the Society of Homeopaths*, December, 18–20

Mearns, D. (1994) *Developing Person-centred Counselling*. London: Sage

Mearns, D. and Thorne, B. (1988) *Person-centred Counselling in Action.* London: Sage

Merry, T. (1999) *Learning and Being in Person-centred Counselling.* Ross-on-Wye: PCCS Books

Morris, E. (1996) Help: Personal and professional development through supervision. *The Homœopath, 60,* 504–5

Norland, M. (1998) A Few Thoughts About Receiving the Case. *The Homœopath, 69,* 10

Page, S. and Wosket, V. (1994) *Supervising the Counsellor.* London: Routledge.

Patterson, C. H. (1964) Supervising students in the counseling practicum. *Journal of Counseling Psychology, 11* (1), 47–53

Patterson, C. H. (1983) A client-centered approach to supervision. *The Counseling Psychologist, 11*(1) 21–5

Pinto, G. (1991) Supervision and support in practice. *The Homœopath,* 11 (3), 83–5

Pinto, G. (1995) In practice: psychotherapy. *Society of Homœopaths Newsletter,* September, 13–4

Pollard, S. (1993) Responding to the challenge: the student's view. *Society of Homœopaths Newsletter,* December, 17–18

Pool, N. (1991) Knowing Ourselves. *The Homœopath, 11* (4), 111–3

Pool, N. (1995) Education and training: psychotherapeutics in the curriculum. *Society of Homœopaths Newsletter,* March, 30

Power, S. (1999) *Nursing Supervision: A Guide for Clinical Practice.* London: Sage

Rice, L. N. (1980). A client-centered approach to the supervision of psychotherapy. In A. K. Hess (Ed.), *Psychotherapy Supervision: Theory, Research and Practice* (pp.136–47). New York: Wiley

Richardson, S. (1981) The patient: prescriber relationship. *The Homœopath,* 2 (2), 61–3

Roberts, E. (1998) The relationship between homoeopathy, therapy and counselling. *The Homœopath, 70,* 46–9

Rogers, C. R. (1951). *Client-centered Therapy.* London: Constable.

Rogers, C. R. (1957) Training individuals to engage in the therapeutic process. In C. R. Strother (Ed.) P*sychology and Mental Health* (pp. 76–92). Washington, D.C.: American Psychological Association

Rogers, C. R. (1969). *Freedom to Learn.* Columbus, OH: Charles E. Merrill

Ryan, S. (1996) The case for supervision in homœopathy. *The Homœopath, 60,* 521–3

Ryan, S. (1997) Pointing a finger at the moon. *Society of Homœopaths Newsletter,* June, 3–5

Ryan, S. (2002) What's in a case? *The Homœopath, 85,* 13–17

Ryan, S. (2003) Personal communication

Sanders, A. (1984) Personal communication

Sankaran, R. (1991) *The Spirit of Homeopathy.* Bombay: Homeopathic Medical

Scaife, J. (Ed.) (2001) *Supervision in the Mental Health Professions: A Practitioner's Guide.* Hove: Brunner-Routledge

Sherr, J. (1986) Personal communication

Sherr, J. (1994) *The Dynamics and Methodology of Homoeopathic Provings.* Malvern: Dynamis

Shipton, G. (Ed.) (1997) *Supervision of Psychotherapy and Counselling.* Buckingham: Open University Press

Sobol, S. (1994) Supervision and support. *Society of Homeopaths Newsletter,* June, 14–16

Society of Homeopaths (2001) *Working Draft: Code of Ethics for Supervisors.* Northampton: Society of Homeopaths.

Society of Homeopaths (2002) *List of Homeopaths working as Supervisors.* Northampton: Society of Homeopaths.

Spring, B. (1990) Homeopathic Politics. Society of Homeopaths Newsletter, March, 47–51

Stoltenberg, C. D. and Delworth, U. (1987) *Supervising Counselors and Therapists: A Developmental Approach.* San Francisco, CA: Jossey-Bass

Townsend, I. (1999a) Supervision: an empowering process. *Society of Homeopaths Newsletter*, March, 32–3

Townsend, I. (1999b) Supervision: long haul, but worthwhile. *Society of Homeopaths Newsletter*, December, 22

Townsend, I. (2001) Manning the lifeboats or sailing the seas with confidence? *Newsletter of the North American Society of Homeopaths*, Spring, 10–14

Townsend, I. (2002) Before the actualising tendency? – Putting the body into person-centred process. *Person-Centred Practice, 10* (2) 81–7

Townsend, I. (2003) Supervision in the service of a profession: a review of the last decade. *The Homœopath* (accepted for publication)

Tudor, K. (2002) Transactional analysis supervision or supervision analyzed transactionally? *Transactional Analysis Journal, 32*(1), 39–55

UCLan (2002) "http://www.uclan.ac.uk/guide2/mission.htm"

van Ooijen, E. (2000) *Clinical Supervision: A Practical Guide.* Edinburgh: Churchill-Livingstone

Villas-Boas Bowen, M. C. (1986) Personality differences and person-centered supervision. *Person-Centered Review, 1*(3), 291–309.

Whitehead, J. (1989) Support groups in Avon. *Society of Homeopaths Newsletter*, September, 26–8

Wood, J. (2001) The reluctant supervisee. *The Homeopath, 80,* 38-9

CHAPTER FOURTEEN

A PSYCHIATRIST'S EXPERIENCE OF PERSON-CENTRED SUPERVISION[1]

RACHEL FREETH

Being a registered doctor in the UK requires adhering to some 14 codes of practice, or 'the duties of a doctor' as the General Medical Council (GMC) describes them (GMC, 2001). These duties are concerned with, for example, providing a good standard of practice and care, maintaining performance and being honest and trustworthy in relationships with patients. Being a psychiatrist requires knowledge, skills and experience in the medical speciality of psychiatry. A psychiatrist is trained to recognise and treat, or 'manage', people with mental illness, psychological, personality and behavioural disturbance. This requires an understanding of 'psychopathology' and the various treatment options that scientific research has developed and attempted to validate. For psychiatrists working in the National Health Service (NHS) it also requires knowledge of the latest management and policy guidelines—both national and local—and the ability to work within and navigate the highly complex system that the NHS mental health services have become.

However, to be the kind of psychiatrist *I* want to be demands much more than the attributes and requirements I have already mentioned. I would describe myself as a psychiatrist who attempts to practise as a psychiatrist in a person-

1. I would like to express my thanks to Mike Worrall, Keith Tudor and Gillian Proctor for their comments during the writing of this chapter. I would also like to express deep gratitude to my supervisor.

centred way. Whether this is possible, and how I attempt to work in a way that is true to myself, congruent with my beliefs, values and ideals, are both questions that raise issues in need of regular reflection. That I have not abandoned this attempt so far is in part due to various supervisory and support networks I have sought out. In particular, it is through receiving individual supervision with a person-centred supervisor.

This chapter, which I hope will be of relevance to other mental health professionals drawn to the Person-Centred Approach (PCA), aims to explore my experience of person-centred supervision and how it relates to my work as a psychiatrist. In this chapter, I describe how person-centred supervision differs from my experience of supervision in the NHS. I then highlight the issues that have become a regular focus in supervision, and in particular some of the tensions and difficulties involved in trying to bring person-centred attitudes and philosophy into the NHS mental health culture. Finally, I will reflect on the supportive aspects of this kind of supervision. I begin by offering a little personal history by way of describing how and why I have come to value the PCA, especially as advocates and enthusiasts of the approach are rarely to be found amongst the ranks of psychiatrists and other mental health professionals.

WHY THE PERSON-CENTRED APPROACH?

My passage through medical school was not a smooth one and on numerous occasions I had serious doubts that I had chosen the profession most suited to me. I realised that I had entered a competitive environment that seemed preoccupied with values with which I felt little sympathy. When I started to work in the NHS I was confronted with a culture and ethos in which any person sensitive to human distress and suffering and who wants to provide care (regardless of cure), unimpeded by politically and economically driven service expectations, agendas and guidelines, could find themselves drowning. Many jump ship to preserve their own health and sanity.

This, combined with my personal experience of depression, has led me to reflect on those aspects of caring and of helping relationships I believe are important and of value in the healing process. Receiving my own therapy both at medical school and several times since has also played an instrumental part in this process of reflection. It has also fuelled an interest in psychotherapy and counselling. This led to my training as a counsellor in the person-centred tradition, something I undertook away from the NHS establishment and the medical profession. In general, though, I regard psychotherapy and counselling as an addition to the resources scientific medicine provides and not necessarily as a substitute.

My particular interest in the humanistic tradition and particularly the PCA could in many ways be a back-lash against the preoccupation with a mechanistic or reductionist understanding of human beings, the overemphasis on science and the so-called 'disease model'. It was also perhaps a reaction against what I perceived as the sterile and impersonal aspects of working as a doctor, particularly in hospitals, where persons are patients (and therefore not persons), or worse, 'cases'. However, it is frequently the sheer pressures of working in an overstretched health care system and being faced daily with illness and death that seem to make it necessary for many doctors and carers to employ defensive attitudes that depersonalise people. As a method of coping, or defensive strategy, it is understandable. Unfortunately, as Mearns and Thorne (1999) put it, 'professional helpers are conditioned not to become "involved" with their clients and advised to remain objective or even gently aloof' (p. 23). Here 'professional detachment' is lauded as the mark of a good professional. Of this I am very critical.

By contrast, the PCA embodies what I believe should lie at the heart of helping relationships. I value its emphasis on viewing human beings as having intrinsic value and extraordinary uniqueness, and its belief in human beings' capacity, given the right conditions, to change and grow. The fact that the approach lends itself to exploration of the spiritual yearnings of human beings, recently explored by Thorne (2002), also attracts me to it. But perhaps what most draws me is its understanding of the need to work at relational depth and to offer the core conditions as the most potent ingredients for healing and growth. I value the emphasis the PCA places on the quality of the relationship in the helping process.

What I try to bring to my role is an extra dimension, the emotional demands of which are extremely heavy. It is in recognition of these extra demands that I have not pursued higher specialist training to become a consultant. Precisely because it is an additional dimension to my work, I recognise my need for extra support and supervision, the likes of which I am unlikely to find within the NHS. My supervision is therefore a private arrangement that I have organised in my own time and at my own expense, although some NHS Trusts may pay for external supervision for some psychiatrists.

NHS SUPERVISION AND PERSON-CENTRED SUPERVISION: A CONTRAST

Good supervision is a scarce resource in the NHS and for many mental health professionals it is neither routinely nor regularly provided. It might also seem astonishing, particularly to those who practise counselling and psychotherapy, that supervision for psychiatrists is a relatively new requirement laid down by the

Royal College of Psychiatrists, and only for doctors in training; it is not a requirement that consultants be supervised. Indeed, it seems that a consultant is one whose practice doesn't need supervision. Furthermore, few consultants, who are traditionally the supervisors, have been trained in supervision (Sembhi and Livingston, 2000). Even more alarming is evidence from one piece of research in which the supervisors, when questioned about their role as supervisors, rated communication skills as fairly irrelevant in that role (Riley, 1998).

In addition, the issue of supervision for doctors is currently overshadowed by the government's preoccupation, which it shares with the medical profession, with 'appraisal' and 'revalidation'. These are processes currently in development. Yearly appraisal is designed as a professional development tool, but many within the profession regard it as a review of doctors' clinical performance and service delivery. Five-yearly revalidation aims to assess a doctor's fitness to practise in order to maintain their registration with the GMC. These processes seem largely a response to reassure the government and the public of doctors' competence in light of the terrible medical scandals in recent years. Examples include the murders committed by GP Harold Shipman and the deaths of children receiving cardiac surgery at the Bristol Royal Infirmary resulting in a major public inquiry and nearly 200 recommendations in the final report (Kennedy, 2001).

For a doctor in training, his or her supervisor, now usually referred to as an 'educational supervisor', is usually the consultant with whom the trainee works. In other words, the boss is the supervisor from whom a job reference will be required and written assessments requested by the relevant training body. This kind of line-management supervision, where there is a clear power imbalance, is not unusual in the NHS generally. Little wonder that it may not feel safe to bring problems or difficult issues, clinical or personal, to the supervisor's attention. The British Association for Counselling and Psychotherapy's (BACP) *Ethical Framework* speaks of the 'obligation for all counsellors, psychotherapists, supervisors and trainers to receive supervision/consultative support independently of any managerial relationships' (2002, p. 7).

My experience of person-centred supervision has also demonstrated to me other limitations of NHS supervision for psychiatrists, and I suspect for other doctors and health-care professionals. For doctors in training, supervision is often focused on acquiring knowledge and clinical skills or can take the form of 'clinical supervision' which Scaife (2001) describes as 'a process for the analysis of performance' (p. 96). It can also take the form of 'case management'. In other words, it is weighted towards having a 'managerial' and somewhat 'educative' function, two of the three functions of supervision described by Kadushin (1976). The third function is the 'supportive' function which, in general, is less well provided, at least for doctors. NHS supervision has rarely provided me with a space to reflect openly on or to off-load how I am experiencing my role, to evaluate my coping strategies or to talk about my thoughts and feelings concerning my relationships with patients and colleagues. What I *do* is given priority over who I *am* and how I *feel*. In my opinion this demonstrates a narrow understanding of the purpose and functions of supervision.

NHS supervision is also driven by the Department of Health strategy of 'clinical governance' which is defined as a 'range of activities required to improve the quality of health services' (Rosen, 2000, p. 551). One of the purposes of supervision in the NHS is to continuously monitor standards to improve care. It is developed as a system of accountability. Hawkins and Shohet (2000) make the following point: 'accountability has become increasingly prominent, as our culture moves towards increased professionalisation. This is paralleled in supervision with its emphasis on accountability and professionalisation' (p. xvii). I regard this as a disturbing trend in which the workers are supervised to increase the efficiency, effectiveness and productivity of the organisation according to the increasingly consumerist values of the NHS. In other words, the emphasis is on performance management and measurable outcomes. Supervision in the NHS seems not to be primarily about the needs of its workers. There is little or no recognition that the workers' needs and well-being matter in their own right. This is probably partly why there is such a recruitment crisis across most of the professions in the NHS, particularly the nursing and medical professions. By contrast, in person-centred supervision my needs and well-being are recognised as important. I have the freedom to do a lot of talking about myself and how I feel. The message I receive from my supervisor is not just that patients matter, but that I matter. This is especially liberating.

Person-centred supervision, unlike my experience of NHS supervision, has never felt threatening to me and I have experienced it as supportive and empowering. I value what Merry (2002) has described as its 'collaborative inquiry approach to supervision [that] acknowledges that both people involved are self-directed and both can contribute equally to the process' (p.174). My supervisor enables me to reflect on my work by focusing on my own understanding and evaluation. I also know that when I am with my supervisor, it is my agenda that is important and that I determine what I bring to supervision according to what I perceive my needs to be. It is important for me to know that this is my time, that it will not be interrupted and that I am receiving my supervisor's full attention.

For me it is also important that my supervisor has knowledge and experience of working in NHS mental health services and that he is familiar with the ethos and culture of the NHS, managerial and political issues, as well as the language of mental illness and treatment. On a practical level it saves a lot of time in that I don't have to explain, for example, how services are constructed or what various diagnostic labels mean to psychiatrists. I am confident that he is able to understand my 'frame of reference' as a mental health professional and psychiatrist with the demands of my role, particularly the pressures of work and the frustrations of working with limited resources. However, it is also important that he has no connection with the NHS Trust in which I work and therefore has no managerial responsibility or accountability for my work.

Another key aspect of person-centred supervision that I deeply value is the attentiveness my supervisor gives to the quality of his relationship with me. This is in stark contrast to some of my ghastly experiences of NHS supervision when I have had little or no rapport with my supervisor and when I have come away feeling that their role as a supervisor is rather a chore to them and that they care little about the quality of their relationship with me.

Recurring issues in person-centred supervision

In this section I describe some of the issues I bring regularly to supervision, and which relate particularly to the tensions and difficulties of trying to bring the PCA into psychiatric settings. Whilst I do have a diploma in counselling, I do not currently practise as a counsellor within my post as a psychiatrist. I have done in the past and have highlighted elsewhere some of the challenges of counselling using the PCA in psychiatric settings (Freeth, 2001). But I do try to work, where possible, in a way that patients may find helpful or therapeutic. Person-centred supervision enables me to reflect on how I attempt this and how my attitudes, beliefs and values impact on my way of working.

Throughout this section I shall use the word 'patient' rather than 'client', despite some person-centred practitioners' discomfort with that term, as this is the convention commonly used in the settings in which I work, particularly in in-patient settings, although the word 'client' is more often used in the community setting.

The core conditions

I find it extremely difficult and challenging to reflect on the attitudes and qualities I bring to my relationships with patients and also with colleagues. However, person-centred supervision greatly assists me in this process. Without it I am sure I would be too encumbered and preoccupied by other professional issues that my aspirations to work in a person-centred way would remain just that—aspirations translating into practice only superficially.

My offering of the core conditions of congruence, empathy and unconditional positive regard is often sidelined by the particular demands and expectations imposed upon me as a psychiatrist and also impeded by the ethos of mental health settings whose values and attitudes I often perceive as anti-therapeutic. I discuss with my supervisor my struggle to offer these conditions, reflecting on 'internal' personal factors as well as 'external' environmental or organisational factors, both of which have an impact.

I also need to bear in mind that for constructive personality change to occur, Rogers (1957) describes six conditions. In psychiatric settings, particularly in hospital, the first condition of establishing psychological contact is especially relevant since many patients are psychotic or acutely disturbed in other ways and their ability to establish and maintain contact is impaired. I do believe that the PCA is just as relevant for people with psychosis and I am aware of Prouty's 'pre-therapy' (Prouty, Van Werde and Pörtner, 2002), although so far I have not developed this way of working in my job. In what follows I focus on the core conditions assuming that psychological contact is established.

Congruence

> Helpers generally support a norm of incongruence. Indeed, perhaps we should be dismayed at the level of incongruence we find in mental health provision. (Mearns and Thorne, 1999, p. 83)

This highlights for me the huge challenge of daring to be freely and deeply myself, being aware of what I am experiencing, as well as being authentic in my relationships.

Being in touch with my inner experiencing is facilitated by my supervisor's attitudes towards me and by providing an environment where I am less likely to feel defensive. This is something crucially missing in mental health settings, in which my capacity to sense deeply what I am feeling is often diminished and where operating from my intellect is routinely a way of coping with the levels of psychological distress I encounter in patients, as well as many other pressures. Often it is only in my supervision that I become aware of, for example, the extent of my feelings of powerlessness, anger or despair, whether these feelings are generalised or in relation to particular patients. It is also hard to listen to my feelings of compassion, tenderness and love, since my working environment does not generally encourage such expression and might be uncomfortable with this type of emotional reaction. My supervisor also enables me to think about my values and beliefs and articulate them more clearly.

The other aspect of congruence—of attempting to be genuine and attending to what and how I communicate—doesn't feature as frequently in supervision as reflecting on empathy or unconditional positive regard. I am generally not afraid of being seen as a person, as human as anyone else, rather than as a professional hiding behind a mask. If anything I need to pay attention to how my desire to be known as a person could potentially lead me to overeager self-disclosure that may be unhelpful to the other. However, there are instances when I need to explore with my supervisor whether and how to express emotions and reactions with which I am uncomfortable, which are blocking empathic understanding and which I would prefer to keep hidden. Examples include when I feel low in mood or very tired. When this is the case my heart sinks to be faced with a clinic or the need to provide an urgent assessment. Other challenges to congruent expression are when I see patients I find hard to like, or emotionally draining to be with. In these instances it can be difficult to know how to handle strong emotional reactions and what might be a congruent response.

Empathy

'Empathy sounds good in theory, but . . .' This is a frequent response from mental health professionals and I am prone to such thoughts myself at times. The questions for me here are why do I aspire to develop empathic understanding and what is it about being a psychiatrist and working in NHS mental health services that interferes with the empathic process? I explore both of these questions in supervision.

It is interesting to note that being a doctor and a psychiatrist doesn't require me as such to empathise with my patients. It is taken as a given that we should care for and respect our patients—'make the care of your patients your first concern' (GMC, 2001). Yet the particulars of that care are not made explicit. It would be interesting to assess the various ways in which the concept of empathy is understood, or not understood, by the medical and allied professions. Empathy is a word much bandied about, but my impression is that it is commonly substituted for something that could be more accurately described as sympathy. It is not generally understood as a 'process', a way of 'being with' and of attempting to understand a person's whole frame of reference, other than for the purpose of uncovering 'psychopathology' and symptoms. Empathy, at least for psychiatrists, is usually taught as a skill and a technique, or a style of response to patients. The primary purpose for mental health professionals 'using' empathy is not usually out of recognition that it is in itself healing and therapeutic, but rather to gain information.

My dilemma is that I am required to gather information as a detached scientific observer in order to evaluate and make judgements about treatment. This also requires me to be directive in encounters with patients, and conscious of pressures of time, particularly when I am in a clinic with a list of patients to see one after another. Therefore, when I also want to give a patient space to tell their own story in their own time, in their own way and just be with them in that, I experience within myself a major conflict of agendas. Empathy at a deep level in psychiatric settings is a rare quality and attitude. The agenda is more often about 'doing' and 'doing to' the patient, 'problem-solving' and 'symptom control'. Professionals are also defended against emotional involvement or pain and in this environment, according to Rowan (2002), 'empathy is very restricted, and all we get is a "limited liability" activity' (p. 26).

My experience of attempting to offer empathy is one of the hardest and most demanding aspects of my work. As a clinician it is not usually expected of me to listen to patients in depth in a therapeutic way. It is not validated as part of my role. That is not to say that my listening and empathy are not appreciated, just that it is not acknowledged that it is a highly conscious and demanding process. The fact that it is neither acknowledged nor supported as part of my work is one of the reasons I feel it necessary to have a supervisor who does value the role of empathy and supports my attempt to develop and offer it.

My supervisor also enables me to examine what in practice makes empathy so difficult and demanding in my particular work setting. I have already mentioned my conflict of agendas. Being able to talk about this conflict helps me to manage it more comfortably. I also use supervision to reflect on my capacity to empathise with particularly disturbed patients, for example, those who are experiencing a psychotic process or whose personalities are deeply damaged. In these encounters, a deep level of emotional involvement carries the risk that I might become overwhelmed or lost in the other person's world. There can be a danger of becoming emotionally identified and here supervision helps me to stay grounded in my own identity. If empathy is also about being a willing participant or temporary companion, then 'one enters into the life of the patient and is affected and sometimes changed by the encounter' (Yalom, 1991, p.13). How much am I willing to be a participant and how prepared am I to be changed by empathic engagement in my daily encounters with patients? To be consistently emotionally attuned to others and to people who experience depths of mental pain and distress is costly. What level of personal cost and vulnerability am I prepared to accept? My supervisor never attempts to provide an answer to such questions but helps me to explore them, which in turn helps me to live with them, usually without clear answers.

Unconditional positive regard

Like the other two core conditions, unconditional positive regard is something I find myself struggling with regularly. With regard to this attitude I use supervision particularly to explore what may interfere with or block my experience of unconditional positive regard for my patients (as well as for my colleagues). I have noticed time and again certain conditions I impose upon my patients, such as whether they are 'getting better' or not. I also experience my attitudes influenced by the ways in which I am positively or negatively perceived by patients and whether I am trusted or not. I notice how my own emotional needs (for example, to be liked and approved of) shape my attitudes. I also notice how, when I feel burdened, I find it especially difficult to offer unconditional positive regard towards those who are likely to place further emotional demands on me. Supervision has provided me with an extremely important space in which I can acknowledge my emotional needs and the impact they have on my relationships with patients and colleagues.

Supervision also helps me to be aware of how easily influenced or 'contaminated' I become by the collective attitudes of other mental health professionals. Patients with personality disorders in particular evoke condemning and judgemental attitudes within staff, as well as feelings of powerlessness. Likewise, some 'difficult to engage with' patients are blamed and condemned for 'not wanting' to get better. With supervision I am more able to stay alert to the danger of 'internalising' unhelpful and judgemental attitudes towards certain patients. In addition it empowers me to stick my neck out and risk being accused of being 'soft-headed' should I dare to express positive regard towards patients who are, for example, aggressive, violent, who know how to manipulate the psychiatric system or who are unable or unwilling to take personal responsibility. That said, like my colleagues I am human and I know my capacity to offer this core condition is all too limited. Here it is important that I don't judge myself too harshly and risk placing on myself the conditions of worth I am placing on others. I need to allow myself to be human and be more ready to forgive myself. My supervisor's attitudes towards me help me to develop greater positive self-regard.

PHILOSOPHICAL, THEORETICAL AND POLITICAL ISSUES

Anyone trying to bring person-centred philosophy, attitudes and values into NHS mental health services is likely to encounter within themselves numerous tensions and conflicts. The PCA is a radical departure from the prevailing philosophies that are dictated by managers, who are in turn dictated to by the government. The PCA is also in conflict with the more commonly used theoretical models of personality development and psychological distress, the 'medical model' of helping and the focus on 'treatment' which underpins modern-day psychiatry. As well as providing a vital opportunity to explore and discuss these conflicts, person-centred supervision also, crucially, keeps me from becoming hopelessly confused and overwhelmed as I try to manage the dynamic tension of holding person-centred values within an organisation with a very different set of values.

I use a significant portion of my time in supervision to explore these issues. I want to feel intellectually secure about what I am doing at work and not act unthinkingly or necessarily according to received medical wisdom. In this regard I want to trust my own experience, this being a quality upon which Rogers (1959) places great value. My supervisor enables my experience to stand out more clearly.

What follows is a brief outline of some of the philosophical, theoretical and political issues I bring to supervision in the hope of achieving greater conceptual clarity. Whilst not being able to reconcile certain differences and conflicts between the PCA and the expected role of a psychiatrist, it is helpful for me to be clearer at least about what those differences are and where the tensions lie. Usually the issues I bring to supervision are in direct response to feeling frustrated, confused or uncomfortable in my work with particular patients. In other words, I am not usually discussing ideas and theory with my supervisor in the abstract.

Origins of psychological disturbance

Thinking about personality development and the origins of psychological disturbance within psychiatric settings rarely incorporates the concept of the actualising tendency and many mental health practitioners would regard it as a naive concept. The actualising tendency is probably misunderstood as implying that people will get better on their own without treatment or practical assistance and without professionals needing to do anything. Perhaps this view reflects partly a fear that the optimistic view of human nature underpinning the PCA threatens the very existence of mental health professionals' jobs.

Debate about the origins of psychological disturbance becomes relevant when decisions are made on treating and managing patients with mental illness or emotional distress. Individual psychiatrists will have their own theoretical leanings and this will influence their decisions about how best to treat or manage a patient. For example, psychiatrists who are biologically-oriented may focus more on mental illness as an imbalance of chemical neurotransmitters and will rely more heavily on the use of physical treatments such as medication. However, the debate about causes is not as relevant as one might imagine. This is because in practice what probably influences psychiatrists and other mental health practitioners most, are the actual resources available to mental health services, despite government promises in *The NHS Plan* (Department of Health, 2000) to give patients more choice about what they want. Treatment with medication to alleviate symptoms will nearly always take precedence over consideration of longer-term psychological therapies. Psychiatric services are increasingly geared towards dealing with the immediate problem in the cheapest way possible, given the resources available, often paying minimal attention to possible causes of disturbance. Unfortunately, since this is also largely a reactive rather than a proactive response, in the long run it is neither cost-effective nor efficient, and short-term improvements are often not sustainable. Psychiatrists are expected to adopt a 'symptom-control', 'problem-management' and 'action-orientated' approach. Therefore, the patient is often seen as a collection of symptoms and problems about which a psychiatrist and mental health services are frequently expected to 'do' something.

Assessment and diagnosis

Rogers did not reject the notion of diagnosis. However, he viewed it in a radically different way from the medical profession in general and from many, if not most, other schools of psychotherapy. For him 'therapy *is* diagnosis, and this diagnosis is a process which goes on in the experience of the client, rather than in the intellect of the clinician' (1951, p. 223).

Assessment with the goal of formulating a diagnosis is a regular source of unease for me given that 'the person-centred approach tends to view these activities as unnecessary and even harmful to the development of a counselling relationship' (Merry, 2002, p. 75). Despite reminding myself that I am not, in my current work place, in a counselling relationship with patients, like most person-centred counsellors I am generally uncomfortable with categorising patients into diagnostic groupings. There are, however, some patients who find it comforting and a relief to receive a diagnosis or be told that they have an illness, the implication of which is often that a chemical imbalance is in part responsible. Here patients might feel less guilty or blame themselves less for their distress. It is important that I am alert to these possibilities.

There are many reasons for my own discomfort with using diagnoses. One is my distaste when I am required 'to sum up a person with a diagnostic phrase and numerical category' (Yalom, 1991, p. 185). Yalom further describes it as 'doing violence to the being of another. If we relate to people believing that we can categorise them, we will neither identify nor nurture the parts, the vital parts, of the other that transcends category' (p. 185).

Other objections to using diagnostic categories include the stigmatising effect of labels and the tendency to respond to people with certain disorders in a stereotyped way and with prejudiced attitudes, especially people labelled with personality disorders. Diagnosis in psychiatry is subjective, based on observation of behaviour and subjective assessment of mood, thoughts and perceptions. This in itself makes the issue fraught with tensions and can lead to disagreement amongst clinicians. Diagnosis is rooted in the 'disease model' which emphasises the existence of a physical pathology. However, in psychiatry the existence of physical pathology is often just hypothesis. The emphasis on a disease process also leaves little room for the belief in the actualising tendency, nor for the humanistic view that human beings are essentially good with intrinsic worth, however outwardly destructive their behaviour might be. I also think sometimes that diagnostic labelling serves the purpose of making the practitioner feel clever and powerful and I have spotted that tendency in myself occasionally. It is also another way of depersonalising patients and keeping them at an emotional distance.

The language of diagnosis dominates psychiatric settings. To me it often feels like an alien or hostile language, even though I am familiar and also in some ways at home with it. I am required to speak it because it is what most mental health professionals, and the medical profession in particular, most relate to. This issue regularly places me in a dilemma of how to speak about patients as people and it requires constant vigilance to be careful about my use of language and the attitudes and values that I convey, not just through the words I choose, but also in how I speak them. This vigilance is tiring. This issue also highlights for me a sense of professional isolation—a sense of being in a foreign land and longing to cross paths with someone who speaks the language of person-centred values. Person-centred supervision, therefore, provides me with a meeting place where I can speak the language of the PCA without fear of being misunderstood or ridiculed. In supervision I can speak about persons, about human beings and not about patients with a diagnosis. I can also speak a language where words such as 'healing', 'compassion' and 'love' are more common currency than words such as 'illness', 'treatment' and 'management'.

Treatment and cure

From assessment to diagnosis to 'applying' treatment, the psychiatrist has been invested in the role of expert who applies his or her expertise in the attempt to 'cure' the patient. Even more disturbing than the notion of 'doing to' the patient, with the patient as the passive and dependent receiver of treatment, is the increasing pressure felt by psychiatrists and mental health services to be *seen* to be doing something, even if what they do is not actually in the patient's interests. This reflects a high level of fear and paranoia within psychiatric services (and social services) about litigation and the threat of being accused of doing nothing to prevent the tragedies that are sometimes inevitable in a free society that attempts to respect individual choice.

Unlike the non-directive approach of the person-centred counsellor, the very directivity of the psychiatric approach makes it unlikely that patients will feel in control. In theory, except for patients placed on a Section of the Mental Health Act 1983 (in England and Wales, 1982 in Scotland) or being treated against their will, patients do have a choice to accept, or not, the treatment offered. But is it really a choice? Patients are sometimes left in little doubt about what the professionals advise and what the professionals think the patient ought to do and what the predetermined goals of treatment are. Patients are under immense pressure to comply, either with the treatment offered or even with thinking about illness as a psychiatrist would, dismissing the patient's own subjective construction of themselves and the world they live in. In fact, the patient's agreement with the psychiatrist's understanding is seen to represent mental health or 'insight' into their illness and disagreement is often seen as proof of 'illness'. It is rare to find attitudes amongst mental health professionals that place emphasis on patients being the experts in their lives and attempting a *genuinely* collaborative therapeutic relationship in which the mental health professional facilitates rather then directs. However, in situations where a patient is acutely disturbed, psychotic or at high risk of harming themselves or others, this issue is particularly challenging and difficult since the approach of mental health professionals will be one of control.

The notion of treatment also raises the thorny issue of there being predetermined goals and outcomes towards which mental health professionals work. The patient can be robbed of being in a 'process' that they dictate, rather than their psychiatrist. The patient can also be robbed of an opportunity to view their experience as a 'journey' that is unique, deeply personal, and from which they can derive their own meaning. Some of my most fulfilling moments as a psychiatrist are when I can be faithful to a patient's process. I was once very moved when I was given a little carved golden scarab beetle a patient brought back for me from her trip to Egypt. In Egyptian mythology scarab beetles are often golden and are considered sacred animals symbolising the sun. However, it was the fact that they bury themselves in the sand for a time before re-emerging that was meaningful to her. She likened this to her own psychological process, to which I had managed to stay faithful. Supervision is also, therefore, a place for me to share positive experiences of such encounters with patients, such as this example. It is important to me not just to use supervision as a kind of dumping ground for problems and difficulties, but also as a place in which I can celebrate heartening and fulfilling experiences.

Although speaking about psychotherapy rather than psychiatry, Sanders and Tudor (2001) assert that:

> If psychotherapy is not to remain stuck in a medical (mental illness)/ pathology paradigm, it needs to develop a view about healing *process* (as distinct from a fixed cure) and to concern itself with health and a vision of human beings and society. (p. 155)

In my ideal fantasy of psychiatric services in the future I would see mental health professionals in very large numbers addressing the same concerns.

The issue of power

I have touched on this issue implicitly many times throughout what I have written so far. However, I would like to address it now rather more explicitly since it is an issue that highlights fundamental differences between the role of a psychiatrist and that of a person-centred practitioner. It is also one that features regularly in my supervision.

Natiello (2001) describes the difficult and delicate task of maintaining one's own power (and expertise) whilst creating a climate where others can claim or maintain theirs. As a psychiatrist this is particularly difficult given the tremendous power invested in me and the readiness with which so many patients disown their own power. Many of these patients have long histories of being disempowered by psychiatric services and professionals. I find it extremely disturbing to encounter so many people who have become dependent upon services and experts with much of that dependence having been created, or at least perpetuated, by the psychiatric system itself.

I have recently begun to explore more my inner conflicts and ambivalence concerning my power as a psychiatrist. Whilst part of me feels highly uncomfortable with power (perhaps because it can fuel patients' suspicions and hostility towards me), another part of me values it. If I didn't value it then I probably wouldn't be able to remain practising as a doctor. The challenge for me, then, is to use my power wisely and in a way that acts in the interests of patients. In doing this I also need to be aware that at the same time I may use my power, without realising it, to serve my own ego and mask my own insecurities. In other words I need to be aware of the tremendous potential for misusing my power, however well intentioned I might be. Supervision plays an important part in helping me keep in my awareness the complexities of the power dynamic as it relates to my relationships with patients and with colleagues. Supervision also helps me consider the organisational context of these relationships and the organisational context of the NHS within which power is so easily misused (Freeth, 2003).

For person-centred practitioners the challenge is to try to work with the concept of 'collaborative power' and to strive towards egalitarian relationships. Natiello (2001) describes this as being 'in radical conflict with the prevailing paradigm of authoritarian power' (p. 11). As an organisation the NHS works from the paradigm of 'authoritarian power'. This is largely the result of governmental influence, leadership and management styles, and the medical profession. The medical model generally works from the position of authority and expertise. Within such an organisation, the challenges and difficulties for person-centred practitioners are immense. Natiello argues that 'real reform in existing institutions requires a paradigmatic shift in attitudes, values, relationship, and leadership style that have prevailed from the beginning' (p. 77).

It is also deeply regrettable and misguided that the issue of power is not a regular source for honest personal reflection for psychiatrists and other mental health professionals through, for example, non-managerial supervision. This is particularly disturbing given that misuse and abuse of power by professionals has done and continues to do untold damage to patients. Proctor (2002) describes how 'psychiatric systems are set up around hierarchical systems of control and power' (p. 4). She also highlights the client's feeling of powerlessness as one of the most significant contributors to their experience of psychological distress.

It is not just my discomfort with my power that I explore in supervision, but also the feelings of powerlessness I regularly encounter in the course of my work. Examples of what creates this sense of powerlessness include responding to the pressures of managerial and political control, and the requirement to respond to more and more policies and targets without the resources to do so. I also feel powerless in my attempts to provide care for individuals whilst being able to do little about the context, such as the family or community, within which that individual lives, and which may be a significant contributor to their psychological disturbance.

It is an uncomfortable paradox to have power, to be perceived as powerful, and yet also to feel so powerless much of the time. Learning to live with this and how it impacts on my work and way of relating is something for which supervision has become crucial.

THE SUPPORTIVE FUNCTION OF PERSON-CENTRED SUPERVISION

Working in the NHS and within the mental health profession can sometimes feel like attempting 12 rounds in a boxing ring. This analogy was offered to me recently by my supervisor and I have elaborated on it. He has become my 'second', the person who waits in the corner of the ring, provides me with refreshment, dries me down with a towel, offers me a bucket to spit in, and gives me vital words of support and encouragement.

It is the supportive function of supervision within NHS health care settings that in general seems to me to be alarmingly lacking. Therefore, even were I to have no interest in the PCA as a way of being as a psychiatrist, person-centred supervision holds for me enormous value for its supportive aspects alone. What I particularly appreciate is the way in which my supervisor attends to the quality of his relationship with me, through offering me the qualities of empathic understanding, congruence and unconditional positive regard. This has a deep impact upon me and it has become vital in sustaining me in my working environment when the NHS culture, like society generally, is preoccupied by the need to blame—and name and shame, as in 'failing' NHS Trusts—and seems to have lost a fundamental sense of trust. The NHS is a hugely powerful organisation in which its workers are more likely to feel criticised and have their weaknesses highlighted than be praised or thanked, and where the workers rarely feel heard, let alone understood.

It has also been vital for me to receive from my supervisor his support and encouragement in my trying to be a psychiatrist working in a person-centred way. I am an idealist and, like many professionals in the NHS with high ideals, I experience pressures and tensions that regularly threaten them. Many of my colleagues would also consider me very naive to have such ideals, although holding ideals in itself is not naive, since it's what you do with them and how you live with them that matters. I often feel disillusioned, despairing, frustrated and angry as a psychiatrist and this is further fuelled when I examine the way I am required to work—a way that compromises the values of the PCA. These emotions I regularly off-load in supervision. This makes it an important safety valve, as well as enabling me to examine my ideals continually and to keep them alive.

I experience my supervisor acknowledging and understanding the heavy emotional burden of what I do. Within supervision I can listen to myself more easily and monitor my own physical and emotional health. In doing this I also need to feel safe and free to talk about my personal life and social circumstances, and to examine what impact my personal life, with its joys and losses, is having on my work. The same goes for needing to consider how my work affects my personal life and how to keep a reasonable work/life balance, this being something that traditionally doctors have not been good at or enabled to do. I am able to explore in supervision when I might need to pay more attention to my own emotional needs, such as the need for more relaxation or fun in life. I also acknowledge my tendency to stretch myself to the limit. Supervision helps me to consider my own work ethic and when I need to ease off and put myself first.

CONCLUSION

Clearly it is unusual for a psychiatrist operating in the NHS to uphold the values and attitudes of the person-centred approach, and perhaps this does make my need for person-centred supervision somewhat of a special case. However, I argue strongly that even were I not trying to practice the PCA, many of the issues I have highlighted are ones which most psychiatrists and other mental health professionals also confront. This would make person-centred supervision extremely useful as a space for all practitioners to think about such issues in an unhurried way. It would also attend to professional development needs and provide a non-judgemental space in which to off-load and feel supported in the highly pressured and emotionally challenging environments of mental health settings.

It is a particular travesty that many, and perhaps most, consultant psychiatrists are neither offered nor receive regular supervision, and that only recently have they become obliged to undergo a yearly appraisal of their work. It is also regrettable that supervision, within the psychiatric profession at least, tends to focus much more on intellectual development in terms of acquiring knowledge and skills. The development of 'emotional intelligence', self-awareness and relational skills and attitudes are left way behind. According to Davies (2000), within the medical profession 'deformation and denial of emotion is endemic and seen as normal for doctors' (p. 50). I agree. For me, person-centred supervision helps to redress the imbalance created by wholly inadequate supervision structures for which, in the psychiatric profession, there are 'remarkably few guidelines' (Cottrell, 1999, p. 88).

One of the fundamental questions I ask myself continually in supervision is this: given that I find being a person-centred psychiatrist so uncomfortable and difficult, why do I continue trying to be one? With the support and encouragement my supervisor gives me I am (just about) sufficiently resourced to keep trying. I also believe that I can use my role as a psychiatrist to speak out more effectively about those things I believe are important, such as the PCA. For the time being at least, I am prepared to try to challenge the system from within, but I need to stay mindful of the personal cost, as well as the risk of developing overvalued ideas of my own importance.

When societal and organisational attitudes and pressures continue to test to the limit my faith in the infinite worth of the human person and in the value of relationship in the healing process, person-centred supervision helps me in 'the awesome task of becoming fully human . . . and embracing the challenge of an existential and spiritual order' (Thorne, 2002, p. 3). When I left my previous job a community psychiatric nurse wrote in my leaving card that she experienced me as 'human', followed by 'call yourself a doctor?' This at least assures me that I am to some degree successful in the task of becoming fully human, of being both a person and a professional, and that being a psychiatrist is not necessarily an impediment to this, even if it often feels like it. Person-centred supervision empowers me in this task.

REFERENCES

British Association for Counselling and Psychotherapy (2002) *Ethical Framework for Good Practice in Counselling and Psychotherapy.* Rugby: BACP

Cottrell, D. (1999) Supervision. *Advances in Psychiatric Treatment, 5,* 83–8

Davies, P. (2000) It never did me any harm: A review of the emotional world of doctors. In H. Ghodse, S. Mann and P. Johnson, (Eds.) *Doctors and their health* (pp.44–51). Sutton: Reed Healthcare Publishing

Department of Health (2000) *The NHS Plan: A Plan for Investment. A Plan for Reform.* London: DoH

Freeth, R. (2001) Challenges of counselling in psychiatric settings. In K. Etherington, (Ed.) *Counsellors in Health Settings* (pp.209–26). London: Jessica Kingsley Publishers

Freeth, R. (2003) Therapy in the NHS: Who's really got the power? *Healthcare Counselling and Psychotherapy Journal, 3*(1), 10–11

General Medical Council (2001) *Good Medical Practice.* (3rd edn.). London: GMC

Hawkins, P. and Shohet, R. (2000) *Supervision in the Helping Professions.* (2nd edn). Buckingham: Open University Press

Kadushin, A. (1976) *Supervision in Social Work.* New York: Columbia University Press

Kennedy, I. (2001) *Learning from Bristol: The Report of Public Inquiry into Children's Heart Surgery at the Bristol Royal Infirmary 1984–1995.* Bristol: The Royal Infirmary Inquiry

Mearns, D. and Thorne, B. (1999) *Person-Centred Counselling in Action. (2nd edn.).* London: Sage Publications

Merry, T. (2002) *Learning and Being in Person-Centred Counselling. (2nd edn.).* Ross-on-Wye: PCCS Books

Natiello, P. (2001) *The Person-Centred Approach: A Passionate Presence.* Ross-on-Wye: PCCS Books

Proctor, G. (2002) *The Dynamics of Power in Counselling and Psychotherapy: Ethics, Politics and Practice.* Ross-on-Wye: PCCS Books

Prouty, G. F., Van Werde, D. and Pörtner, M. (2002) *Pre-Therapy.* Ross-on-Wye: PCCS Books

Riley, W. (1998) Appraising appraisal. *British Medical Journal: Career focus,* 317

Rogers, C. R. (1951) *Client-Centered Therapy.* London: Constable

Rogers, C. R. (1957) The necessary and sufficient conditions of therapeutic personality change. *Journal of Consulting Psychology, 21*(2), 95–103

Rogers, C.R. (1959) A theory of therapy, personality, and interpersonal relationships, as developed in the client-centred framework. In S. Koch (Ed.) *Psychology: A study of a science, Vol.3. Formulations of the Person and the Social Context* (pp.184–256). New York: McGraw-Hill

Rosen, R. (2000) Improving quality in the changing world of primary care. *British Medical Journal, 321,* 551–54

Rowan, J. (2002) Three levels of empathy. *Self and Society, 30*(4), 20–7

Sanders, P. and Tudor, K. (2001) This is therapy: a person-centred critique of the contemporary psychiatric system. In C. Newness, G. Holmes and C. Dunn (Eds.) *This is Madness Too: Critical Perspectives on Mental Health Services* (pp.147–60). Ross-on-Wye: PCCS Books

Scaife, J. (2001) *Supervision in the Mental Health Professions: A Practitioner's Guide.* Brighton: Brunner-Routledge

Sembhi, S. and Livingston, G. (2000) What trainees and trainers think about supervision. *Psychiatric Bulletin, 24,* 379–81

Thorne, B. (2002) *The Mystical Power of Person-Centred Therapy: Hope Beyond Despair.* London: Whurr Publishers

Yalom, I. D. (1991) *Love's Executioner and Other Tales of Psychotherapy.* London: Penguin Books

ABOUT THE EDITORS
AND
CONTRIBUTORS

PENNY ALLEN started her working life as an Occupational Therapist in a small psychiatric unit in Sheffield, specialising in creative therapies. She has lived in Sheffield ever since, with a husband, two children and a dog. She continued to work in the field of mental illness in in-patient, day-care and community settings for 20 years. A career break led to a training in person-centred counselling and later in supervision. During the 1980s Penny attended an IPR workshop led by Norman Kagan and subsequently ran an IPR workshop with colleagues from Sheffield. This led her to see IPR as a useful and essentially person-centred aid to self-reflective practice. She has worked at the Sheffield University Counselling Service, and now has an independent practice as a counsellor and supervisor. She also works for Temenos as their Training Supervision and Placement Co-ordinator.

ROSE CAMERON was born near Inverness and grew up in Edinburgh. She studied English and art history at Stirling University and Georgetown University in Washington DC. She now lives in Manchester, where she has been in private practice as a counsellor, supervisor and trainer for the last ten years. She has a long-standing interest in subtle energy work, and as a trainer, seeks to promote energetic self-awareness amongst therapists. She has been aware of the energetic interactions people have with each other since childhood, but had to use made-up names for them until her training as a healer introduced her to the energetic paradigm. Realisations shared by participants during a workshop led her into helping supervisees and clients become aware of their energetic process. She has written a number of pieces about subtle energy awareness for person-centred publications, and welcomes enquiries at energyawareness@quista.net.

RACHEL FREETH works for Gloucestershire Partnership NHS Trust. She works in Gloucester with a large community mental health team and also has responsibility for patients in hospital. In 1998 she gained a diploma in counselling at the University of East Anglia after taking a year out of psychiatry. Since then she has tried to integrate person-centred values and philosophy into NHS psychiatric settings. She is associate editor of HCPJ (Healthcare Counselling and Psychotherapy Journal), and psychiatric advisor to OCIC (Oxford Christian Institute for Counselling). For recreation she enjoys singing with North Cotswold Chamber Choir, and, to counteract a rather sedentary lifestyle, she runs several times a week. She lives currently in Oxfordshire, but will be moving shortly to Gloucestershire with her partner Ilse, and their cat.

DEBORAH GIBSON is a qualified art therapist and person-centred therapist. Initially an artist and jewellery designer and maker, she arrived, via community arts, in the world of counselling, psychotherapy and art therapy. Seemingly living a life of transition, she has changed direction from the psychodynamic model that was the theoretical base of her first training to the person-centred approach. She now works as a person-centred art therapist, counsellor, trainer, tutor and lecturer. Having worked in community mental health and in primary care, she currently works in a project working with survivors of sexual abuse.

PAUL HITCHINGS M.Sc. is a chartered counselling psychologist and UKCP registered psychotherapist. He maintains a private practice in West London as a supervisor and as a psychotherapist for individuals and couples. He also works as a tutor at The Metanoia Institute where he teaches on the Integrative Psychotherapy, Supervision and Couples therapy programmes.

GREG MADISON is an existential-phenomenological and Focusing-oriented therapist practicing in various settings in London. He is a visiting lecturer at Regents College School of Psychotherapy and Counselling and is involved in teaching and supervising advanced psychotherapy and counselling psychology students. He is an accredited mediator and is involved in training lawyers and others in mediation skills. Greg also offers training in Focusing and is currently completing his PhD on the topic of "Existential Migrants", exploring the experience of 'home' for those individuals who chose to leave their homeland to live in foreign places. Greg can be contacted at gregmadison@mac.com.

TONY MERRY I am currently Senior Lecturer in Counselling and Psychotherapy at the University of East London. I have been invoved in the Person-Centred Approach for about thirty years, and I have written a number of books and journal articles about various aspects of the theory and practice of person-centred psychotherapy. Though I work in London, I live in the Herefordshire countryside, which is where I prefer to spend most of my time.

SENI SENEVIRATNE is a psychotherapist of mixed racial heritage (English/Sri Lankan) who was born and brought up in Yorkshire. Her understanding of issues of race and culture has been informed through her personal experiences, her political activism and through 25 years involvement in the statutory and voluntary sector as a teacher, trainer and community development worker. She was a founding member of Ashiana Asian Women's Refuge in Sheffield and continues to raise awareness through training and campaign work on the impact of domestic abuse. She is currently employed as a therapist with Sheffield Women's Counselling and Therapy Service and Barnsley NHS. She also works as a freelance therapist, supervisor, trainer and consultant. She is a writer and has published a wide variety of poetry and prose and edited resource packs and anthologies.

IAN TOWNSEND is an educator, homeopath, and person-centred supervisor. As Senior Lecturer in the Faculty of Health at the University of Central Lancashire Ian is Course Leader for one of Europe's two undergraduate degrees in Homeopathy. His particular interest lies in utilising supervision to explore and support the emergence of the authentic self from the interplay between the personal and the professional in the development of the practitioner. Ian learnt his homeopathy in the 1980s as a member of the Darlington Collective, a radical experiment in co-operative adult education. He then practised in Derbyshire and Yorkshire for over 17 years. Founder-director of the Darlington and Sheffield Schools of Homeopathy, he has also taught at many of the independent Colleges in England and Scotland. Ian has a Masters Degree in Education, and post-graduate qualifications in Clinical Supervision, Person-Centred Supervision, and Person-Centred Group Facilitation. He has delivered supervision workshops in the UK and Norway, written widely on the subject, and is Editor of the Society of Homeopaths Code of Ethics for Supervisors.

KEITH TUDOR has worked for 25 years in the helping professions in a number of settings. He is a qualified and registered psychotherapist and has a private/ independent practice in Sheffield offering therapy, supervision and consultancy. He is an Honorary Fellow in the School of Health, Liverpool John Moores

University. In 1993 he co-founded Temenos, an independent training organisation, which runs courses in person-centred psychotherapy and counselling, and supervision. He is a widely published author in the field of psychotherapy and counselling, and mental health and has pubished five books: *Mental Health Promotion* (Routledge, 1996); *Group Counselling* (Sage, 1999); editor, *Transactional Approaches to Brief Therapy* (Sage, 2002); with Tony Merry, the *Dictionary of Person-Centred Psychology* (Whurr, 2002); and with others, Embleton Tudor *et al.*, *The Person-Centred Approach: A Contemporary Introduction* (Palgrave, 2004). He is the series editor of 'Advancing Theory in Therapy' (published by Brunner-Routledge).

JOANNA VALENTINE works in the National Health Service as an internal Organisational Development and Leadership Development Consultant and Facilitator. She is a professional member of the Institute of Personnel and Development, holds a Masters Degree in Management Learning and has over 20 years experience within her field in the public, private and voluntary sectors. She began training in the person-centred approach with Temenos in order to enhance her facilitation skills, and stayed to complete her Diploma in the Person-Centred Approach to Organisations because she was inspired by her experience of using the approach with teams. She has worked extensively with clinical teams and with clinical leaders, and is interested in supervision as a model of professional reflective practice.

MIKE WORRALL read English at Oxford, worked for the Probation Service and trained in the person-centred approach at The Metanoia Institute in London. He works in independent practice in Oxford, and is an occasional trainer at Temenos in Sheffield.

AUTHOR INDEX

SUBJECT INDEX

PCCS Books
The largest list of Client-Centred Therapy and Person-Centred Approach books in the world

Client-Centred Therapy and the Person-Centred Approach
Essential Readers
Series edited by Tony Merry

Client-Centred Therapy: A revolutionary paradigm
Jerold Bozarth

Experiences in Relatedness: Groupwork and the person-centred approach
Colin Lago & Mhairi MacMillan (Eds)

Women Writing in the Person-Centred Approach
Irene Fairhurst (Ed)

Understanding Psychotherapy: Fifty years of client-centred theory and practice
C.H. Patterson

The Person-Centred Approach: A passionate presence
Peggy Natiello

Family, Self and Psychotherapy: A person-centred perspective
Ned L. Gaylin

Contributions to Client-Centered Therapy and the Person-Centered Approach
Nathaniel J. Raskin

Rogers' Therapeutic Conditions: Evolution, Theory and Practice
Series edited by Gill Wyatt

Volume 1: Congruence
Gill Wyatt (Ed)

Volume 2: Empathy
Sheila Haugh & Tony Merry (Eds)

Volume 3: Unconditional Positive Regard
Jerold Bozarth & Paul Wilkins (Eds)

Volume 4: Contact and Perception
Gill Wyatt & Pete Sanders (Eds)

PCCS Books

The largest list of Client-Centred Therapy and Person-Centred Approach books in the world

The Tribes of the Person-Centred Nation: A guide to the schools of therapy associated with the PCA
Pete Sanders (Ed.)

The Client-Centred Therapist in Psychiatric Contexts: A therapists' guide to the psychiatric landscape and its inhabitants
Lisbeth Sommerbeck

Steps on a Mindful Journey: Person-centred expressions
Godfrey T. Barrett-Lennard

Learning and Being in Person-Centred Counselling (second edition)
A textbook for discovering theory and developing practice
Tony Merry

Person-Centred Practice: The BAPCA Reader
Tony Merry (Ed)

Trust and Understanding: The person-centred approach to everyday care for people with special needs
Marlis Pörtner

Classics in the Person-Centered Approach
David J. Cain (Ed)

Client-Centered and Experiential Psychotherapy in the 21st Century:
Advances in theory, research and practice
Jeanne C. Watson, Rhonda N. Goldman & Margaret S. Warner (Eds)

Pre-Therapy: Reaching contact-impaired clients
Garry Prouty, Dion Van Werde & Marlis Pörtner

Voices of the Voiceless: Person-centred approaches and people with learning disabilities
Jan Hawkins

To Lead an Honorable Life: Invitations to think about Client-Centered Therapy and the Person-Centered Approach
John Shlien

Journal

Person-Centered and Experiential Psychotherapies
The journal of the World Association for Person-Centered and Experiential Psychotherapy and Counseling

---

Visit our website for news of the latest releases www.pccs-books.co.uk
UK customers call 01989 763900 for discounts